THE
AGE OF
DETERRENCE

THE
AGE OF
DETERRENCE

THE AGE OF DETERRENCE

by George E. Lowe

Little, Brown and Company · Boston · Toronto

Published simultaneously in Canada
by Little, Brown & Company (Canada) Limited

PRINTED IN THE UNITED STATES OF AMERICA

To John F. Kennedy
Traditionalist

Contents

THE
AGE OF
DETERRENCE

THE
AGE OF
DETERRENCE

Introduction

The *Age of Deterrence* IS A HISTORY OF THE DEVELOP-
ment of strategic theory from 1952 to 1963. Thus it can be
considered an intellectual history of strategic ideas advanced by
the American defense establishment during the 1950's and early
1960's. I do not pretend that this is a definitive work, nor
would I claim to be completely objective in selection of material.
However, I have tried to select representative statements from
both Utopian and Traditionalist viewpoints.

A *Utopian,* in the realm of strategic theory, is anyone who
makes little or no distinction between the traditional uses of
force and the new dimensions of nuclear violence. Fascinated
by the expectations of nuclear technology and frustrated by the
repeated treachery and continued militancy of our Communist
opponents, he feels that all weapons should be usable and "legitimate." Because we are patently superior in modern weaponry
as well as morality, we should have no compunction about using
this superior military power to force our adversaries to relax
their global pressures on the Free World. The Utopian has regarded atomic weapons as "conventional" for over a decade. He
believes that the real problems of American foreign policy are
more susceptible to technological solutions than to old-fashioned,
traditional diplomatic ones. Furthermore, since thermonuclear
war is a real possibility, we should be prepared to fight and *win*
such a war regardless of the cost to our society and institutions.
Therefore, the Utopian is essentially a revolutionary in the fashion of George Orwell's *1984.*

A *Traditionalist,* in the field of strategic thinking, is anyone who, although granting the need for an effective military establishment, is convinced of the absolute necessity for using no more force than necessary to implement foreign policy decisions made by the constituted civilian authorities. The Traditionalist visualizes the basic role of nuclear weapons as deterring World War III or protecting the vital interests of a nation. In all other contingencies, non-nuclear conventional force, unconventional tactics, or traditional diplomatic pressure should be applied. The Traditionalist is essentially a conservative in the grand manner of conserving that which is best from the past and cautiously evolving new forms and institutions to meet the problems of tomorrow.

Since this study is basically a specialized variety of contemporary intellectual history, the utterances and writings of individuals, publications, and institutions are highly significant because they indicate a position in the continuing strategic debate. For the most part these positions, once taken, tend to remain constant throughout the decade. Because I am primarily interested in strategic ideas, this analysis has been limited to the strategic concept known as deterrence. The vast majority — indeed, practically all — of the strategic thinking in and out of the military has centered upon deterrence and deterrents. Both Utopians and Traditionalists agree that thermonuclear weapons deter total war. The argument or debate arises over what else thermonuclear weapons can deter. The answer makes Traditionalists or Utopians of us all.

I confess to being a Traditionalist, probably because of nearly six years of active duty in the Navy, two years in the Foreign Service, and a bedrock conviction that the Korean War was a noble conflict for American fighting men. The main thrust of my research was directed initially at attempting to prove that there existed within the Navy a doctrine of limited war that coincided rather closely with Army views on this strategic touchstone. This original line of research was eventually expanded to cover the much broader topic of Army, Navy, and Air Force views on deterrence. The ideological conflict among the services over the nature of war and strategy serves as the continuing thread on which *The Age of Deterrence* is developed.

The basic disagreement between Traditionalists and Utopians revolves around the use of force as an instrument of American foreign policy. The Utopian makes little or no distinction between nuclear and non-nuclear weapons, maintaining that ultimately both would be used for the same purpose: total military victory. Therefore, no restrictions should be placed on their use nor meaningless political and moral distinctions drawn. To do so would give aid and comfort to our enemies, who are short on technological capacity but long on manpower (Communist "hordes" to the Utopian). Therefore, to be fainthearted when it comes to nuclear weapons is to hand world Communism a needless advantage and deprives the United States of its most effective and modern weapons.

Fascinated by these technological marvels, the Utopian looks with loving fondness on "aerospace" weapons systems, especially manned ones. Utopians demand the creation of the glamorous-sounding "aerospace dominance" (an updating of the old airpower dominance) and vainly search for the Absolute Weapon, hoping for a unilateral technological breakthrough. This all-conquering aerospace force, numbered in tens of thousands, would consist of a "mix" of manned bombers, fixed-based missiles, and manned orbiting bombers, along with the associated, highly elaborate command and control equipment and systems. Utopians would then attempt to implement a military philosophy called counterforce, which masquerades as a deterrent strategy but contains strong overtones of an aggressive thermonuclear war–winning strategy.

Behind the façade of a respectable and traditional deterrence posture lies a temptation that many Utopian theoreticians and policy-makers find hard to resist: the threat or use of thermonuclear war as an instrument of foreign policy. Resurrecting John Foster Dulles's "brinksmanship," the new high priests of strategic theory and analysis have begun to construct force levels and a command and control structure that could be utilized in some future contingency if the duel at the brink got out of hand and the world were plunged into thermonuclear war. Utopians earnestly believe that by proper targeting, tight command and control procedures, and the "right" weapons systems, strategic forces can and should be used for deterrence and, if deterrence fails, for fighting and *winning* the resulting thermonuclear "exchange." SAC commander-in-chief General Thomas S. Power, one of the last of a long line of Utopian generals stretching back to Billy Mitchell, has remarked: "Deterrence is more than bombs and missiles . . . deterrence is the determination of the American people to prevent and, if necessary, fight and *win* any kind of war, whether hot or cold, big or small."

In other words, Utopian strategists believe that thermonuclear wars are not only thinkable but can and will be "won" provided enough scientific thought and analysis is cranked into the creation and maintenance of our strategic nuclear forces. Thus the Utopian answer to the age of mutual thermonuclear deterrence is to condemn it and attempt to create instead thermonuclear forces necessary to implement a "war-winning," relatively "bloodless" strategy called counterforce. If this counterforce of missiles and bombers is massive enough, they claim, it will cover all possible contingencies. Thus, if America builds sufficient hydrogen bombs and the proper kind of delivery vehicles, all outstanding international problems can be resolved — in our favor. Limited, local, or regional war will easily be handled by the strategic thermonuclear deterrent, for "the dog that takes care of the cat can handle the kittens too."

Such Utopian beliefs are not new. The dark and bloody battlefields of northwestern Europe were the seedbed for Utopian doctrine during and after World War I. Out of the slaughter on the Western Front came a new concept: leap over the stinking trenches with the airplane and hit the enemy where he works and lives. If his front-line troops are not starved for food and ammunition, home-front morale, wrecked by incessant bombing, will force the government to sue for peace. Thus a few brave, highly skilled knights can be substituted for the millions of farmers' sons and city poor slugging out the war on the ground. The country with the most mechanics and strongest industry will win future wars, not the nation with the largest land armies.

This, then, has been the Utopian dream for nearly half a century: a cheap and easy air blitz, favoring the most technologically advanced nations. Among the theorists of this new military strategy were Lord Hugh M. Trenchard, General Billy Mitchell, General Giulio Douhet, Major Alexander P. De Seversky, Winston Churchill, Sir John Slessor, Air Marshal Kingston McClourty, and Air Force Generals Orville A. Anderson, Robert C. Richardson, III, Dale O. Smith, and Thomas D. White. The theory's popularizers were Herman Kahn, Bernard Brodie, John Foster Dulles, C. J. V. Murphy, Dr. Edward Teller, the Rand Corporation, the Stanford Research Institute, General Bonner Fellers, the Richardson Foundation, Stefan T. Possony, Richard Fryklund, Earl Voss, Albert Wohlstetter, and Henry S. Rowen.

Throughout their many articles, books, speeches, and testimony several assumptions appear repeatedly: "War is Hell," but since evil aggressor nations insist on starting it, we must give them back double measure. We must create a force so powerful that it will enforce peace for all time and guarantee a state of *Pax Americana* or *Pax Aeronautica*.

The Anglo-American bomber fleet would do for the twentieth century what the British battle fleet had done for the nineteenth. Western democracies are singularly equipped to maintain their technological superiority because they have such a lead in complex technical equipment, which is vitally important to create such a superior bomber force that no nation can ever catch up to them. Furthermore, the average American is such an excellent mechanic that in this aspect of human skills we will be forever ahead.

Since the 1940's, Utopian claims as to our areas of superiority have changed. We were first superior in industrial base, skilled mechanics, and pilots. With the advent of the B–17, followed by the B–29, B–36, B–47, and B–52, our superiority lay in the

bomber vehicle itself and its elite crews. With the invention of
the atom bomb, we had a double superiority: the plane *and* the
bomb. When the Russians exploded an atomic weapon in the fall
of 1949, our superiority was expressed in terms of having the
original bombers and superior *numbers* of bombs in our stockpile. Then, with the advent of the hydrogen bomb, our superiority lay in vast numbers and "cleaner" thermonuclear weapons
and a superior organization — the Strategic Air Command.
When this was countered by the Russian development of a
droppable hydrogen bomb, we responded by building more delivery vehicles and re-honing SAC. With the arrival of nuclear
plenty, we allowed ourselves the luxury of basing a strategy on
the use of tactical nuclear weapons, which we could produce in
greater quantities than our opponents, and we banked on our
highly superior social institutions.

Once again, as our supposed technical superiority is about to
be canceled out, we are falling back on the neutron bomb, the
orbiting bomber, and the doomsday device with the high assurance that these will tip the scales our way once again. And
Major De Seversky in *America: Too Young to Die!* offered a
new panacea, "an unpenetratable defense system through new
uses of electronics — a field in which we do lead (because we
can outproduce anyone)."

Likewise, Dr. Stefan T. Possony darkly warned, in the tradition of the infamous bomber and missile gap hoaxes, that sinister
forces in "the Pentagon" purposely were creating a "nuclear
firepower" gap. Under the stewardship of Defense Secretary
McNamara, "the Pentagon" is deliberately slowing down our
aerospace progress and thereby preparing America for a "nuclear and technological Pearl Harbor." When this happens, according to the very Utopian Dr. Possony, "there is no doubt
that we would be defeated or could win only at the price of
excessive American casualties."

Soon a newer cure-all will be advocated: the construction of
extensive underground blast shelters. Here is one competition in

which the Russians never will catch up with us: pouring concrete and digging holes. These Utopian concepts, although they look defensive in nature, are really offensive because they appear to make thermonuclear war survivable and "winnable" and could conceivably set the stage for a future pre-emptive war.

In the thermonuclear–ballistic missile era, accepting the first blow entails fixed-based missile sites absorbing the aggressor's attack and having sufficient strength left over to inflict unacceptable damage on the attacker. Utopians interpret "unacceptable damage" to read "win" the thermonuclear exchange. This can be done only by a counterforce, for a force that cannot win and prevail cannot deter. And if deterrence fails, all Americans assuredly would want to "win" the resulting thermonuclear war. Thus the Utopian sees only imperfect, tentative peace eventuating in a catastrophic war. Balanced forces, they believe, are vestiges of the prehistoric military world before Hiroshima. Any attempt to impose new air-atomic strategy on the old-fashioned conventional approach is doomed to failure and will take the nation down to defeat. Utopians firmly believe that if the proper type and number of hydrogen bomb–carrying delivery systems can be built along with the proper shelters and underground storage and recovery supplies, *all* possible world contingencies can be handled by nuclear weapons backed up by relatively few continental-based forces, fleshed out with "indigenous" ground troops *and* the national will to use these nuclear weapons.

A shorthand statement of the theoretical modifications of Utopian strategic concepts includes: strategic bombing (1945–1949), air-atomic power (1949–1952), new look (1953), massive retaliation (1954–1957), limited nuclear war (1954–1961); counterforce (1958–1963), controlled thermonuclear war (1962), and controlled peace (1963).

Traditionalists often are accused by Utopians of having their heads stuck in the mud and their minds riveted to old-fashioned concepts and weapons because Traditionalists draw a very sharp distinction between nuclear and non-nuclear weapons. The Traditionalist regards this difference, even if it is mainly psychological at fractional kiloton levels, as a vital "firebreak," which as long as it is preserved is the best guarantee that some minor border incident does not escalate into total nuclear exchange. The Traditionalist, then, is interested in setting up as many "hurdles" as possible — military, political, economic, moral, and psychological — before being driven to use nuclear weapons, for he fears that an entirely new situation will be created when the first nuclear is fired in war. Or as Thomas Schelling of the Center for International Affairs at Harvard expressed it: ". . . and even those who have argued that nuclears ought to be considered just a more efficient use of artillery will surely catch their breath when the first one goes off in anger."

This fear scarcely troubles the Utopian; indeed, he welcomes using nuclears and would have America and the West deliberately adopt a policy of immediately escalating all regional conflicts to the nuclear level. The Utopian maintains that the West could do this with relative immunity because of our massive nuclear superiority. The Traditionalist prefers to meet the enemy at his level of provocation with a measured amount of usable force. In other words, the Utopian would use nuclear technology at the slightest pretext, whereas the Traditionalist would meet the challenge with the ground soldier or marine, conventionally at first but backed up by the capability to "go nuclear" if so ordered.

Furthermore, Traditionalists are no longer sure that either total wars or limited wars can be won absolutely. They believe the purpose of thermonuclear weapons is to *prevent* total war, and they prevent it by adopting a defensive "strike-second" posture. Although aiming their thermonuclear weapons at the enemy's governmental-industrial base, they differ from Utopians by considering it impossible to "win" a nuclear exchange. But should deterrence fail and total war come, they would aim at the same strategic targets as the Utopians and with the same amount of precision. Traditionalists maintain that limited wars, by definition, cannot be carried to unconditional surrender but must be fought with the realization that these less than total wars are always highly political. Thus the political situation after the fighting ends must be kept constantly in mind, and destruction for destruction's sake must be avoided scrupulously.

The Traditionalist obviously is no pacifist, but neither is he a warmonger. He regards thermonuclear weapons as something unique in history and fervently believes that man must do his utmost to prevent the next conflict from being the last.

There has been no outstanding Traditional theorist, but rather a host of commentators on twentieth-century war who have laboriously constructed an alternative theory to victory through airpower. They include: B. H. Liddell Hart, Walter Millis, Hanson Baldwin, Samuel P. Huntington, Robert E. Osgood, T. E. Phipps, John Coyle, J. Robert Oppenheimer, Donald G. Brennan, Oskar Morgenstern, Admiral Sir Gerald Dickens, Admiral Anthony Buzzard, C. P. Snow, P. M. S. Blackett, Alastair Buchan, Generals Taylor, Ridgway, Gavin, and Medaris, Captain Ralph E. Williams, USN, Admiral George H. Miller, Admiral Arleigh Burke, Hans Bethe, Ralph E. Lapp, James E. King, Jr., Paul H. Nitze, Dean G. Acheson, George Kennan, Hans J. Morgenthau, Ferdinand O. Miksche, and Raymond Aron.

These Traditionalist writers and thinkers, like their counterforce counterparts, had modified their ideas in light of the new weapons, but by the summer of 1963 had come back full circle to their original position before the H-bomb. In 1948 they believed that traditional forces were needed in addition to the atomic bomb. They granted that atomic weapons were important, but they were convinced those weapons had not eliminated the need for land and sea forces. Korea reinforced this belief.

The advent of nuclear plenty, occurring at the end of the Korean War and at the beginning of the Eisenhower Administration, forced a temporary flirtation with the idea of using tactical atomic weapons to cancel out the supposed Communist manpower advantage. It soon became apparent that what the United

States could accomplish in technology, the Russians were capable of duplicating, or, as C. P. Snow put it:

The overriding truth is a bleak one, if one is living in the physical presence of gadgets and spends one's creative force developing them: that societies at about the same level of technology will produce similar inventions. In military technology in particular, where the level of the United States and the U.S.S.R. is very much the same and where the investment of scientists and money is also similar, it would be astonishing if either society kept for long anything like a serious, much less a decisive, technical lead.

It is overwhelming odds that one country will get its nose in front in one field for a short time, the other somewhere else. This situation, fluctuating in detail but steady in the gross, is likely to continue without limit. It is quite unrealistic, and very dangerous, to imagine that the West as a whole can expect a permanent and decisive lead in military technology over the East as a whole. That expectation is a typical piece of gadgeteers' thinking. It has done the West more harm than any other kind of thinking. History and science do not work that way.

By 1957–1958 it had become clear that tactical atomic weapons would cancel themselves out, and proponents of balanced forces soon realized that modern technology had made it impossible to find a long-range advantage in weapons gadgetry. Although agreeing that a thermonuclear deterrent was absolutely essential, Traditionalists wondered if there were not an upper or finite limit to these total war weapons. They questioned whether we were building "overkill" into our nuclear arsenal — that is, the ability to obliterate all targets more than once. Why not construct a limited, invulnerable thermonuclear force and concentrate on mobile land forces backed by proper sea and air support? This was a shift away from technical gadgetry toward geographically oriented factors in response to the changing nature of the Communist challenge.

A grand strategy can either be formulated to deter total war, stabilize all other crisis situations, and make constructive but traditional use of the time gained, or it can attempt to deter war through a massive superiority in thermonuclear weapons and at the same time prepare to "win" any resulting thermonuclear exchange brought about by deliberately risky and obviously provocative but highly tempting foreign policy "initiatives." The first path is essentially a traditional-conservative one, and the second reflects a reactionary-revolutionary strategy. It is my thesis that our nation should make the choice for stabilized deterrence and arms control. This means: (1) creation of a finite number of invulnerable true deterrents; (2) modernization and addition to the limited war forces; (3) increased paramilitary and unconventional warfare capability; (4) engagement in a radical and revolutionary economic, political, and ideological effort to make the most effective use of the time gained by the tri-level military stabilization; and (5) minimal civilian defense measures largely of an "insurance" variety.

But if the choice is made for a destabilized "winning" strategy and accelerated thermonuclear arms race, the course is also obvious: (1) unlimited numbers of hardened, fixed-based missiles; (2) new weapons specifically designed for counterforce; (3) greatly accelerated arms race in space; (4) enormous civilian defense, recuperation, and rehabilitation programs; (5) tremendous governmental regimentation; (6) reduction of U.S. troops in Europe to a "trip-wire" force of one division; (7) a neo-isolationist "go-it-alone" foreign policy; and (8) abrogation of the Test Ban Treaty.

The limited Test Ban Treaty of 1963 has sharply silhouetted the choices between these two grand strategies. The history of how the world arrived at the first cessation of the nuclear arms race since that awful December day in 1942 at the University of Chicago's Stagg Field is intimately linked to the struggle over strategic doctrine within the United States government and its armed forces. The Age of Deterrence, which is slowly replacing the era of the Cold War, is made possible by the brave and largely unsung battles of lonely Traditionalists, utilizing all the weapons of an open society in order to create, publicize, and lobby for an alternative doctrine to the official strategy, which — dominated by the atom and the bomber — has been largely

Utopian in origin and implementation since 1945. The story of the struggle for this traditional strategy is the *raison d'être* of *The Age of Deterrence*.

Domaine de Saint-François d'Assise
La Celle St. Cloud, France
August 6, 1963

1

Traditionalists and Utopians in Defense Policy

SITUATED NEXT TO THE BUSTLING INLAND SEAPORT OF Iwakuni on lower Honshu, Japan, is a United States naval air station. Thirty miles up the winding bay is Hiroshima. The efficient electric train makes the trip to that historic city in about forty minutes. A few miles north of Iwakuni stands the skeleton of a very large steel plant, which at first glance appears to be under construction. Upon closer examination and questioning of the local populace, one learns that the rusting girders are the remains of a steel plant destroyed by carrier planes from Admiral Halsey's Task Force 38 operating off southern Honshu during the summer of 1945.

The rebuilt and revitalized Hiroshima has risen phoenixlike from atomic ashes. This city, as all the world knows, was one of two strategic targets atomized by the Twenty-first Air Force with resulting casualties of over 100,000. The modern museum of horrors erected near ground zero preserves for posterity the indiscriminate nature of strategic bombing and leaves no one in doubt that this form of warfare was indeed "baby killing."

These two examples — the rusting steel plant at Iwakuni and the ravaged town hall memorial at Hiroshima — are symbols of two radically different concepts of war and military strategy.

This conflict exploded in the summer of 1949 but went down in history simply as the fight for the B–36, or the "Revolt of the Admirals." It is, however, a continuing struggle not yet ended between Utopian and Traditionalist strategic concepts. The central issue of the sixties is one of "enough" thermonuclear power to *deter* a total war or "enough" to *win* a thermonuclear war. Defense organization, weapons systems, and force levels will ultimately be determined by the resolution of this issue.

There are three varieties of Traditionalists. The Liberal and Conservative Traditionalists are generally found in the political field; the Military Traditionalist is usually non-political in uniform, but he can be either a Conservative or Liberal Traditionalist when out. The Traditionalist prefers to take technology in his stride, realizing that technological advancement tends to cancel out on either side of the Iron Curtain. He places great stress on tradition, esprit de corps, bravery, the strength of free individuals fighting for an open society, and geography. He feels we are not as fat and contented as we look and that through inspired leadership we can have once again that lean and virile look of a society on the make.

His model is the Eighth Army under General Ridgway, stabilizing the front after the retreat from the Yalu, or the First Marine Division under General O. P. Smith, slashing its way from Chosin Reservoir through twelve Chinese divisions, decimating eight beyond repair.

The Traditionalist attempts to prepare for a wide spectrum of warfare by equipping his forces with increasingly "modern" weapons, revitalizing old tactics, and attempting to limit the use of force by the erection of an invulnerable deterrent shield. The Utopian, on the other hand, still believing that thermonuclear wars can be won, attempts to create "prevailing" thermonuclear weapons systems.

There have always been and probably always will be representatives of both Utopian and Traditional strategic views in our armed services. This is so because, stripped of service loyalties and temporary weapons fascination, the dichotomy reflects the universal difference between monistic and pluralistic views of society, the world, and history.

The very nature of contemporary military force, with almost unlimited amounts of power available for immediate use once the political word is given, coupled with the existence of an aggressive set of Communist antagonists, tends to breed frustration in military leaders. In a democratic society this restlessness cannot be directed easily into "normal" revolutionary channels, a course open to brother officers in Korea, Turkey, and Vietnam. Some officers crack under the strain and attempt to go beyond the accepted limits of our tradition; the result is the spectacle of Major General Walker, a Military Utopian turned Conservative Utopian Militarist, perverting the vital military professionalism so necessary in an unstable world and in a pluralistic society.

Another and more legitimate outlet for military energies is, in Robert Lovett's words, "advising on military policies and . . . preparing detailed, strategic plans as part of the complex of specialized advice from which an over-all national policy can be evolved." In addition, only the military is capable of supplying the expertise for a continuing critique of war contingency plans, developing new weapons and tactics, and training troops under its command.

Each of the three services has its peculiar flavor, philosophy, and way of life. The older services, Army and Navy-Marines, have, because of their almost two centuries of existence, a greater amount of tradition intermingled with their nuclear weapons and ballistic missiles. The decade-and-a-half-old Air Force proceeds by the original motto of its Air University: "Unhampered by Tradition." All three services are parochial institutions, basically inner-directed, and utterly dependent upon the good will of the American people and Congress for their annual allowance of over fifty billion dollars. Their entire highly structured institutional life flourishes or withers depending upon their share of the annual budget pie. It is a truism that the sharpest interservice quarrels take place when the budget shrinks and that eras of good feeling occur when there is something for everybody. As a result there is an enormous amount of effort, time, and money spent by the services in convincing their constituents, the American public, that the country needs them. There are various ways to catch the public's eye: shiny new gadgets and marvelously complex weapons systems, actual or theoretical use of military force in carrying out the foreign policy of the nation, and humanitarian, public service, and educational efforts.

Each of the services tries to demonstrate to the American people that its weapons and its organization are essential to the continued existence of the Republic; each service tries to identify its organization with the total needs of America. That service which does the best public relations job will most likely be favored with the largest share of the finite budget dollar. This fierce competition for public acceptance is, in reality, a competition for continuing defense appropriations. Since each service is convinced of the righteousness of its own particular view of history and war, it is inevitable that clashes, conflicts, and infighting are continually taking place. These differences are real, honest, bitter, and tremendously important to the services and to the nation. Unfortunately, the public, with help from within the services and interested outside observers, classifies and magnifies these conflicts as "interservice wrangling" and demands that they be eliminated.

The Traditionalist views our society as a pluralistic one, and from this flows a pluralistic view of strategy. To the Traditionalist, military force is an essential element, but only one element, of an effective national strategy. Factors other than purely military, such as economic, political, psychological, ideological, and financial, are readily accepted by the Traditionalist as playing an important part in shaping a broadly based national strategy. As would be expected from a philosophy so broadly based, the Traditionalist is distrustful of radical new ideas, weapons, or cure-alls that promise a ready, single solution to extremely complex political-military problems. This distrust has manifested itself in the nearly half-century conflict between the Traditionalist and the Utopian over the uses to which the airplane should be put. Army-Navy Traditionalists have consistently visualized the airplane as complementary to the control of the land or sea. The Utopian heretic saw the airplane in the form of the bomber as a completely new weapon, which would dominate and supplant old-fashioned land and sea weapons and create a new form of warfare leading to a new strategic concept and eventually to complete and total victory to the nation first mastering the command of the air.

Army and Navy strategists visualized the airplane in the form of a fighter bomber working in close harmony with surface forces. They created the doctrine of close air support that Hitler used so effectively in 1939 and 1940. Utopian strategists imagined the airplane in the form of a multi-engined bomber working independently of the obsolete land and sea forces. The Traditionalist's opponents were the enemy's tactical military forces, whereas the Utopian's targets were the enemy's strategic forces, which meant obliterating the opponent's industries and cities. Both attempted to affect the enemy's will to fight, both could cite historical chapter and verse, and both felt their way was gospel. Put in another way, the Traditionalist placed his faith in geography, history, and tradition, whereas the Utopian gambled on accelerating technology and innovation.

Occasionally some member of one of the services or an outside scholar attempts to integrate his service doctrine into a grand national strategy that will effectively tie the national purpose to the service's future. If this happens, the service that is the recipient of such good fortune becomes the dominant one. The time must be ripe for such a tour de force. Any national strategy to be truly effective must be broadly based, capable of covering all contingencies, military and diplomatic, yet keep within finite budgetary bounds and, almost as importantly, stay within the limits of the American dream.

Strictly speaking, there have been only three such fortunate coincidences in the field of American political-military strategy since the Civil War, although we may be on the verge of a fourth. The Army under Grant and Lincoln emerged as the savior of the

Union, and for nearly a quarter of a century Army service was a prerequisite for a successful political life. While no great strategist was thrown up by the war (except perhaps Emory Upton), the lessons of this first modern conflict were not lost on European generals and British admirals.

Americans at the turn of the century discovered Alfred T. Mahan, an obscure Navy captain who some ten years previously had made friends with two young politicians, Teddy Roosevelt and Henry Cabot Lodge. Mahan in 1890 had written a revolutionary theory of sea power that perfectly suited the expanding and ebullient nation. During our "splendid little war" Teddy Roosevelt gained his military experience at San Juan Hill, and the United States acquired its empire. The Navy became the nation's first line of defense in those first good years of the twentieth century. World War I saw the Army under Black Jack Pershing gain credit for the victory over Kaiser Bill. There was too much normalcy in the twenties to allow military men to gain prominence in American politics; in fact, throughout the 1920's and 1930's, thanks largely to historical revisionism, militarist generals and avaricious munitions makers were deemed the source of war.

During this armistice period a challenger arose to the Navy's quitclaim of the American taxpayer's pocketbook: the multi-engined heavy bomber. Its prophet, Billy Mitchell, in and out of uniform proclaimed the bomber's virtues. His resulting court-martial was the first in the long and continuing series of sensational strategic struggles between Traditionalists and Utopians. Unfortunately for Mitchell, a naval champion in the form of FDR came to power, and as long as he lived Traditionalists were assured executive protection. Roosevelt championed the Traditionalist viewpoint that was to be instrumental in delaying the creation of the United States Air Force until 1947. FDR declared:

One additional word about aircraft. Recent wars, including the current war in Europe, have demonstrated beyond doubt that fighting efficiency depends on unity of control.

In sea operations the airplane is just as much an integral part of unity of operations as are the submarine, the destroyer, and the battleship, and in land warfare the airplane is just as much a part of the military operations as are the tank corps, the engineers, the artillery, or the infantry itself. Therefore the air force should be part of the Army and Navy.

The Utopian position has never been better stated than by General Douhet, the Italian airpower theoretician, when in May 1928 he wrote:

The Army and the Navy can no longer seek to solve the problems resulting from the aerial factor by incorporating more or less substantial aerial means in the land and sea force. Even from their present viewpoint, this would be a mistake. The Air Service in relation to the Army and to the Navy is overwhelmingly more important as to functions, organizations and methods of employment.

Modern sea power matured gloriously in the Pacific War with the perfection of the fast carrier task force, which seemed to bear out the faith that Admiral John W. Reeves and FDR placed in it.

World War II saw the three services struggling, not only against the Germans and Japanese, but for postwar strategic position as well. Liberating Europe and destroying Hitler's Wehrmacht were the tasks of the United States Army with help from the Navy and Army Air Forces. Whether Hitler could have been defeated solely from the air is a question of some interest but no importance, since he was actually defeated by infantry and armor in the traditional way wars have always been won: the lowly infantryman occupying the home of the enemy. The Pacific War was essentially a Navy show with an assist from the Army and Army Air Forces. The dramatic ending of World War II soon after two atomic bombs were dropped tended to obscure the fact (in postwar strategic discussion) that the United States Navy through an offensive blockade had crippled the warmaking power of Japan.

It was left to the Eighth Air Force based in England and the British Bomber Command to attempt to prove the validity of the Mitchell-Douhet-Trenchard theory of victory through strategic air bombardment. This theory was conceived but never fully implemented during World War I by Lord Trenchard, the first Chief of Staff of the independent Royal Air Force. Two million tons of bombs were dropped on Germany, but the best that can be said for Douhet's theory in World War II is that old Scottish verdict — "Not proven." The key principle of the European air experience — pinpoint daylight bombing of industrial-military targets — was applied by the Twenty-first Air Force against Japanese targets, and it also failed. General Le-May rescued the entire B–29 operation by his famous, or infamous, low-level fire-bomb raids. It remained for the atom bomb and the jet engine to revitalize the floundering doctrine of Mitchell, Douhet, and Trenchard.

The grand strategy of World War II was a mixture of strategic concepts but weighted heavily toward the Traditionalist doctrine of destroying enemy military forces. The 1943 meeting of Churchill and FDR at Casablanca resulted in two major decisions: unconditional surrender would be announced as the war aim of the Allies, and the British and American bomber commands would be given the go-ahead to prove or disprove their theory of victory through strategic air bombardment. Traditional armies from the East and West finally crushed the Wehrmacht, but the illusion of victory through bomber airpower remained undiminished. The Navy, with an assist from ground troops and Air Corps B–29's, brought Japan to her knees, but the dramatic ending of the war after Hiroshima and Nagasaki added to the Utopian illusion that bomber-delivered atomic weapons would be the determining weapons of the future. Ladislas Farago, in his book *Burn after Reading,* discussed a Traditionalist plan

conceived in O.N.I., pushed by Capt. E. M. Zacharias and supported by Navy Secretary James V. Forrestal, [that] would have ended the war in Japan without the atom bomb *and* without the landing of troops. Before the bombs were dropped on Hiroshima and Nagasaki, the Japanese leaders had indicated that they were ready to surrender,

Farago claims, and all it would have required was a short, psychological campaign to show them how they could save face.

That campaign was started, but was not allowed to run its course, which its supporters felt would have shown hard results by Sept. 1, 1945. Japan surrendered on Aug. 14, 1945. "To save two weeks," writes Farago, "the United States introduced history's most savage weapons into human conflict, and thus endowed war with an unprecedented horror. The United States did this at a time when a small band of dedicated men was ready to demonstrate that conflicts could be ended in an intellectual sphere by non-military means."[1]

Ironically, the two services, Army and Navy, whose strategic theories had been successfully implemented during World War II, were the very ones that felt the cold breath of unfriendly public opinion. The Air Force, which became independent in 1947, had a monopoly on the public imagination, the atom bomb, and more importantly, the bomber to carry it. With the beginning of the Cold War in 1948 and the clear identification of our Eurasian enemies, it seemed to many that only the bomber and atom bomb stood between us and oblivion.

As a result public acceptance and defense appropriations began to flow in increasing amounts to the newly independent Air Force. All the elements of a total political-military strategy were available except a theorist: the weapon, the organization, the strategic theory, and the military doctrine.

And so the years 1947 through 1962 represent the flood tide of a doctrine that was as questionable when it was institutionalized as when it was first enunciated in the 1920's, unproved in World War II but accepted as an unquestioned article of faith after the war by most Americans. It has shaped the mainstream of our defense policies since 1945. The unexpressed premise was that wars can be won by directly attacking and destroying the vital urban-industrial heart of the enemy. Once this heart is destroyed, his outlying extremities — land, air, and naval forces — will wither on the vine. Utopians of all political persuasions fervently believe in victory through airpower, achieved by strategic air bombardment once command of the air is attained.

This doctrine is basically a single weapon, single service, single strategy, single chief of staff approach to the complicated business of modern war. This monistic viewpoint afflicts everything the Utopian touches. He thinks in absolute terms of black and white, war or peace, victory or defeat. To carry out his single-minded strategy, the Utopian desires to reorganize the Defense Department, eliminate the Joint Chiefs, merge the services, and jettison all past traditions. What is needed, he feels, is a single-mindedness of purpose backed by a ruthless efficiency so that all the nation's resources can be directed into the creation of an all-powerful thermonuclear force capable of resolving any or all situations in our favor by the sheer weight of numbers. Part and parcel of Utopian strategy is preventive war, although it is usually advocated under the disguise of such terms as "first strike force," "pre-emptive war," or "exercise of the initiative."

The Utopian strategic mansion has rooms for many diverse groups: Democratic liberals, Republican conservatives, right- and left-wing extremists, and militarists in and out of uniform; anyone in fact who is looking for a quick and simple solution to horrendously complex political-military problems can find a home in the Utopian camp.

A common denominator running through this broad coalition is its almost unlimited faith in the superiority of technology, especially American technology. The Utopian, in C. P. Snow's words, tends to be "drunk with gadgets." "Any choice he makes — particularly if it involves comparison with other countries — is much more likely to be wrong than right." Snow regards such individuals as a great menace, for "the nearer he is to the physical presence of his own gadget, the worse his judgment is going to be."

The Utopians have tapped a deep wellspring in the average American. As D. W. Brogan in late 1961 wrote in the *New York Times:* "To Americans, taught that all important advances in modern science and technology were American in origin (few were), the sudden triumphs of Russian technology were too bad to be true." The Utopian offered the quick, easy, 100 per cent American solution to our problems and American commitments: Utilize the atom bomb ("the ultimate weapon") carried to the Asiatic heartland by the epitome of American industry — the long-range heavy bomber.

Postwar American defense policy has been dominated by Utopian-minded individuals who would rather substitute technology and gadgetry for manpower and the traditional forms of armed force in hopes of gaining a quick and easy victory over the forces of evil in this world. In a nutshell, American defense policy in the postwar years has been motivated and directed by a fascination with atomic explosives and the means for their delivery. In the process the emphasis on atomic gadgetry has semiparalyzed our foreign policy.

By and large our directors of strategic thinking have been blinded by Utopian guidance. A combination of atomic gadgetry, flashy jet aircraft, and magical missiles, buttressed by incestuous, government-sponsored "think" factories, has contributed to what Brogan has called the illusion of American omnipotence. When this illusion was challenged by Soviet missile and space feats, the resultant frustrations were great. The tendency has been to respond exactly the way the Russians prefer: more of the same nuclear gadgetry, which the Communists have found relatively easy to counter while continuing their forays into the Free World from behind the Iron and Bamboo Curtains.

Traditionalist pleas for more conventional arms and a greater stress on geopolitical factors went largely unheeded in the mad race to pile up thermonuclear weapons. Utopians convinced themselves, despite the logic of technological facts, that the United States could create a first strike force that would be used only for retaliatory purposes, and that the Russians could be convinced the motivation behind the creation of this force was wholly defensive.

In most strategic thinking, especially Utopian created or inspired, there is a weird doublethink or mirror inversion principle, which is commented on by John C. Polanyi in the December 1961 *Bulletin of the Atomic Scientists:*

. . . Perhaps the most striking impression that remained after 10 days [at a Moscow arms control conference] was that of symmetry of fears on either side. Not infrequently one had the feeling that one was arguing with one's own reflection in a mirror. It was as plausible that the Western powers might launch a surprise attack on the Soviet Union to forestall a surprise attack that they feared the Soviet Union was on the point of unleashing against them, as was the reverse occurrence with the Soviet Union as aggressor.

The obsession with very large numbers of strategic delivery systems carries with it the inevitable doctrine of the first (or war-winning, pre-emptive) strike and forces the Utopians to openly advocate, or at least flirt with, the doctrine of preventive war. Utopians have not yet given up the anachronistic concept that all wars can be won in the sense that World Wars I and II were and that even thermonuclear wars can be made livable and the threat thereof used as a continuing instrument of national policy, providing of course proper measures are taken in the years before the thermonuclear exchange.

It is often lamented that the last good idea formulated in the political-military field was containment, authored by George Kennan in 1948. It is frequently alleged that containment has failed, which is partially true, but the reasons for its limited success are not the ones usually given: internal subversion, "little men," and "soft on Communism." The fact is that the containment policy was never allotted the proper type of usable military force with which to contain world Communism. Truman, from 1948 to July 1, 1950, attempted to carry out Kennan's Traditionalist insights with Utopian weapons systems: the B-29, the B-36, and the atom bomb. This was attempting to use the unusable atomic force to implement a policy that by its very nature had to be backed up by ground, naval, amphibious, non-nuclear, conventional, and guerrilla forces. Containment's great success, Korea, was compromised by liberal Democrats, Utopians in Truman's inner circle, and Conservative Utopians outside the administration.

Korea, in many ways more than World War II, was the true

test of the American fighting man, and a superior soldier he turned out to be. In World War II we generally had too high a superiority in manpower and materiel to bring out his true fighting qualities. During Korea the forces were more nearly balanced, as is the nature of limited war, and the Traditionalists had a field day.

During this limited war the cherished doctrines of the Utopians were decimated one by one. Strategic air warfare was not decisive. A series of Chinese victories proved that a modern army can fight without air cover. Tactical air, Marine and Navy variety, was the most effective type of close air support. The bitterly contested fruits of the B–36-versus-carrier struggle of 1949–1950 seemed to turn to ashes before the very eyes of the air-atomic supremacists as the Chinese Communists rewrote the book of modern war.

And worst of all from the Utopian viewpoint, the atom bomb was not used; in fact, all sorts of limitations were placed on airpower. These shackles, however, gave the Utopians an alibi with which they managed to take captive a Conservative Traditionalist — President Eisenhower. China blindness, the ever-present desire to cut billions from the budget, personal power motives, and extravagant election promises — "Let Asians fight Asians," "liberation," "rollback," "unleashing Chiang" — all conspired to promote the new look and massive retaliation. The Military Utopians were overjoyed, for at long last airpower had an Administration that seemed to understand it.

2

1953—The Genesis of the New Look

T HE REPUBLICANS WON THE ELECTION OF 1952, IN WHICH four of the major issues were Communism, Corruption, Korea, and China. Eisenhower went to Korea, and on the way home aboard the cruiser *Helena* bumped into Admiral Arthur Radford at Iwo Jima. Eight months later Radford became chairman of a new and slightly different Joint Chiefs of Staff. The power and influence of the chairman had been inflated — over the opposition of both Traditionalists and Utopians — by Reorganization Plan No. 6, which increased his responsibility over the work and personnel of the Joint Staff.

Why Radford, the brilliant Navy partisan and bitter foe of the B–36, became chairman of the Joint Chiefs of Staff is explained in Robert Donovan's book, *Eisenhower: The Inside Story:*

> Eisenhower felt that the new chairman should be an officer who was in sympathy with the notion of a broadened strategy in Asia, which Radford surely was. . . . the Republicans had been charging for years that the Roosevelt and Truman administrations had concentrated too much on Europe and too little on Asia, and Eisenhower was looking for a chairman of the J. C. S. whose record would indicate an urgent interest in the Far East.

The first year of the Eisenhower Administration was one of transition for East and West. Stalin died in March, and his heirs turned a more friendly face toward the capitalist world; peaceful coexistence became the party line. One immediate result of the thaw was the abortive June revolt of the East Germans. Despite brave words about "rolling back the Iron Curtain," a dynamic new alternative to containment, the new Administration failed to react. Admittedly the risks of intervention were great, but our relative nuclear striking power was probably never greater. However, Utopians have traditionally regarded Asia, not Europe, as the testing ground, the litmus paper, of any successful policy.

In the settlement of the Korean War, Secretary of State John Foster Dulles thought he had proof that the bold new policy his Administration was to unveil would work. First, Chiang Kai-shek was "unleashed" to harry Red China's southern flank and, secondly,

the Administration decided that if its efforts to gain an armistice failed, it would bomb Chinese bases and supply sources in Manchuria and China, blockade the mainland coast, and possibly use tactical atomic weapons "to provide a tremendous beef-up in the United Nations punch." Dulles conveyed this decision to Prime Minister Nehru of India in late May, 1953, on the assumption that Nehru would pass the message on to the Chinese Communists.[1]

Dulles never claimed publicly that these new actions forced the Communists to agree to the truce, "but he believed it to be the plausible conclusion."[2] Seen in the light of 1953, the Korean Truce was a laboratory to carry out the unborn policy of massive retaliation, or at least the tactical nuclear aspect of that strategy.

One fact, from a man who had an excellent pipeline into the Eisenhower Administration, seems to give irrefutable proof that the Eisenhower Administration believed it was the threat to use "the bomb" that brought about the truce. Sherman Adams thought so and said so in his book, *First Hand Report: The Story of the Eisenhower Administration.* Air Force Reserve Colonel C. J. V. Murphy, General Vandenberg's former speech-writer and an early publicist of the Eisenhower military-political policy, claimed a squadron of F–84G jets was sent to Japan armed with tactical atomic weapons to carry out Dulles's threat. Thus it seems that Dulles had placed the weapons five thousand miles nearer the front in case he decided to recommend their use. This action could be referred to as tacit massive retaliation.

But by the spring of 1954 the doctrine was already passé. Three months after its announcement it still had not been invoked to save Dien Bien Phu. Indeed, Dulles soon stopped mentioning it, but his enthusiastic supporters among Military and Conservative Utopians continued to mouth it as the greatest statement of policy since George Washington's Farewell Address.

Drummond and Coblentz in *Duel at the Brink: John Foster Dulles' Command of American Power* noted that

amazingly, he is known to have been completely taken aback by the flood of letters he received from the American clergy — men with whom, as a leading lay churchman, he had long worked closely — bitterly upbraiding him for his announcement of a policy of "massive retaliation." He was shocked that they construed his formula as immoral. He never anticipated it. He couldn't understand it. At the time he remarked . . . "But I never threatened 'massive retaliation.' I only said we must have 'the capacity for massive retaliation.'"

Dulles, the Liberal Utopian at his finest, was a lineal descendant of Woodrow Wilson, but Dulles was armed with SAC and the H-bomb to make the world "safe for Democracy" and for Godfearing men everywhere. Massive retaliation started its long downhill slide to oblivion the day it was announced. Ironically, the first Russian H-bomb, and a "droppable super" at that, was disclosed at the same time Admiral Radford assumed command of the Joint Chiefs of Staff. The moment the Russians gave proof of their thermonuclear delivery capabilities (first, by jet bomber at the very time Dien Bien Phu went under for the last time, and, second, in October 1957 by a powerful missile booster) Dulles's policy of building a containment wall against Soviet and Red Chinese expansion, backed by the military force of the Strategic Air Command, was doomed to failure. This failure explains the deep frustration of Dulles's last years as he toured vainly about the Free World attempting to stop the leaks in the dikes he had built against Communism.

In 1953 liberation, total war, and preventive war were all part of the Utopian viewpoint, for Dulles had committed himself and his party to rollback or liberation.

Some of the more extreme Utopians of 1953 appeared to be preparing for a nuclear showdown. Typical of this group was Colonel Kieffer, an active-duty Air Force reservist with the Chief of Staff in the Pentagon. He wrote one of the most amazing, violent, fire-eating, and bloodthirsty books of the decade, *Strategy for Survival*. It had the tone of a fundamentalist Baptist preacher, the hatred of an Eastern European expatriate, and the violence of a modern Douhet. For example:

Through us must run the blood of a democracy, and by our efforts this democracy must be preserved. This thought must be transmitted to all who believe in democracy, and on it we must base our plans for the coming conflict with Russia.

Neutralism is not quite appeasement; it is in some respects even worse. . . . We do not desire him to disarm, to do our will, or to be destroyed; we merely insist that when the war is finished, he no longer continue to exist in the same political and cultural state he enjoyed prior to the war . . . it probably would be better for all of us if we were to shoot summarily the Red leaders where we find them rather than go through the fiction of any kind of trial. . . . In short, democracy may be best served by immediate elimination of the Communist leaders rather than by a long drawn-out legal farce. . . . [We must plan for our victory] in the interest of the welfare of future generations and the whole people. . . . However, time is swiftly running out, and every day lessens our chances of delaying war beyond a few months from the original Soviet target date. . . . Now is the time, perhaps too late but nevertheless not hopeless, to stop her if we wish to survive. . . . To win we must be superior to Russia in every aspect of air warfare. . . . When will the inevitable war with the Soviet Union begin? . . . It started 5 years ago [1948] but few recognized it. . . . Sooner or later, strong men will arise among us, men who have the courage to say *no*. [Then] the Communist march to easy victory will cease. . . .

She cannot stand up under shooting-war tactics launched against her by the Democracies. Therefore, our chance of survival depends upon the very thing we fear — the shooting war.

What the exact relationship was between Colonel Kieffer's thinking and the official Air Force command is open to conjecture. However, two years later Brigadier General Dale Smith wrote a book on American military doctrine from the high vantage point of the Operations Coordinating Board, a part of the National Security Council. General Smith clearly reflected Air Staff enthusiasm for the doctrine of massive retaliation, and his book on United States military doctrine had a great similarity to Kieffer's work. Both had unlimited faith in the ability of the United States as an atomic power to force its will on the Soviets.

On the eve of the new look and massive retaliation, *Air University Quarterly Review,* the official publication of the Air War College at Maxwell Field and the source of Air Force doctrine, published in the winter issue, 1953–1954, an article by Brigadier General Bonner Fellers. He mourned the fact that United Nations ground forces in Korea were never permitted to seek a decision that could easily have been achieved if "higher authority" had been willing to press its terrific air advantage. Playing the casualty "numbers racket," the general claimed that the Air Force in the previous two years had lost 801 aircraft and 1262 airmen killed, wounded and missing, while ground forces had lost 138,551! Therefore, it was obvious that air action was far less costly "in blood and treasure than was ground action." Switch to airpower, and "great reduction in the size, composition, and cost of our surface land and sea force" would be possible.

How can such thinking be explained? Walter Millis, in a lecture at the Naval War College in the spring of 1953, compared the Air Force plan for beating Russia through strategic airpower to the Prussian land warfare theory that to win one must employ overwhelming force in the first moments of the war, sacrificing every political, or even moral, consideration to the military necessity for doing so. Millis reflected:

This seems to me now to possess not only the virtues, but also the fearful defects of the Prussian model. Perhaps this is a prescription to win the Third Global War, if it comes; but it is certainly to my mind a prescription to make impossible anything less than a Third Global War, a probably frightful total devastation with quite unpredictable final effects.

If Air Force doctrines — as they have been expounded to the public, at any rate, in recent years — had actually ruled from 1945 to 1950, we could never have met and held the enemy in the limited operation in Korea. We would have been obliged either to abandon that peninsula and go to work on Moscow with nuclear weapons, or else to abandon the peninsula, period, probably finding ourselves a few years later not only going to work on Moscow with nuclear weapons, but Moscow going to work on us.

Captain George H. Miller pursued a parallel line in his essay, "Shall We Blow Them Up?" In the *United States Naval Institute Proceedings* for February 1953, a caption asked: "Is time on the side of the Communists, or can we afford protracted negotiation as well as they can?" Miller thought we could, for talk does not kill and the idea of human liberty is in the long run irresistible. Some impatient Americans after twenty months of Korean negotiations said, "Why don't we get the war settled? If they won't agree with us, let's send enough force over there to deliver a knockout blow!" "Whom shall we knock out?" Captain Miller wondered. "Are we willing to risk expanding the war, even to the point of a worldwide conflict[,] in order to deliver our 'knockout blow?' Is an expanded war with its increased casualties, its huge cost, and its attendant uncertainty a satisfactory sop to our impatience?" We are, he reminded, "an impatient people. . . . Impatience is an expensive luxury."

Captain Miller was worried about "what kind of military strength will be required to meet our worldwide commitments over a long period of years?" Dulles's and Radford's answer was the old Utopian solution, air-atomic power with a minor stress on mobile conventional forces. Captain Miller's answer was just the opposite: A military establishment geared to fight a war within the next year or two will not be too effective in 1970.

A political aggressor, who is aware of any date toward which our military buildup is oriented, need only wait a few years longer before attacking to insure that our costly stockpile of weapons is obsolete.

Captain Miller saw the danger of creating provocative deterrent forces in 1953, and he pleaded that we should look at our own military forces to determine: "Would it serve to deter or provoke us?" He warned that it must be clear to others that we have no intention of attacking them, and a rigid re-examination of our external policies must be continued toward that end.

If our readiness and willingness to use military strength in limited situations remains clear to them, a direct military clash between the United States and Russia may be avoided. . . . Destruction solves nothing in the struggle for human liberty. For in the process of destroying others, we also destroy part of ourselves.

Although the new Secretary of Defense, Charles Wilson, could not be considered a complete Traditionalist, he was never a single-weapon, single-strategy man. His first reaction to defense problems was to have a smaller version of Truman's balanced forces. In fact, there was initially a Wilson–Air Force battle over the number of Air Force wings Wilson would allow. Then, on August 3, 1953, shortly after the "new chiefs" took office, Wilson joined the Utopians in favor of the new look. This seemed to be occasioned by the Russian H-bomb and Eisenhower's decision to adopt the new look as the only way the budget could be balanced.

In 1953 it was a brave officer who spoke out against the impending, almost total reliance on one form or another of nuclear weaponry. Admiral Carney, Chief of Naval Operations, was almost apologetic in a speech launching the U.S.S. *McCain* at Boston on October 12: "If we retain some of the older types of weapons and techniques in our locker it is neither because we are resisting progress nor because we have been denied the funds for modern weapons to put in the arsenal. . . . There is no use shooting quail with the artillery."

Walter Millis was convinced that tactical nuclear weapons and a cutback in conventional weapons were "illusory" concepts. "The idea that tactical atomic artillery [or air squadrons] can replace ground divisions is unsupported by any practical experience; and the whole subject of the effect of atomic weapons used tactically on a ground battlefield is still so inadequately explored and so full of unknowns as to offer no good basis as yet for policy. The idea that America might soon retire from the front lines, removing her troops and leaving in their place only a pledge to bring up reinforcements when needed . . . is again quite unreal."

General Ridgway in a speech at Cleveland on November 10, 1953, stressed a related theme the Army would reiterate time and time again: "There is still one absolute weapon — the employment of which dominates every consideration of national security — the only weapon capable of operating with complete effectiveness — of dominating every inch of terrain where human beings live and fight, and of doing it under all conditions of light and darkness, heat and cold, desert and forest, mountain and plain. The weapon is man himself."

But Bonner Fellers argued: ". . . if the United States limits its action principally to air war, American combat casualties would be relatively light."

Korea was advanced as a perfect example. The Air Force, which killed so many hundreds of thousands of Communists, suffered only 1364 casualties or one per cent of the total, illustrating that if the most modern weapons were placed in the hands of our fighting forces, American lives could be saved while enemy losses mounted.

How would we win? The Utopians' way — new gadgets. "Most fortunately we have developed new weapons which have again returned the advantage in striking potential to the United States. These new weapons are the hydrogen bomb and the new B–52 bomber. So far as is known, Russia has no weapons comparable to those two new ones which we possess."[3]

Thus we have the Utopian strategy in embryo. Its real origins are in the Finletter Report of 1948, the B–36 hearings of 1949, and before that, in De Seversky's book, *Victory Through Air Power*. The central thesis was deceptively simple: (1) Churchill and others have said the greatest deterrent to war is the A-bomb in American hands, for it had saved Europe from the Slav. (2) United States scientific and manufacturing genius has produced two magnificent new weapons — the jet bomber and the H-bomb — and only they can save the Free World from the billion Chinese and Russian Communists. (3) The Communists have massive amounts of manpower; we have a massive technological lead. (4) Therefore, the military strategic course is simple. Adopt the new weapons, throw out the old, draw a line and say to the Communists, "You cross that and we'll vaporize you all" — then hope they cross that line so you can use these marvelous new gadgets on the new barbarians from the Eurasian steppes.

This may sound fantastic, but in the light of history the policy of massive retaliation, which adopted these assumptions, *was* fantastic. It was based on technology in an era of the most rapid technological change the world has ever known. It was based on the assumption that a single set of Communist tactics (North Koreans crossing the thirty-eighth parallel) would remain the future pattern of Red aggression. It was a single-weapon approach, completely fitting for a political administration that was largely single-interest. It was a simple solution in a period of highly complex international events, such as the rising nationalism of underdeveloped nations. It was the overt articulation of an underlying technological premise, which, while perhaps valid at one time, had been bypassed by Russian technology.

The Red Army temporarily and effectively neutralized the American nuclear monopoly and gave Russian science the time to develop its own nuclear delivery systems. International Communism used this time to vary its tactics from overt aggression to indirect aggression. The dominant United States answer was like a power play in football: sheer power over right tackle. When the game called for more deception plays, we answered with more of the same: bigger bombers and bigger bombs.

The Military Utopians and their Liberal and Conservative supporters have consistently attempted to downgrade the Korean War experience — each for their own reasons: Military Utopians because it confounded so many of their pet airpower theories, Conservative Utopians because of the "halfway measures adopted," and Liberal Utopians because they wanted to forget the entire campaign that had such tragic political overtones.

Air University Quarterly Review, Winter 1953–1954, in discussing the public view of the Air Force, said that in Korea "of course the outbreak of aggression could have been halted in its original tracks by air forces with atomic war-heads, but that would have reversed the military thesis [balanced forces] that had been adopted."

It seems probable that the strategic overtones of the new look had British origins and were publicized in this country by *Fortune* magazine for its own purpose of creating a more dynamic American foreign policy. It can further be contended that the Military Utopians utilized the Luce press as long as it furthered their interests and vice versa. This mutuality of interests was very apparent in the similarity between the treatment Utopian publications, like the *Air University Quarterly Review* and *Air Force,* gave to the recently concluded Korean War and the closely parallel "No More Koreas" position that the Luce publications took in late 1952 and continued throughout the decade. The result has been an extended triangular love affair between Military Utopians, Republican proponents of "beyond containment," and the Luce press. The self-interests of all three groups were fused in a common desire to revise basic American military thinking and foreign policy into a "Greater America Policy." This coalition lasted from January 1953 to January 1961, and while effective, it had enormous influence on such political-military concepts as the new look, massive retaliation, clean H-bombs, centralization of the Defense Department, "liberation," the B–52, B–58, and B–70, Strategic Air Command, Curtis LeMay buildup, the smearing of Oppenheimer, brinksmanship, deification of John Foster Dulles, Lewis Strauss, and Edward Teller and, as always, the touchstone of orthodoxy and patriotism — China Policy.

A curious thing is that after eight years of incessant hammering on these themes the nation could move, even slightly, out of the web that Henry Luce had spun. The real disservice done to American political-military policy was that such reiteration of a technologically oriented strategy made any modification of strategy exceedingly difficult and seem almost akin to appeasement.

The first of a series of *Fortune* articles (January 1953), which would in time become apologias for the Eisenhower strategy, appeared in the first months of the new Administration. C. J. V. Murphy became the key link among the three groups of a coalition attempting to saddle the nation with the Utopian strategy. According to Murphy, Churchill in the spring of 1952 "faced up to one of his greatest decisions in a decision-ridden career." A financial crisis in Britain necessitated a cutback in defense. Churchill wondered if there were not "a better way of coping with the Soviet threat — a cheaper and at least equally effective alternative to the prevailing policy of piling up in the West the entire catalogue of military armaments?"

Then Churchill, so the story goes, remembered his "highly privileged briefing" by the Strategic Air Command at the Pentagon in January 1952, and recalled that "the potentialities of this form of warfare, based on atomic weapons, had not figured heavily in NATO calculations." Churchill was so impressed with the Strategic Air Command briefing that he went straight home, convinced "that the West possessed, in the combination of atomic weapons and air power, a military resource that as long as it was steadily developed and perfected, assured the Atlantic coalition the balance of military power in the critical years ahead." And so it came to pass that Sir John Slessor for Air (who later recanted); Sir William Slim for Army, and Sir Rhoderick R. McGrigor for Sea worked out the central thesis of the new strategy — a pure amalgam of Douhet, Mitchell, and Trenchard.

According to Murphy, the three British chiefs concluded that "the advent of atomic weapons plus air power has already revolutionized the character of modern war; that the American superiority in these and other related weapons, if prudently bulwarked and extended, assures the West the upper hand in any general war that might come in the next few years." To carry this out the West would have to revise "the traditional emphasis" on "large aggregations of ground forces." Murphy then described the supposed British view in terms of American military strategy. Murphy's three basic assumptions reduced to their essentials were: (1) Any future major war will consist of an initial, and probably decisive, massive nuclear exchange. The United States is far ahead in the capability of delivering such an attack. (2) Since we have the atomic advantage, we should limit our "ready forces" to those "required to cope with and survive the initial crucial blows," which we can do because of our capacity for "instant retaliation." (3) If we are going to carry out this strategy, we shall need a "high degree of selectivity" in the long-range development of weapons systems. These are so expensive that if we do not want to bankrupt ourselves, we must reshape "military forces around weapons systems to further only the most essential national tasks; and the allocation of resources and practices accordingly."

Thus we see that future wars will be total nuclear wars in which the most efficient delivery will spell the difference between defeat and victory. To make sure that we keep up our "efficiency of delivery" so that we can win total nuclear war, we will need constantly to develop better bombers and more powerful bombs. This is the number one priority, and all traditional forces, ideas, and institutions must be sacrificed to this ever-pressing goal.

Eisenhower, pledged to cut defense costs by twenty billion dollars, needed a major economy that only air-atomic power could offer. "If really big savings are to be achieved, they will come about only through the exercise of a ruthless selectivity in future development of military forces." What we needed, according to Murphy, was a careful reappraisal concerning the full scope of United States strategy and force levels "in light not of service traditions but of the specific tasks imposed by the cold war. It is about time."

The unfortunate thing for the Eisenhower Administration and the West was that either Murphy was advocating a strategy designed for the most unlikely type of future contingency, a Russian first strike on the United States homeland, or he was advocating the creation of a first strike force to utilize the United States "atomic advantage" in a pre-emptive strike against the U.S.S.R. Perhaps he and other Utopians felt that even if the Soviets were provoked to attack, our professional elite force would "win" the exchange, providing we excelled in the arms race that this implied. Murphy conceded the need for conventional forces to handle "Korea-type peripheral actions . . . until our atomic advantage has developed to a point where it may be judged in our general interest, with the concurrence of our allies, to use its leverage for a diplomatic showdown with the U.S.S.R. This did not mean using the bomb; it means using its power for bargaining."

The H-bomb used as a substitute for ground forces is "a far more potent weapon against troop concentrations than the present atomic bomb," but Traditionalists and some scientists stood in the way of such an ambitious undertaking. They would obviously have to be taken care of. The Army-McCarthy battle and the Oppenheimer hearings were two examples of the attempt to silence dissenting views over strategy and the use of nuclear weapons. The Navy had been effectively humbled in the B-36 hearings of 1949; the Army and scientific community would be taken care of in 1954. Too bizarre? Let us continue to look at the record.

The first public assault on the mind and strategy of J. Robert Oppenheimer appeared in an unsigned article written by *Fortune*'s defense correspondent, obviously C. J. V. Murphy.

He had hinted at the coming persecution in the January 1953 issue of *Fortune:*

There is also a powerful move, supported by many influential scientists and tacitly approved by Mr. Truman, to create, as a quasi-independent enterprise, on the Manhattan Project model, a continental air defense system. [It would cost 25 billion dollars over a five-year period and there is a question if it is really necessary. The only thing it would accomplish would be to] fasten a superstructure of atomic strategy on top of a traditional land-sea strategy based primarily upon conventional weapons.

Oppenheimer had been one of those "influential scientists" associated with Project Charles, which had led to the Lincoln Air Defense Laboratory at Bedford, Massachusetts. He believed in a number of things that Utopians at this time did not: (1) He opposed the initial use of the H-bomb and wished to refrain from mass area bombing, (2) saw the necessity for expanded air defense, and (3) advocated the tactical use of atomic weapons delivered by diversified means including aircraft carriers.

Murphy, in "The Hidden Struggle for the H-bomb" (*Fortune,* May 1953), told the story of Dr. Oppenheimer's alleged persistent campaign to reverse United States military strategy. Murphy began the campaign (which *Time* correspondents Shepley and Blair would complete in their book eulogizing Dr. Teller and the H-bomb) with:

But the most serious aspect of the struggle has so far escaped public attention: whether a strategy shaped around the "retaliatory-deterrent" principle embodied in the Strategic Air Command shall be discarded, or at least dramatically modified, in favor of a defensive strategy wherein the U.S. atomic advantage would be confined to short-range tactical forces designed to engage other military forces in the field.

Murphy accused Dr. Oppenheimer of being the "prime mover" in this attempt to downgrade SAC:

. . . he and his followers have no confidence in the military's assumption that SAC as a weapon of mass destruction is a real deterrent to Soviet action. On the contrary, they believe that, by

generating fear in the Kremlin, it has been a goad to Soviet development of counter-atomic weapons. They argue that it has aroused
misgivings in Western Europe; and that a renunciation of atomic-
offensive power by both major adversaries is essential to an ease-
ment of world tension.

Murphy also claimed that Oppenheimer violated the Project
Vista Charter, which in early 1951 limited the original Air
Force study to new weapons for ground warfare and defense of
western Europe. By the summer of 1951 the Air Force was
conscious of a change in atmosphere. They blamed this lack
of enthusiasm on Oppenheimer because the Vista group had
been conferring with him, and he had even written a crucial
introductory chapter to the report. There was an Air Force
"explosion" because Oppenheimer "had transformed Vista into
an exercise for rewriting U.S. strategy," an exercise introduced
by veiled suggestion that Air Force doctrine was based on the
slaughter of civilians.

As if this were not bad enough, Oppenheimer thought tactical
atomic air forces and relatively small ground forces could hold
western Europe against the Red Army without SAC! This really
meant that part of the atomic stockpile would have to be divided
up: one-third to the ground battle, one-third to air defense, and
the remainder to SAC. Further, Oppenheimer believed that if
war should come to western Europe, the United States should
try to keep it limited by announcing "it would withhold SAC
from action."

Recall that when Murphy wrote this article, the Strategic Air
Command and Air Force were being squeezed by the first
Eisenhower defense budget. If there were an across-the-board
cut and at the same time a demand for tactical air for Europe,
SAC would suffer. Splitting up the atomic stockpile was not
appreciated by SAC, since it felt it had proprietary rights over
it. Indeed, in 1948–1949 SAC had savagely fought the Navy to
prevent it from breaking into its monopoly. The H-bomb was
just around the corner and to have bomber delivery aircraft cut
back at this time would be dangerous, especially when the H-

bomb was the *ultimate* weapon. With this new weapon true strategic bombing was possible on the battlefield, on the cities, or on the airfields.

Furthermore, the new chairman of the Joint Chiefs of Staff, Admiral Radford, was not quite unknown to the Air Force, for he had spearheaded the brilliant Navy counterattack against the B–36 and strategic air warfare in 1949. And to make matters worse, in a time of defense cutback Oppenheimer and fellow eggheads wanted to spend billions on air defense, making the defense pie that much smaller. All these factors and more must have been behind the desire and design to ruin Oppenheimer.

On November 17, 1953, William Liscum Borden, ex–B–24 pilot, amateur military strategist (*There Will Be No Time*), and inner circle member of the Atomic Energy Commission, acquired access to the Oppenheimer security file and arrived at the conclusion, which was relayed to Eisenhower, that Oppenheimer was "more probably than not . . . an agent of the Soviet Union."[4] This was an effective way to silence strategic dissent at the crucial time of the unveiling of a new and radical strategic doctrine. The argument sketched here was the perennial struggle in military strategy between the Traditionalist and the Utopian: a conflict over the nature of the deterrence concept. *What were the deterrent limitations of the H-device exploded in November 1952? What were the possible military applications of this new bomb? How would it change the world balance of power?*

Here was unlimited destructive power that *must* have some practical military uses. If one bomb had the power of a million tons of TNT, the Utopians argued, then traditional doctrine and old-fashioned wars were obviously a thing of the past. Korea could be forgotten as an anachronism. The future belonged to the nation that best utilized these new weapons and first promulgated a national strategy taking these new weapons into consideration. We could actively enforce our will, backed by the H-bomb and superior delivery capability.

The new Administration appeared sympathetic. The Military Utopians were on the brink of their finest hour. All that was

needed was "professional competence and national determination" to develop an air weapon that had the capability to destroy
"the economic and social fabric of a nation" and to accomplish
it at "relatively reasonable and sustainable cost." Or as one air
colonel enthusiastically put it: "We now refer to 20 KT bombs
as the hand grenades of the A-bomb family. From this sort of
comparison it should be obvious that in any effort to destroy a
nation's war-making capacity through air attack, or to destroy
military installations or concentrations of military forces, the
A-bomb represents the most revolutionary advance in offensive
capabilities of all times." Therefore, to seize upon World War II
successes and failures "is not only inadequate but dangerous."[5]

The Russian H-bomb explosion occurred about the same
time Arthur Radford took charge of the Joint Chiefs of Staff.
Then in mid-August 1953 the Air Force confirmed the production of a Russian turboprop B–36 type long-range strategic
bomber. Secretary Harold E. Talbott told an Air Force Association convention in Washington that the Air Force "is virtually
certain they are in production."

Aviation Week claimed the H-bomb meant the "renewal of
USAF monopoly of the means for delivering" these weapons. "It
is doubtful that H-bombs can ever be reduced to a size that a
carrier plane could deliver, because the H-bomb contains an
atomic bomb as its trigger mechanism."

In September 1953 Robert Hotz wrote in *Aviation Week:*

It is apparent that the U.S. and Russian strategic air commands are
now the opposing queens on the international military chessboard.

All the other pieces on the board will be devoted to protecting
them from the enemy or to clearing the way for the full use of
their power against the foe. Both will be the top-priority targets in
any future war.

Neither opponent can afford to attack the other while the retaliatory power of the other's hydrogen and atomic fleet remains in
existence.

On October 3, 1953, Hotz reported that the Air Force had
ordered an "H-bomb fleet." Air Force Secretary Talbott indi-

cated that the decision had been made to build the "large fleet of hydrogen-bomb carrying Boeing B–52 stratofort jet bombers" and that the production would involve a "maximum production effort." The next week *Aviation Week* reported that "LeMay is strongly interested in development of an intercontinental jet bomber that can do the job of atomic bomb delivery without aerial refueling." Evidently the Military Utopians recalled the old truism that Congress was never happier or more generous with appropriation dollars for the Air Force than when they were voting money for a United States–based intercontinental bomber. Bonner Fellers agreed: "For the most part, our air strength should be kept in the heart of America — in Omaha and the Dakotas and Oklahoma and Texas — where it belongs."[6]

Before Radford could announce the new look, a nasty national struggle took place. In the early part of the Administration it was General Vandenberg versus Defense Secretary Wilson, when Wilson came up for an across-the-board cut, which Humphrey, Dodge, and Kyes rejected because it would not save enough money. As a result of this impasse, a basic strategy shift was originated in the famous Operation Solarium paper, which was groomed to replace NSC 68, a key political-military guidelines paper of the late 1940's, as the controlling document through 1957 at least. There is evidence to indicate that the basic decision was taken by the National Security Council (or an influential part of it) to convert the entire military strategy in gradual stages to atomic weapons. In a few years it was hoped to have a completely equipped nuclear defense force. Of the new chiefs only Ridgway seemed violently opposed, although there is some evidence that Admiral Carney fought the strategy as well. What is not always understood is that Dulles's massive retaliation was planned to be a complete atomic strategy from H-bomb to tactical nuclear weapons, to handle any range of provocation or aggression — no more Koreas, no more relying on conventional forces to stop aggression, just use the "nukes."

C. J. V. Murphy, attempting to "make history" in *Fortune,*

July 1953, discussed Eisenhower's views on United States weaponry:

> Military men who have worked with the President have this impres-
> sion: [The Soviet Union could not challenge the U.S. for five years.]
> This judgment rests, in large measure, upon U.S. superiority in
> atomic weapons, now being compounded by the thermonuclear
> weapons. . . . Because of this ace in the hole, he believes that
> the Truman military program can be safely scaled down, over the
> next two years, while the new Joint Chiefs of Staff under Admiral
> Radford re-examine the basic assumptions of U.S. strategy and
> redress national military forces in light of the new technology of
> weapons.
>   . . . It is interesting to note, too, that Churchill and Eisenhower,
> on assuming the direction of their respective governments, both
> arrived at the same decision in much the same political context;
> massive military programs inherited from predecessor administra-
> tions; increasing fiscal deficits; and a recognition that the force at
> present being produced at such strain only partially reflect the new
> technology.

One of the first uses of the words "new look" appeared in
Murphy's column, "Defense and Strategy," where he confided
to his readers that the new chiefs "have actually been engaged
for many weeks in the 'new look' at U.S. strategy and forces
provided by Defense Secretary Wilson." Murphy then related
that the new chiefs were deviating from their professional ethic
by considering the dollar cost of defense. Under these "different
ground rules" the Chiefs were "charged by presidential directive
with re-examining the defense establishment in all of its aspects
. . ." The Chiefs would be on their own "without benefit of
the usual staff" at a price tag of around 30 billion dollars. It was
a tough job, Murphy related, keeping "one eye on the Kremlin"
and the other on "Joe Dodge and . . . George Humphrey."

Murphy pushed home his main thesis that if the budget were
to be cut, then the new weapons made it impossible not to adopt
a new strategy. "A really 'new' look at the new weapons and
their effect on military economics is, of course, what the Air
Force has been urging for some time, and General Twining may

be expected to press that point of view." Only Ridgway was fighting the inevitable.

Humphrey, Kyes, Dodge — Conservative Utopians all — spoke out on the importance of discarding "outmoded" military doctrines and weapons. Keyes said, "We can no longer afford to prepare for every conceivable kind of war." Humphrey in the NSC "prodded his colleagues on the necessity of fitting forces to strategy and strategy to new weapons." Fortunately for the future of the United States (and the United States Air Force), Murphy said, economic pressure was forcing Radford and the Chiefs to agree. Radford held out for a gradual change rather than for a violent surrender of the "conventional" weapons system. The Admiral was reluctant to "grasp so soon the apple of discord."

"In recent weeks," Murphy went on to assure his readers, "there have been intimations that the NSC has under study a clear statement of this government's position on the employment of atomic weapons, in defense of its national interests and treaty obligations." Sounding much like Joseph Alsop, Murphy intoned, "It is about time the government had a position on this subject. Given the policies evolving in the highest councils of government, the continuing heavy investment in atomic weapons, it is difficult to believe that the Army or the Navy will be able to justify much longer their current claims upon nearly two-thirds of the U.S. military budget." The great question was: Would Wilson force a showdown with the JCS? Or would Eisenhower step out of his role of moderator? Maybe a new Finletter Commission was necessary to effect the shift because of Wilson's "inexperience in these recondite matters" and Radford's "long naval attachment." We needed men to think in "global terms" to devise a new strategy worthy of these new weapons. Murphy did not have long to wait.

Admiral Radford delivered three speeches in December 1953 spelling out the new look. The first one at West Point took the students on a global tour of the world's hot spots. He informed them that "war-by-satellite" technique can be frustrating, told

them about the "human sea tactics" of the Red Chinese and
their lavish use of manpower, and expressed hope about the
"forces of Freedom" winning in Indochina and stopping Communism there and everywhere.[7] That evening the Admiral talked
to the American Ordnance Association on the "FY 1955 Interim
Look." He took a "long look into the future in order to project
long-range military strategy and objectives, and provided guidance for technological advancement." We need forces to combat a "three-prong system of operations: politico-economic,
military, and psychological-propaganda." The program will be
evolutionary, but "new weapons lead of course, to new techniques of warfare." "The U.S. will maintain national air power"
superior to anyone. Yet other forces are needed. "Our security
. . . cannot be entrusted to an unbalanced . . . a unilateral or
a bilateral . . . concept of forces . . . The Armed Forces will
go through a process of evolution as a result of their own imagination and creative efforts; and counterrevolutions will undoubtedly be imposed on us by the inventiveness of others."

Then on December 14, 1953, at the National Press Club he
produced the new look. It was based, Radford told the reporters,
on Eisenhower's April speech calling for plans for the "long
pull" instead of a "year-of-crisis." By stressing airpower and
air defense, we would save manpower. There is always the threat
of atomic war, and "hot spots" will be with us for a long period.

"If we maintain a strong armed posture . . . a counteroffen-
sive capability along with mobile, combat forces in readiness,"
the Kremlin will be convinced that "neither a global nor a localized war will be to their advantage." Political, military, and economic factors have all entered in because we must keep our
national economy strong. The new look will last for ten to
twenty years. The admiral warned, ". . . we cannot be strong
everywhere simultaneously." Balanced force does not mean an
artificial even dollar split between the services, for today's emphasis is on modern airpower. It will continue to grow stronger
and be superior because it is composed of "national" airpower.
"Today, atomic weapons have virtually achieved conventional

status within our Armed Forces." They all can use them. Our Strategic Air Force and naval carriers are "without peer in this world." Our superiority in national airpower plus allies, and collective strength in other forces will enable us to "look to the future with confidence and resolution."

At last the new look had been spelled out and the rough outlines glimpsed of the new strategy that Dulles described so completely four weeks later.

An *Aviation Week* editorial for December 21, 1953, said: "It is considered significant that Radford and the Administration finally and definitely have thrown over this artificial and discredited stopgap of the Truman Administration [balanced forces], devised mainly to create harmony among Air, Navy, and Army, rather than to build up our national defense."

John Norris, military correspondent of the *Washington Post,* correctly appraised on December 31 that the new look "is based on the use of tactical atomic weapons against military targets if necessary to counter a serious but limited future aggression." It represented a basic change of policy because "heretofore, United States policy has contemplated employment of atomic weapons only in a third world war and in retaliation against an all-out enemy attack."

Norris went on:

Republican chiefs also believe they can convince Congress, the country and the free world that there is nothing "immoral" about the selective use of small nuclear weapons, aimed with reasonable precision on military targets. They will stress the distinction between such weapons and the strategic atomic bombing of cities.

However, there is bound to be some opposition to the strategy, if for no other reason than the reliance on such weapons might serve to encourage their use and the possibilities of backing into an all-out atomic war. It could, however, serve as a lever to bring about a real world settlement with the Communists.

3

1954—Massive Retaliation Full-Blown

RADFORD'S STATEMENTS PREPARED THE WAY FOR DULLES'S famous massive retaliation pronouncement of January 12, 1954. The new look, if carried to completion by 1956–1957, would create the type of military forces needed to implement massive retaliation. Radford and Dulles worked in tandem to overhaul the grand strategy of the United States. It might have been successful against a less resourceful enemy than world Communism. But Khrushchev, backed by Russian science and industry, soon nullified the basic premise of the deterrent doctrine: continuing United States air-atomic dominance.

The doctrine died symbolically at the news conference in which Dulles said we would not save northern Indochina because it really was not vital after all. Instead, we created the Southeast Asia Treaty Organization to prevent any further Red aggression in Asia. The actual death of massive retaliation was that split second when President Eisenhower overruled his vice president, the chairman of the Joint Chiefs of Staff, his Secretary of State, the Air Force Chief of Staff, and the Chief of Naval Operations in agreeing with General Ridgway and deciding not to intervene in the Indochinese war. Eisenhower, like Truman before him, had refused to introduce the tactical atomic bomb into Asian warfare again. Because there was not enough conventional force for jungle warfare, he did nothing.

Still, the great military debate in 1954 was over the policy of massive retaliation. The Utopians were in the saddle riding hard. The Atomic Energy Commission under the stern hand of Lewis Strauss offered no alternative strategy, even though Thomas E. Murray made a valiant attempt. The Army was intimidated by its fight with McCarthy. The Navy under Admiral Carney was cautious, trying to co-exist with Admiral Radford and to digest the atomic revolution and its new carriers. The Department of Defense had been stormed by the Utopians. State, of course, was not interested in formulating a strategy other than the Dulles doctrine. Only the White House had not been completely captured. And here was the fatal flaw, for on three different occasions within the first year after the birth of massive retaliation, President Eisenhower, a Conservative Traditionalist at heart, overruled the Utopians in his cabinet and executive branch. In the final analysis it was President Eisenhower who torpedoed massive retaliation: in Indochina in April, Quemoy in September, and at the Tachens in January 1955. He gave the coup de grâce to a deterrent strategy at its weakest point — its credibility. Once the credibility had been destroyed, it was exposed to the world as either a massive bluff or a massive luxury.

One thing will nullify a deterrent strategy faster than anything else: outward evidence of an unwillingness or a reluctance to carry out the threat inherent in the strategy. Deterrence is largely a psychological ploy residing in the minds of the protagonists. It is an ever-changing estimate of what one of the protagonists will or will not do in any given situation. If there had been the slightest doubt raised in the Communist mind by Dulles's atomic warnings on Korea in 1953, it was effectively nullified by the actions of the Eisenhower Administration in 1954–1955. Asian real estate *was* lost to the Communists despite the threat of massive retaliation. The Communists continued to flout our thermonuclear advantage in 1954 with much the same impunity they had enjoyed since World War II.

Perhaps because of this there were not a few hints that some members of the Eisenhower Administration during 1954 were thinking in terms of a preventive war or its newer version, preemptive war. The urgency for this alternative strategy was heightened by the technological breakthroughs of both major powers. The United States caught up with the Russians in the development of a dry, droppable H-bomb and continued in its production lead of B–47 jet bombers. The Russians at a May Day flyover unveiled before the world a long-range jet bomber, Bison, capable of delivering an H-bomb and a medium range jet bomber, Badger, capable of carrying nuclear explosives to B–47 bases surrounding the U.S.S.R. In effect, the Soviets had given clear warning that they had either nullified, or were about to nullify, American nuclear superiority.

As if in reflex reaction there appeared an outpouring of preventive war speculation: some of it very open, some couched in safe language. The pressures were immense. Eisenhower and Wilson continually admonished against "atomic bomb rattling" as if to quiet the world's fear that a local incident would be used as a pretext for a preventive atomic attack against the U.S.S.R. It was well known that "mere" loss of an aircraft was not sufficient in the thermonuclear age to cause a war. What was needed was a "moderate" border incident like the Japanese-Russian exchanges of 1936–1939; then SAC could be unleashed in all good conscience.

There were many who realized that once the United States monopoly in atomic striking power was lost, it was lost forever. Thus 1954 seemed like the last chance for a successful "knockout" blow against Soviet Russia. Gordon Dean opened the year with a veiled appeal for action in the *Bulletin of the Atomic Scientists* (January 1954): "We are faced with the ugly fact that within two years she will have the capability to virtually destroy us if she moves first. . . . Can we as a nation and can the now free world permit the Soviet to reach this position of power?" He wished the United Nations members knew and appreciated the power of the H-bomb, for if they did, "it might lead them to ask what I am asking today — whether the free world can tolerate such power in an aggressor nation."

Dean gave tacit approval to the new look and massive retaliation by agreeing that should another Korea happen, we "simply cannot resist with tanks and artillery and other orthodox weapons of war and thousands of American men. . . . Wars cannot be effectively fought by any country whose hands are tied behind its back and that aggression cannot be crushed without the employment of the most crushing weapons." He closed with an outspoken plea for preventive war: "Again I ask, can we as a nation and can the nations of the now free world permit the Soviet to reach the position where if it chooses it can completely annihilate this country? Time and the unwillingness of the free world to stop the clock combine to give her this power. This, very bluntly, is the great problem of 1953–1954. It is the more disturbing since the solution cannot be found simply in treaty or unilateral assurance."

In response, Hanson Baldwin continued his often lonely campaign against preventive war in the January 1954 issue of *Combat Forces Journal*. Baldwin's article was the first of a series of Army-sponsored attacks on the new look and massive retaliation that continued from 1954 to 1960. Baldwin noted that neither isolationism nor a world order by agreement is a viable alternative. He then asked, "What about the opposite extreme, world order by conquest — a preventive war? Hit Russia with our atomic stockpile before she becomes too strong and attacks us?" Such a war, according to the *New York Times* military analyst, was based on the fallacious assumption that war is inevitable and settles things with a quick and easy victory.

Thomas E. Murray of the Atomic Energy Commission also protested: "Perhaps the greatest strain on our physical and moral fiber will be to restrain a national impulse to try to get it over with, by resorting to that ultimate remedy of a spiritual bankruptcy of mankind — preventive atomic war."[1]

The prospect of preventive war was implicit in Dulles's doctrine of massive retaliation and the more enthusiastic Military

Utopians were quick to spell out their interpretation. One popularizer was Brigadier General Dale O. Smith, USAF, who at that time was assigned to the Operations Coordinating Board of the National Security Council. Since basic strategic decisions were made in the NSC during the fall of 1953, the presence and writings of General Smith are of more than academic interest. Although his book had the all-encompassing title, *U.S. Military Doctrine: A Study and Appraisal*, in reality it was an apologia for massive retaliation. The following excerpts are included in detail to show how massive retaliation favored a policy of the "initiative" and how very sympathetic to it the Military Utopians were:

A policy which permits America to play by its own rules in pursuit of its own national objectives provides positive and purposeful guidance at a time when such guidance is most needed by all citizens. . . .

If a housewife is bothered by flies in her kitchn . . . she has several courses of action. She may kill them one by one with a fly swatter — a time-consuming and limited action of no lasting benefit; the flies continue to swarm in the open doors and windows — or she may put up screens to contain the flies and attack them with an insecticide, thus conducting a limited war. But this limited war breaks out every time the screen door is opened. And the flies persistently find ways to penetrate the kitchen. Always hovering at the barrier of containment, the flies find small holes and openings to invade. With this strategy, there is really no peace. Now as a final solution . . . if the flies persist in invading, the housewife may have to do something about the stable behind the house. That is the source of the flies; that is where they breed, eat, and grow. This does not mean that the stable must in every case be blown to Kingdom Come with bombs. There are many other ways to keep flies from breeding there. . . .

Military necessity has tended to dictate the choice of weapons, and when their use becomes habitual, questions of weapon morality are forgotten. The course of wisdom would be to prepare to use atomic weapons to the limit, with lightning speed on the draw. We all pray for that day when war can be reduced in fury or eliminated. But until then we must be ready and poised to defend our country through the use of weapons which promise success. This is the course of a higher morality.

Thus the Utopian general created his case for seizing the initiative, whatever the pretext, and launching the first thermonuclear strike. Such homely analogies as "flies in the kitchen" and "fastest gun in the West," with their nostalgic overtones of a simpler America, masked the attempt to change our national policy into initiating an aggressive war.

One of the year's biggest preventive war scares was provoked by Admiral Carney on May 27 in a speech called "Today's Alternatives" before the National Security Industrial Association in New York. It came shortly after two events which, when joined, tended to favor preventive war: strategic necessity, represented by the defeat in Indochina, and fading military superiority, represented by the Russian fly-by of the long-range jet bomber. These two events seemed to lend an air of desperation to some United States military circles throughout 1954.

Vice President Nixon, in a famous off-the-record speech, had suggested the possibility of sending United States ground troops into Indochina. Eisenhower had spoken of the Domino Theory, and Dulles had fumed as Ho Chi Minh moved closer and closer to that isolated jungle fortress, Dien Bien Phu.

It was in this emotionally charged context that Admiral Carney warned that Indochina was at "flood tide" and we must fight "harder for what we believe." We stopped them in South Korea. If we didn't stop them in Indochina, all of Southeast Asia would be next. The Communists could move anywhere from their "centralized position."

In actuality, the problem is not one of coming up with a succession of minor strategies to cope with brush fires. The real and fundamental problem is to develop a strategy which is a true long-range counter to the centralized overall strategy which is directing the moves in the campaign for communist expansion.

Getting down to brass tacks, the simple alternatives are these: To do nothing, to rush around plugging the dike, or to take measures to lower the pressure against the dike.

Then he added that we were approaching a fork in the road. One road was smooth and ended in oblivion; the other was rough, but it "goes on and on." Communism had eight hundred million people and was "constantly expanding." He closed with the question, "Do we want to turn into the smooth dead end or take the rougher road that offers us a good destination if we can negotiate it?"[2] By negotiating the "rougher road," the Admiral was widely thought to be suggesting a preventive war.

Eisenhower reacted moderately and at a cabinet meeting on June 4, 1954, urged his administration in the future to be very careful of foreign policy material in speeches. He told the cabinet he had suggested to the Joint Chiefs that foreign policy speeches by men in uniform were undesirable.[3]

Admiral Carney's speech was also repudiated by the press, but more forcibly the *Washington Post* remarked:

In so many words the argument in favor of a preventive war is being developed from an increasing number of sources. Sometimes the argument is denied when the author is confronted with the plain meaning of what he says. This applied to Admiral Carney, who, it seems, complains privately that his speech of May 27 was misunderstood. . . .

The warmongers talk of destroying communism, not of setting up anything in its place; and their arguments are merely an unconscious recognition of the physical facts of warfare in the atomic age.

Those people who would risk all in a preventive war have one thing in common. This is lack of faith both in the institutions of liberty and in the evanescense of antiliberation regimes.

In the *Washington Post* on July 13, 1954, Marquis Childs commented, "Here at home he [Dulles] might cope with a number of conflicting views, including a widening conviction that a preventive war may be the only answer to the increasingly serious threat to America's security from communist imperialism."

Childs was referring to remarks such as those of General Thomas D. White, who, in the spring *Air University Quarterly Review,* raised the rhetorical question: How much more can we accomplish in the cause of peace if we are prepared to employ our new air forces under a policy of initiative?

A British officer, writing in the same *Review* that summer, was much more explicit:

We ought, I suggest, to use the next few years, before the Communists have a sufficient stock-pile of "H" bombs, to regain the diplomatic initiative. We cannot be satisfied with a status quo which leaves whole nations at the mercy of the Red army and the Secret Police. We must find means, short of war, of compelling the Communists to relinquish their hold on the countries that they now occupy, and force them to withdraw behind their own frontiers. . . .

And so, under the shadow of air power wielding weapons of terrible potency which, by God's grace, we shall never have to use, we may hope to face the enslaved peoples of the world, and keep the peace until the canker of Communism, as some day it surely will, has passed away. We should, therefore, I suggest, reject the spurious morality that shrinks from the acceptance of the master weapons that science has given us, and embrace the higher morality that bids us take advantage of their existence to abolish the new slavery, and exorcise from the world the evil ideology that threatens twentieth-century humanity.[4]

Preventive war was in the air that summer of 1954, and Marquis Childs, as always vigilant, became quite specific in isolating various preventive warriors. He stated that "certain Air Force generals, conspicuously Curtis LeMay, chief of SAC, have from time to time openly advocated a preventive strike that would destroy or at least permanently cripple Russia's war-making centers."

Dulles, according to Childs, held that no one can set himself up as God in launching an atomic war that can mean "the devastation of most of the works of man and the mass death of millions of human beings." But Childs revealed the existence of a National Security Council study, which probably explained the outburst of preventive war talk in the last half of 1954. This study claimed that "the ratio of military strength . . . is shifting in favor of [the Soviet Union.] This means, . . . that defense of the United States in an atomic war would be far more difficult two or three years from now. . . . If at one blow, the threat of America's destruction from an atomic attack would be removed, then that blow should be struck." This was the view of military men who considered it the "only realism in the light of the Communist peril."

Two weeks later a voice from the Orient cried out for a preventive war against Communist China. Syngman Rhee's plan was simple: use his and Chiang's troops, backed by the United States Navy and the United States Air Force. This would probably bring Soviet ground and air forces to the aid of China, "but that would be excellent for the free world, since it would justify the destruction of the Soviet centers of production by the American Air Force before the Soviet hydrogen bombs had been produced in quantity."

A fortnight after Dr. Rhee's gratuitous advice, which was fortunately rebuffed by a "wall of silence in Congress," Chen Cheng, vice president of Nationalist China, added a new wrinkle to the debate over whether or not to launch a preventive war. Mr. Cheng said, "A disastrous atomic war between the Western world and the Communist bloc could be avoided." The way to do it was through localized wars or "limited action," which might prevent the final arrival of an all-destructive atomic war. He was quite definite that the way out of our dilemma was to crush the Communist bloc of nations before they were strong enough to launch an atomic war.

Aviation Week (August 2, 1954) added another voice to the growing clamor, basing its reasoning on Russian progress in bombers, missiles, and nuclear weapons, "which have the Pentagon planners deeply concerned over the diminishing rate of U.S. superiority in these critical fields." As a result there was more and more serious talk of the advisability of a "preventive war" against the Communist bloc, aimed at crippling their atomic airpower striking force while the United States still enjoyed a significant advantage in quantity and quality of long-range bombing weapons. Proponents of the preventive war philosophy argued that if the United States allowed the Communist bloc to approach parity in atomic airpower, the results would be disastrous because "the Communists will have the advantage of striking the first and perhaps decisive blow."

Ex-Ambassador and Conservative Utopian W. C. Bullitt, a close friend of Chiang and Radford, pressed home the case for immediate preventive war in the *Washington Post* (August 10, 1954). America was "in mortal peril" because Russia was "constructing hydrogen bombs and intercontinental bombers as fast as it can in order to inflict on us a nation-wide H-bomb Pearl Harbor." Bullitt argued that America would be destroyed unless "we either destroy the production centers of the Soviet Union before they produce enough bombs and bombers to annihilate us, or swing the world balance of power strongly against the Soviet Union, so that when it possesses those weapons of annihilation, it will not dare to use them." Today's alternatives "are either to reply to the next Communist aggression by dropping our bombs on the Soviet Union or to await a Soviet H-bomb attack, knowing that we shall wait ourselves to death."

One suspects that if the truth is ever known about this period in our history, we will find that preventive war was under active consideration by the government. It was probably a limited preventive war against selected Chinese targets, but if the Russians moved in, this intervention could have been used as the pretext needed to strike Russia. Dulles had a study prepared to prove the extent of actual Chinese participation in the Indochinese war. If sufficiently detailed and blatant, it would have made direct United States intervention in Indochina to save Dien Bien Phu much easier. It would have justified attacks against South China to prevent supplies from moving southward and thus prevent a repetition of sanctuaries and limited war as in Korea.

The point is that Indochina was a perfect pretext to launch a much wider strangulation move around Red China. There is also evidence that Eisenhower overruled his State and military advisers in September 1954, when the Communist Chinese began shelling Quemoy and the "fire eaters" wanted to blast the gun emplacements on the mainland. Failure to act in either Dien Bien Phu or Quemoy was bound to reinforce the Chinese Communist image of America as a "paper tiger" and undo much of the lesson of Korea. Thus massive retaliation as a deterrent strategy withered on the jungle vines of Southeast Asia.

The drive for preventive war was greatly accelerated by Russian jet bombers and Russian development of the H-bomb. Many Utopians felt that all of these factors — growing strength of the hated Red Chinese, accelerating Communist technology, declining American prestige and sagging personal reputations — could be recouped by one massive thermonuclear first strike against the seedbeds of evil in Russia and China.

The mounting demands for preventive war finally forced President Eisenhower at an August 11 press conference to repudiate the idea categorically. The *New York Times* the next day interpreted President Eisenhower's remarks as reaffirmation of

our traditional policy which has outlawed war, except in self-defense and resistance to aggression. . . . But the President is right in constantly reiterating this policy, because the advocates of "preventive war," though small in number, have become so vocal as to put the United States in the wrong light before the eyes of the world. . . .

As President Eisenhower pointed out, a "preventive war" is unthinkable because, by whatever name it is called, it would still be war, and an atomic war to boot. It would mean that in fear of future dangers we would be courting suicide and the annihilation of our civilization — a policy not of wisdom but of desperation.

The *Washington Post* on August 13 likened the call for preventive war to "Swift's modest proposal" and hoped that the President would be able to still "the present hubbub . . . for a time."

The historian Richard Hofstadter, in a letter to the *New York Herald Tribune,* reminded his readers "that the policy of the United States is prevention of war not preventive war."

General Twining, at the Air Force Association convention in Omaha on August 20, 1954, backed Dulles's policy of massive retaliation and rejected *preventive* war and limited conventional warfare. His fellow delegates agreed with General Twining and said, "We cannot accept preventive war as a solution." Instead, they unanimously adopted *pre-emptive* war as their answer to the Soviet threat. Both preventive and pre-emptive wars envisage striking first in order to cash in on the great premium inherent in the first nuclear strike. The essential difference between the two concepts is one of time. For example, a preventive attack would be one launched by the United States against China in order to prevent Red China from becoming a mortal threat to our security at some *future* date. A pre-emptive attack, on the other hand, would be an American first strike against the Soviet Union (after Russia had acquired atomic weapons) that would anticipate a Russian aggressive blow against us. In other words, we would pre-empt the Russians by getting in the first or "forestalling" blow.

The reasoning behind the delegates' decision was a revealing insight into the mind of Military Utopians: (1) There was no evidence that coexistence was possible. (2) The "time of total danger" was fast approaching "when it is possible to destroy a nation's capacity and will to retaliate, or even resist further aggression, by a single, large-scale surprise attack." (3) Only our ability and willingness "to take decisive action during the present period might still resolve the issue between world freedom and world slavery without precipitating the catastrophe of all-out nuclear warfare." (4) Time was working against the Free World.

The Association then called for the United States to exploit our superiority in airpower and nuclear weapons "in our reaction to continued local aggression, sponsored, supplied, and directed by the Kremlin." We should act sensibly in Southeast Asia soon because "for a relatively brief period, the Soviets may be unprepared for all-out war, and the Free World can react decisively to aggression with small risk of precipitating an all-out conflict."

Our dilemma, the Association concluded in words similar to those of General Dale O. Smith, was much like that faced by the town marshal in the old West, who, confronted by men of evil ways, upheld law and order primarily through his ability to beat such men to the draw. Carrying this analogy into the H-Age, the Air Force Association fabricated a doctrine eventually known as pre-emptive war. "Since the Free World can reach for its gun only *after* the enemy has drawn his, we must be prepared to draw faster and shoot straighter, or be eliminated in the process."

John Foster Dulles finally committed himself in November of 1954. "Any idea of a preventive war is wholly out of the question as far as the United States is concerned," Dulles said. President Eisenhower had made it "unmistakably clear" that preventive war "would be abhorrent to him. . . . It is not in any sense part or parcel, even remotely, of United States foreign policy." Dulles added that he did not want to create the impression that "the way to favor in this or any other administration is to be an advocate of a preventive war against the Soviet Union. That I say, is not and, as far as I can forecast, never will be any part of the United States foreign policy."

In early December both Generals Ridgway and Gavin spoke out against preventive war. Ridgway maintained that the hope of world peace rested in diplomatic negotiation by our statesmen backed by military strength. He insisted that war was not inevitable and that such a belief was "inconsistent with our professed principles and dangerous to the cause of liberty." Addressing a Sigma Chi luncheon, Ridgway said preventive war "would hardly accord with our repeated declarations that our primary purpose is the preservation of an honorable peace, that our principles forbid deliberate recourse to aggressive war. History records some unpleasant examples of aggressive wars ending in ways the aggressor neither planned nor expected."

General Gavin, at the Sixth Annual Student Conference at the United States Military Academy, called for a flexible defense force, rejected preventive war, and stressed the danger of putting all our resources into a single weapons system.

But on December 2, 1954, in the *New York Times,* Hanson Baldwin pointed out that "many in the Air Force believe the price of survival means beating the enemy to the first atomic punch."

Klaus Knorr of Princeton University summed up the realistic argument against pre-emptive attack on the basis of United States and Russian capabilities by late 1954:

It is unimaginable, for obvious reasons, that the United States should plan to start an atomic preventive war. Nor would doing so make sense now that the Soviet Union may be able to retaliate instantly and in kind. Why should we want to initiate hostilities which are bound to lay waste to our cities and fatally cripple the economic capacity of this country? If this were a possible strategy, moreover, it would most likely be a possible strategy for the Kremlin as well, and to concede this is to shatter the doctrine of deterrence.

Knorr's observation was a vital one. The usual definition and distinction between the two varieties of aggressive war is one of timing. You wage a preventive war because at some future, relatively faroff date the enemy will be prepared by modern technology to destroy your land. Thus you take action to prevent this from ever happening. A devastating atomic attack by the United States on China today would be an example of such a war.

Pre-emptive war, on the other hand, is an anticipatory attack upon an enemy when you have irrefutable proof he is about to attack you. Since you "know" absolutely he is going to attack you at five in the morning, you hit him at four in order to deprive him of the first strike premium. This involves, of course, reading your opponent's mind through a highly developed intelligence system. It would, however, have to be a much more efficient and effective system than past American intelligence efforts. From Pearl Harbor to the Ardennes Forest to the Yalu, Suez, and Cuba, American intelligence has not been able to predict accurately major military events, and there is no evidence to suggest that future efforts will be any more successful. In fact, one must conclude that pre-emptive attack is a fraud, perpetrated by those who wish to mask and sanitize their real motives.

The year 1954 marked the midpoint in the postwar conflict over strategic doctrine. Utopian strategy had reached its acme after a nine-year struggle for recognition. As the Utopians surveyed the decimated and routed opponent from their peak in Washington, it must have seemed that they would be the custodians of the dominant strategy forever. Not only had the new Administration seemingly bought the Utopian strategy, but new technological breakthroughs, such as the lightweight H-bomb and the B–52 intercontinental bomber, were rapidly coming off the production line. A Korean-type war would never again becloud the issue, for the new Administration was pledged to prevent conventional limited wars. A new and positive foreign policy was in the wind, and it would be carried out by all varieties of nuclear weapons.

The downcast Traditionalists held on to their principles, continued their appeal to history, and waited. For a while it seemed as if the most important lessons of Korea were lost in the orgy of budget slashing and prevailing nuclear madness; but international events like Indochina and the Offshore Islands forced a sense of reality upon the Utopians, making them face up squarely to the use of conventional ground troops in Southeast Asia. The resulting decision rejected both nuclear and conventional intervention and adopted instead a policy of retrenchment lasting until 1961.

Moreover, Russian technological developments forced the Utopians to modify their strategy. The atomic submarine *Nautilus* and the carrier *Forrestal,* appearing at the beginning and end of 1954, were symbolic reminders that in these ships resided not a modification of the Utopian position but a completely new strategy.

Two of the key formulators of the alternative strategy during 1954 were the old Traditionalist standbys, Hanson Baldwin and Walter Millis. Professors Samuel Huntington and Dexter Perkins, Lieutenant Commander Samuel Stratton, Commander

Ralph E. Williams, Jr., and Lieutenant Carl Henn, Jr., also made important contributions to the developing doctrine.

Baldwin's article in the January 1954 issue of *Combat Forces Journal* represented the beginning of a long Army dialogue on the nature of war, massive retaliation, and the new look. Out of this discussion the doctrine of limited war slowly matured. Baldwin brilliantly restated his traditional principles, now doubly reinforced in his mind by the destructiveness of the new weapons:

It is one thing to recognize frankly the risk of war and another to regard it as inevitable. . . .

And if war should come, its objective should never be merely destructive; the objective should be construction through destruction. . . . It does not mean a world crusade against communism. . . .

I cannot emphasize too much the dangers of a great crusade with force of arms against communism everywhere. . . . It [global war] means victory but not complete destruction; it does not mean a Carthaginian peace — a peace of fire and sword, slaughter and complete devastation.

I find myself increasingly concerned by the ideological motivation of too many of our actions. McCarthyism and the fear of a Red under every bed have confused many of us; there are too few thinking clearly in the terms of realizable goals. Passion too often holds the reins. . . .

The atomic bomb does not solve political problems; promiscuous devastation is no substitute for a valid objective. . . . Moreover, the unlimited use of atomic and hydrogen weapons by the United States — to blast Moscow and Kiev off the map, for instance — would certainly lead to political frustration and might lead to military defeat. . . .

Can we in America insure our atomic security by atomic attack, or indeed by any technical military defense that we can devise? Is "victory" to be measured by unequal piles of rubble where our cities once have been?

Such a war of unlimited means, I submit, achieves no valid political objective; it could result in mutual defeat.

Atomic restraint, weapons restraint — a strategy built deliberately upon such restraint — seems to me to be an indispensable part of any policy which hopes to achieve by a major war with Russia. . . . Whether we like it or not the world must return to the days of limited wars or "advance" to chaos. . . .

Ideological crusades tend to end in unlimited wars of unlimited means with unlimited arms which usually end in unlimited destruction and despair.

By October 1954 Baldwin had refined his ideas, partly as the result of Dien Bien Phu and the new Russian jet bombers of the May Day Moscow air show. His remarks in the *Bulletin of the Atomic Scientists* were directly opposed to the Eisenhower Administration's attempt to make atomic arms conventional:

Our aim, therefore, should be to shun atomic warfare, primarily because such warfare would inevitably lead to total and unlimited war from which no "victory" and no stable political results could be expected by anyone.

To achieve this aim, we must, paradoxically, maintain two fundamental capabilities — the capability of waging an atomic war unequaled in destructiveness by any opponent and the equally important capability of waging a victorious war without utilizing atomic weapons.

Alluding to the defense of Europe and to the failure of the NATO allies to bring conventional ground forces there up to the 75 divisions deemed ideal by Dean Acheson and others in 1950, Baldwin commented:

The reluctance of Europe to pay the bill required for raising the conventional forces necessary to win a non-atomic war, and the increasing neutralism of Europe, [results] in part from the threat of the Russian atomic stockpile to Europe's cities. Because of the paucity of conventional means of victory, the strategic planners are forced to plan in terms of atomic weapons; because of the threat of those weapons to cities and hence the declining will-to-resist of our allies, the planners talk in terms of tactical use.

Hanson Baldwin then described the phenomena of "nuclear escalation," which would become a household word in 1961–1963:

But this is neither realism nor courage. We must face the fact that the United States armed services and NATO must be able to win and must plan for victory without the use of atomic arms. Unless such plans and preparations are made, the cities of Western Europe will certainly be in ruins, for who can draw a dividing line and determine what is the tactical use of atomic weapons, and what is strategic?

In early 1954 the editors of the *Combat Forces Journal* requested Walter Millis to write an article expressing his Traditionalist views on the new Radford-Dulles strategy. Millis began his commentary with the observation that after 1946 the United States "held the Soviet cities and their inhabitants in hostage . . . for the good behavior of the Red Army." But when we were challenged by a direct ground assault in Korea in June 1950, the "only thing which could save us from a shattering defeat was ground troops, conventionally armed, which we were just able to scrape together in time. The atomic bombs were useless. Throwing them at the great Russian and Chinese cities would have been as militarily futile, so far as the battle lines in Korea were concerned, as it would have been barbaric and dangerous." Millis noted correctly that rearmament in 1950 was "recreating the conventional forces" needed to handle limited situations like Korea or Indochina.

We had to escape the thralldom of a weapons system too big and too dangerous to use in anything but the last extremity. This denied us the power to take military action in the various minor crises out of which the last extremity might easily come, as well as denying us the power to react in a major crisis in any but one way — a way which the enemy might easily discover means to circumvent or nullify.

One Traditionalist approach to the nuclear deterrent is to limit its use to responding to a direct assault against the homeland. Lieutenant Carl L. Henn, Jr., argued for this restrictive view in the *U.S. Naval Institute Proceedings* of February 1954.

It is of pressing importance that we clarify what is meant by "air power", . . . especially in view of the support given to this type of police force by so many distinguished statesmen. . . . There is little question that the feasible, swift, and devastating retaliation that strategic air power confers upon its possessor is a fierce weapon in the event that the situation requires such tactics. The situations which a collective security system must face, however, are not always cases that call for immediate death dealing blows against a particular state. Even in cases of surprise attack by a potent aggressor force, retaliatory bombing from the air is an entirely inadequate measure in itself. One of the important lessons of the battle of Korea has been the reaffirmation of the need for adequate ground strength. Even in this atomic age of unbelievable technology, it still takes soldiers on the ground to stop invading armies.

Lieutenant Henn did not accept the Utopian doctrine of air control or air policing, which had been developed since the 1920's. On the contrary, he maintained that strategic air is of little use for international police action.

Those responsible for flouting the law must be punished without exterminating masses of innocent people.

The strategic air weapon, especially when armed with atomic bombs, is a total measure. As such, it will achieve its maximum effectiveness only if it is used as a last resort with the full political and moral support of the vast majority of the nations and the peoples of the world for a cause which commands their utmost respect. The temptation to identify the speed of a fleet of military bombers with fast corrective action in world political affairs is an illusion that must be resisted wherever it is found. It is far more likely that such measures would create many more problems than it is contended that they would solve.

However eloquent and rational scholarly articles may appear, they are of little value unless the political and military leaders they are directed toward take cognizance of the insights advanced. Admiral Carney, the Chief of Naval Operations, discussed the Navy's views on war and by implication criticized the new look at the Naval War College:

The title of this speech ["The Role of the Navy in a Future War"], raises another pregnant question: What sort of war do we have in mind? If we are honest with ourselves, we will acknowledge that there are big wars, little wars, general wars, localized wars, Marquis of Queensbury wars, and savage, ruthless wars; atomic wars and, perhaps, non-atomic wars. What can we expect? . . .

If the answer is "Atoms!" that is one thing. Were the criterion to be "No Atoms!" we are militarily right back where we started.

I cannot, nor can anyone else, forecast the blueprint for an ultimate show-down of the nations now in ideological conflict. It is entirely conceivable that we might see a limited use of atomic weapons. We might see, and probably will see, a continuation of the so-called brush fires. Or — we might see, as has so far been the case with chemical and bacterialogical warfare, a nuclear stalemate with both sides refraining for fear of retaliation.

Confronted with great uncertainty in this respect, I see no alternative but to hedge our strategic bets, ready to push into the future, but also prepared to meet, and rely on, the methods of the recent past. . . .

Consequently, . . . I would say that something new and something old are both needed in the military locker.

General Ridgway took an even more traditional viewpoint than did Admiral Carney, perhaps because of the fact that the Army had been most severely affected by the new look and massive retaliation. The ground soldier was a symbol of Korea and, as such, officially despised. Yet, Ridgway insisted that the infantryman was

emerging ever more clearly as the ultimate key to victory. The need for a strong Army and the importance of ground warfare remain as great as they ever were. In fact, the advent of new weapons and the increased importance of air power have but given new meaning and wider scope to the dimensions of land warfare, without changing war's nature and basic objectives.

The most penetrating Traditionalist analysis of the effect of the new weapons and implied criticism of massive retaliation was an article by Commander Ralph E. Williams, Jr., entitled "The Great Debate: 1954," which received the Naval Institute's Gold Prize. Commander Williams predicted that the squeeze between cutting expenses and developing new weapons would be resolved in favor of the latter to the detriment of balanced forces. "As the field of maneuver thus narrows with the approach of the coming fiscal year, we are likely to see a contest between two opposed strategic concepts revived with an asperity unknown since the days of Billy Mitchell." This debate concerned "nothing less than the place and purpose of war in the pursuit of the objectives of a democratic society." Williams explained that

the inherent weakness of the air-atomic concept and the cause of
its incompatibility with sound national objectives arise out of the
fact that its weapons cannot be used at all except in total war.
And total war in the light of today's weapons capabilities means
the irretrievable loss of all objectives of every nation involved in it.
None of the belligerents could ever win such a war; most of them
could not even survive it. . . .

If, by our concentration on a single weapon, we reduce our
other military capabilities to the point where we can make no adequate reply to an act of limited aggression, we can, when confronted with such an act, have only two alternatives: We can
capitulate, and stand idly by, watching our position in the world
being nibbled away, or, perhaps stung by frustration and humiliation of successive defeats, we may invoke our atomic power and
in so doing extend the conflict to a scope and level of intensity
totally unwarranted by the circumstances of the aggressive act.

After Chairman Lewis Strauss's 1954 April Fool's day announcement that an H-bomb can take out "any city," the mutuality of atomic destruction became even more apparent.

The H-bomb caused a slow but apparent change in the way
Utopians and Traditionalists looked at war. In one sense it
merely reinforced their past positions. Utopians saw either a
"phony war" like the Cold War, which they and their conservative supporters labeled World War III, or a total thermonuclear
holocaust. Traditionalists, realists but not pacifists, sought refuge
in the concept of limited war. Making this jump, they logically
tried to rationalize both limited, total war (finite deterrence)
and "limited," limited war.

Hence in October 1954 Colonel George A. Lincoln could
discuss "the nature of war" at the Naval War College. "The
advance of military capabilities for destruction may soon make
'keeping ahead of the Russians' in military technology much
less meaningful. Twice total destruction, if opposed by total
destruction, still does not give security."

By the end of 1954 Secretary of the Navy Charles S. Thomas
had begun to distill the doctrine of balanced deterrence.

For if we channel our military effort to counteraction against only
one type of possible military aggression — as we had begun to do

just prior to Korea — we ignore the threat of other types of military aggression which can be just as defeating and just as conclusive. Moreover, in doing so, we permit any enemy to concentrate sufficient strength toward neutralizing or circumventing our single strength. Thus in these days of supersonic planes, nuclear weapons, and guided missiles we must still have soldiers and sailors, rifles, tanks, grenades and bayonets, antisubmarine ships and landing craft as we so recently saw in Korea, as well as global bombers and massive retaliatory weapons. This is especially true when it is remembered that our fundamental philosophy gives to our opponent the initiative of choosing when, where, and what type of war they can be.[5]

But the best theory of war, deterrence, and the place of the military services in the conduct of foreign policy are meaningless unless the military weapons system and force levels are "in being" to support the alternative strategy. Put in other words, even the most sympathetic and inventive Traditionalist policymaker will find his possible courses of action paralyzed by weapons systems that are "in being." So powerful are modern weapons systems that they influence political and international events long before they become truly operational. The adoption by one Administration of weapons systems that are basically single purpose — deterring total war against the United States homeland — can set a future Administration's feet in concrete.

This is why the Truman Administration's choice from 1945 to 1950 to emphasize the intercontinental bomber must be considered a fundamental decision, which, when coupled with the desire for economy and the Korean War hangover, made the adoption of massive retaliation by the Eisenhower Administration so much easier. In one sense it was inevitable. Kennedy would have found himself a similar prisoner of the big bomber and hardened, fixed-based missile and the strategy of counterforce if it had not been for a pair of weapons systems completed in the Eisenhower Administration from keels laid in the Truman Administration. Mrs. Eisenhower launched the *Nautilus* in early January 1954, but since it lacked immediate deterrent value, no service in-fighting resulted. This struggle was postponed until

1958 to 1960 when the full potential of the Polaris as the prime deterrent of the Western world was realized. Instead, the conflict in 1954 over weapons systems centered as it had from 1948 to 1950 over the U.S.S. *Forrestal*, the reborn and remodified U.S.S. *United States.*

Carrier air under the benevolent protection of Admiral Radford and selected Republican and Democratic Traditionalists prospered primarily because of naval air's fine showing in the Korean War and, to a lesser extent, because of the diversified lightweight atomic weapons that could now be carried by jet planes launched from aircraft carriers. The real basis of the Navy–Air Force conflict in late 1954–1955 was over the delivery of the H-bomb. After the March Pacific tests the United States Air Force once again had a monopoly of deterrent delivery. The first "droppable" H-bombs were so heavy that only land-based aircraft could carry them, but it was inevitable that their weight would eventually be scaled down. The new carriers were so large and the bomb-carrying and range capabilities of the new jet bombers so great that it was only a matter of time before an alternative weapons system capable of carrying with it an alternative strategy would be developed. This would be especially true if the Navy were allowed to build *Forrestal* carriers at the desired rate of one a year for a decade.

Senator Leverett Saltonstall complained that "all too often in the discussion of national air power, Naval and Marine aviation are overlooked and ignored, yet in terms of active aircraft our naval and marine aviation represent more than one-third of our total airpower." The big blowup over carrier air, as previously mentioned, took on the aspects of a transatlantic debate. In December 1954 the Air Force brought Field Marshal Montgomery to the United States for a short lecture tour that coincided with the launching of the U.S.S. *Forrestal.* Monty of El Alamein took special delight in downgrading the new aircraft carrier. Assistant Navy Secretary for Air James H. Smith, Jr., stalked the British general much the same as the Republican truth squads followed Harry Truman in 1948 and 1952.

In November, Smith warned that the increase in enemy weapons would make "our immovable home bases vulnerable to sudden overwhelming attacks which could prevent our counterattack." To prevent this, he maintained that our counterattack potential must be dispersed on our "moving bases." By December 7, 1954, Smith was saying that flat tops were key weapons in this country's "massive retaliation strategy." Their cardinal virtue, as he saw it, was their ability to operate on the high seas as mobile bases for attack planes without violating another nation's sovereignty.

At his special news conference Smith reminded the correspondents that Monty was an Englishman and a ground soldier, whose horizons were limited to Europe and the Mediterranean. The aircraft carrier was vitally needed to defend the vast reaches of the Pacific and as a mobile and relatively invulnerable base for attack planes carrying atomic bombs.

Thus to some it looked as if another doctrinal fight between the Navy and the Air Force was about to begin over the best way to deliver thermonuclear weapons. Few realized at the time that the *Forrestal* was an interim solution to the problem of the mobile, sea-based deterrent. The real answer was launched at Groton, Connecticut, on January 21, 1954, with the world's first atomic submarine, the U.S.S. *Nautilus*. At the launching Admiral Carney said: "As a sailor, I recognize this ship as the beginning of a new chapter in the history of sea power. Revolutionary thing that she is, the technicians and tacticians will strive to wring the greatest military advantage from the latest product of American genius."

Joining the Navy in its fight for balanced forces, were the Army and most of the atomic scientists. Harold C. Urey, discussing the defense issues of 1954, gave some advice to his fellow atomic scientists. He felt that the United States should, if the situation ever arose, force Russia to make the first decision to use atomic weapons in western Europe. He warned against "the false economy of depending on atomic weapons alone in our ground and air military forces."

The Army Association took a very definite and, at the time, courageous stand for limited war: "Our national objectives include the limiting of war. If we must fight, it should be for an end that will increase the chances of peace and eliminate the seeds of further conflict. Military men must join with statesmen in a new crusade — a wise and deliberate campaign to keep the scope and horror of war at a minimum."[6]

General Ridgway, carrying on in the tradition of General Marshall and General Bradley, spoke out for the truly professional soldier in a democratic society.

Except, perhaps among certain barbarians, war is never an end in itself. . . . History provides examples in which "saber-rattling" precipitated rather than prevented war.

The purpose of war, when it occurs, is for one contestant to impose its will, by force, upon the other. . . . The method by which this end is achieved has remained fundamentally the same throughout history. That method is the defeat of the enemy's armed forces. . . . A policy which depends for effect upon military capability becomes nothing but bluff — and obvious bluff — when the military capability for backing it up is patently inadequate. . . .

The soldier's responsibility lies in the professional military field. His over-riding responsibility is to give his heart, objective, professional military advice to the civilian authorities over him. . . . The military . . . keep in mind that he is called in only when other methods have failed. The statesmen should remember always that the soldier's effectiveness in supporting any national policy is only as great as his capability.[7]

By late 1954 the awareness of limitations on massive retaliation and reliance on atomic weapons had spread beyond the Army. Besides partisan political criticism in which Adlai Stevenson and Chester Bowles were the most vocal, some civilian strategists began to criticize the Dulles doctrine. This dissenting criticism would grow over the years until it became the new orthodoxy, making converts of most of the strongest lay strategists, publicists, and politicians.

But, as we have previously indicated, 1954–1955 was the high point of the Utopian air atomic doctrine. Most key men in high places had accepted the new strategy.

Three books about events of 1954 attempted to solidify Utopian doctrine: *Strategy for the West* by Sir John Slessor, *Power and Policy* by Thomas K. Finletter, and *U.S. Military Doctrine* by Brigadier General Dale O. Smith. Additional support was given by *Fortune, Air Force, Air University Quarterly,* and *Aviation Week.*

Sir John Slessor was one of three men C. J. V. Murphy credited with creating Britain's new look; thus, by inference, he was the godfather of our own new look. Slessor's ultimate goal, unlike that of most Conservative Utopians, was not root and branch elimination of world Communism. Instead, he maintained that

we have no God-given mission to destroy Communism. . . . [Rather the object in our strategy for the West is] to drive [militant] Communism back behind its own frontiers and keep it there. [Our strategy should not be a] negative policy of mere containment. It does *not* mean building a sort of Maginot line of armaments and sitting behind it awaiting attack. . . . It *does* mean having a liberal, consistent, politically aggressive and *common* policy based on spiritual values, that we are brave enough to pursue because we are strong enough not to fear; a policy that is wise and patient, far-seeing and unselfish enough to prove that the Western way of life is better than the Communist way of life.

Slessor's definition of winning a war was more Traditional than Utopian. "It means not merely forcing an enemy to lay down his arms and accept terms, but *being successful in creating world conditions more favorable to yourself than if there had never been a war.*" Slessor thought that since the Kremlin stood to gain by a conventional war, we should never abolish the atom bomb that had eliminated it. In his words, *"War has abolished itself."* "Air power has turned the vast spaces that were her prime defense against Napoleon and Hindenburg and Hitler into a source of weakness. . . . One thing is clear beyond doubt: We can no longer afford the attempt to superimpose the new atomic strategy on top of the old conventional strategy. . . . We must maintain atomic air power to prevent war; we must therefore depend upon it — and we can safely" as the primary agent for the defeat of our enemy if the deterrent fails. If another Korea happens, "we might have to take very drastic action — more than we did in Korea. There is no basic reason why we should not use atomic weapons. . . ."

Like most Utopians, Slessor had no use for the limitation of wars. "Nor in another Korea need there necessarily be another Yalu, another sort of touchline over which the ball is out of play for us but in play for our enemies. . . . The United Nations airmen deserve the highest credit for their discipline and forebearance in the almost intolerable conditions of the Yalu touchline." Airpower was not decisive in Korea because it was a limited war, and "airpower in its fullest sense is an *unlimited* instrument. . . . [The] real strategic function of the air [is] to keep small wars small. . . . Nevertheless if further economies must be found in defense expenditures, it is impossible to resist the conclusion that they must and can be found in the sea service. . . ."

He continued, "There is no suggestion that one should or could ever have forces specially maintained and organized for 'small wars.' If they happen, we shall have to draw on our strategic reserves for the forces we need. . . . So the dog we keep to deal with the cat, so to speak, will be able to deal with the kittens. . . ."

Slessor closed with his solution for Berlin called the "Berlin Guarantee" based around an Air Locarno. Suppose Russia is about to seize Berlin. Order full mobilization of your entire bomber command, then warn the aggressor that specific cities will be our targets. If the enemy still crossed the line, we should "strike instantly and in overwhelming force."

On the other hand, Finletter's *Power and Policy* was a plea for a counterforce of B–47 and B–52 jet bombers armed with thermonuclear bombs to keep the peace. Like most Utopians Finletter was obsessed with the so-called "numbers racket." The brunt of his argument was that Russia was building bombers faster than we were, and by 1956 the "superiority in the air-atomic power which to date has been ours will shift from us to

Russia." When this happened Russia would be able to stage a sneak Pearl Harbor and take out most of our major cities and industry as well as our retaliatory atomic air. The surprise attack would leave us so weakened that Russia would be able to survive our "enfeebled counterattack."

Finletter's solution to prevent this was simple: build, defend, and disperse so many bombers that the Communists would know we could absorb a Russian first strike "and then go on to destroy the Russian state in counterattacks." If we had the proper air-atomic forces, such a Soviet surprise attack would be "national suicide." Finletter warned that it was possible to have this kind of United States retaliatory air-atomic force, but "it will be extremely difficult to have it. We will not have it without a radical change in our present military policies and a searching restudy of our existing foreign policy."

So important was our air-atomic counterforce that it must have number one priority in our military establishment. "It must have the first call on the dollars available to the military services. Only when the needs of this retaliatory force are fully satisfied would we allocate money to other military tasks."

Finletter wanted to cut United States ground forces in Europe to "four or even three . . . divisions" because the great defender of Europe and the United States was "atomic-air." Finletter agreed with the Eisenhower decision to withdraw United States divisions from Asia in 1954. "So far as United States forces are concerned there is no reason why a thin line of khaki in Korea could not be maintained with one U.S. division of ground troops, or even less, and with no U.S. naval forces or U.S. land-based or carrier air." In other words, air-atomic power could cover all contingencies by devastating U.S.S.R. or Red China if they crossed the barrier into the Free World.

Thus Finletter made the same case in 1954 that he did in 1948. To Utopians, neither the Korean War, the advent of the Russian long-range striking force, nor the H-bomb changed the formula for United States security. The answer was always the same: overwhelming United States air-atomic retaliatory striking force.

The most impassioned and disturbing book on Utopian doctrine during 1954–1955 was *U.S. Military Doctrine* by Brigadier General Dale O. Smith, USAF. It was a paean of praise for the strategic and military wisdom of John Foster Dulles and President Eisenhower, who had officially "accepted" Utopian ideas on the nature of modern war. General Smith's book is a monument to the highwater mark of the Mitchell-Douhet-Trenchard theory of warfare.

General Smith dogmatically asserted, "The concept of total war still holds sway, regardless of the cold war and Korean experiences of limited conflict," and he quoted Clausewitz with relish to prove his point:

If war is politics by violence, reasoned Clausewitz, then that nation which is the most violent will win. "War is an act of violence pushed to its utmost bounds." Therefore, warfare should be fought not on the attrition principle, but on the shock principle; not as a wearing down of the enemy, but as a mass attack at his source of strength; not as a rapier thrust, but as a bludgeon blow. The strategy of the rapid mass attack at the source of the enemy strength grew out of this theory of warfare and gained more credence with the years, particularly with the intellectual acceleration imparted by Marshal Foch. . . .

Now the new era [of atomic warfare] is upon us, like it or not. We cannot wish it away. We can only deter this kind of warfare by being prepared to wage it with more skill than any enemy. A policy such as instant retaliation should be most discouraging to a warlike neighbor. And with this in mind, another statement of D. H. Mahan bears review: "Carrying the war into the heart of the assailant's country . . . is the surest plan of making him share [the war's] burdens and foiling his plans." Air power can do this at the outset. Massive, instant retaliation, then, becomes a strategy of air celerity. . . .

General Smith's specific strategy, called air siege or strategic bombardment, incorporated many of the ideas of Colonel Kieffer, Thomas K. Finletter, Sir John Slessor, the experience of World War II, and the criticisms of the Strategic Bombing Survey. He advocated the destruction of selected industrial, troop, communication, and power targets, all demolished after we had achieved air dominance by the pre-emptive destruction of the enemy's air force in the air battle.

The general closed his book with a patronizing dig at the opponents of the brave, new, exciting strategy.

Dissident elements abound, and hoary traditions nourished by ancestral fears of men-at-arms may weaken this brave policy. Some men will undoubtedly hold grimly to the romantic notion that glory in future war can only be secured through tried-and-true strategies of the past. Still others will urge that we withdraw into a shell, gird our borders with thousands of radar-missile-fighter walls, and forget the rest of the world. Hand-wringers will prophesy the end of civilization if we resolutely stand up to the great principles which made our civilization. But it can be surmised with some confidence that the enlightened American public will adopt this dynamic new policy as its own and bring it into reality.

During 1954 there was a great partisan political debate over the new look and massive retaliation. Adlai Stevenson, Chester Bowles, and Dean Acheson dueled with John Foster Dulles, Vice President Nixon, and Admiral Arthur Radford. But the Military Traditionalists were not overt in their criticism because massive retaliation was the official policy, even though President Eisenhower in March and April 1954 asked reporters not to use the term and suggested that his strategy was not new after all. The President's actions were consistent in that they never gave any indication that he would carry out, or had any intention of carrying out, massive retaliation. In fact, the modification of massive retaliation, beginning with John Foster Dulles's article in *Foreign Affairs* in April 1954, can be partially attributed to President Eisenhower's disenchantment with the implications of the doctrine. The President was, after all, a Military Traditionalist turned Conservative Traditionalist, and the grandiose schemes some of his Utopian advisers visualized flowing from massive retaliation were alien to the old general.

But there were many in and out of his Administration who were hypnotized by a strategy that seemingly answered all our economic, political, and military problems. C. R. Smith, president of American Airlines and a general in the Air Force Reserve, delivered a "layman's" address on United States strategy, which was published in *Air Force* in January 1954. It was almost a "pure version" of the latest Utopian doctrine: The H-bomb makes it inevitable that any future war will be fought with these weapons, and it will be a short war. Army and Navy are not needed. The British fleet has been replaced by "the American strategic bomber force and its atomic weapons" as the new deterrent. If we hope to save ten billion dollars, then there "is no evading the conclusion being forced upon us. It is that the deterrent force represented by atomic weapons and the capacity to deliver them is also the only sure war-winning force."

Similarly, in discussing the coming new look, Roger M. Kyes of the Department of Defense spoke on a favorite Utopian theme: "We must reassess our strategic planning and logistics in the light of technological advances, and have the courage to discard the outmoded procedures and weapons which will no longer serve more than tradition. We can no longer afford to prepare for every conceivable kind of war. We can no longer afford the luxury of the status quo in strategic planning."

Lloyd Norman critically analyzed the new look in the February 1954 issue of *Combat Forces Journal* and called it a "shotgun wedding of two incompatible military ideas." One of these was the "glistening, still untried atomic (hydrogen) air power theory" versus the "traditional surface theory" that the enemy must be conquered on the ground. Norman maintained that this strategy was created by the administration's desire for a " 'long pull' military strategy that would balance the federal budget, nurture the national economy, and still provide a reasonable posture of defense." Senator Barry Goldwater had another, more accurate analysis of the genesis of the new look:

The use of this nation's Air Force as a retaliatory weapon, one that would by its strength dissuade our enemy from attack, is far from a new concept in the field of strategy. General Vandenberg . . .

held strongly to this concept, and all his efforts were directed to such an objective. . . .

The truth is that the new look in the Air Force has been in process of formulation since World War II. . . . To a great extent the new look is merely an acceptance of the old look.

Air Force General Twining readily accepted the Utopian program, attacked the limiting of any future wars or tying down ground troops, and advocated the use of "new air weapons . . . in minor wars, if we have to fight them." The implication of Twining's remarks was clear enough: in any future peripheral action like Korea, nuclear weapons should be used.

The unbounded faith in technology that has so characterized Utopians was given a tremendous uplift with the news of the March 1954 H-bomb tests. One *Aviation Week* editor waxed eloquent on the relation of the H-bomb to the airplane. The H-bomb represented the ultimate in fire and blast power that science could unlock from the atom.

The H-bomb tests gave new life to the future of the heavy bomber because the first bomb was so large that only the B–36 or B–52 could carry it. Thus the same drama of 1948–1950 was about to be played over again. This time, instead of a carrier-bomber battle, the issue was cast in more politically partisan terms of bomber gap and missile gap, which developed into the defense issue in the political campaigns of 1956 and 1960.

The aviation press happily discovered that jet bombers and atomic weapons were, in the long run, not only cheaper than the "old ways" but were the only "sure war-winning" force.

In April 1954 *Aviation Week,* reacting to the H-bomb, said:

The one thing that seems certain is that the power to retaliate instantaneously and crushingly is the surest restraint upon aggression. . . . There is no escaping the conclusion being forced upon us. It is that the deterrent force represented by atomic weapons and the capacity to deliver them through the air is also the only sure war-winning force. Science has doomed the old ways.

Never has the airplane been such a vital military requirement as it is today.

One of the most significant news conferences of the twentieth century took place soon after the spring Pacific H-bomb tests. The Chairman of the Atomic Energy Commission declared that the H-bomb could be made as large as desired, "large enough to take out a city, to destroy a city."

"How big a city?" a reporter asked.

"Any city," Admiral Strauss replied.

"Any state" would be more accurate in the era of super-bombs.

Air Force by April 1954 was calling for the evolution of the "megaton fighter" and a wide use of tactical nuclear weapons in limited wars. "It's been said that nuclear weapons are immoral. But so is war itself. . . . If this [tactical nuclear attack] had been done 'early in the game,' might it not have actually served to reduce the total number of casualties eventually suffered by both sides? A number of military experts say 'Yes.' " Thus the old argument over whether or not to use nuclear weapons in Korea was revived, and the use of nuclear weapons in Indochina tacitly received the magazine's blessing.

Air Force Chief of Staff General White gave his official appraisal and approval to the new strategy in the *Air University Quarterly Review* in an article entitled, "The Current Concept of American Military Strength." "We have recognized that our atomic weapon developments form the only effective counter to the overwhelming mobilized manpower of the Soviet. Our Air Force with its ability to deliver nuclear weapons has been recognized as an instrument of national policy. The basic theme of this policy is described by Secretary of State Dulles 'to depend primarily upon a great capacity to retaliate instantly, by means and at places of our own choosing.' "

Represented in this theme is an awareness of the simple but subtle fact that modern air forces can be a controlling influence in the world power situation.

On page five of White's article was a picture with the caption, "Role of Total Air Forces under a Policy of Initiative," which detailed how the Military Utopians interpreted their seeming mandate to solve all foreign policy problems with airpower. Major aggression from the U.S.S.R. would be resisted by the firepower potential of the long-range Air Force; minor satellite aggressive wars would be checked by the firepower potential of deployed theatre air forces.

To prove that the doctrine of air control was feasible, the staff of the *Air University Quarterly Review* studied an incident in the Korean War called "The Bridges at Sinanju and Yong-midong"; the lesson for Indochina was obvious. The article explained how the "air forces bought a piece of real estate 100 miles behind enemy lines and ruled it for 11 days," which for air theoreticians contained a major implication in doctrine and planning. It "exhibited the capability of modern air forces to seize, occupy, and control a ground area as surely as these objectives had been traditionally accomplished by ground forces." The *Air University Quarterly Review* protested that the "present repugnance against the use of atomic weapons in Korea," prevented the result from being achieved "more easily and economically."

If the Utopians and their supporters hoped to carry out the new strategy, the organization which made this possible, the Strategic Air Command, would have to be given a further buildup.

In the May 1954 issue of *Fortune* John McDonald's article, "General LeMay's Management Problem," was accompanied by the general's picture captioned: "one of the most brilliant commanders in modern military history." The article went on to puff SAC:

This relatively small complex of elite flyers, bombers, bombs, and bases at home and abroad is the mid-twentieth equivalent of the nineteenth century British fleet; on SAC "in being" rests the enforcement of what amounts to a global Monroe Doctrine on behalf of the free world. SAC's estimated 175,000 officers and airmen, comprising only about 5 per cent of the total U.S. defense establishment . . . have counterbalanced, and held at bay on pain of the inferno, Soviet Russia's 3,200,000 mobilized ground troops.

McDonald told his business audience they would like the cost accounting efficiency of SAC, for "SAC is a Spartan organization" that should appeal to hardheaded businessmen. Good management of SAC, therefore, consisted of building it to the required target-hitting capability for the "least amount of money." LeMay gives you the "best military economy . . . at reasonable cost." The article closed on a note of military isolationism in the request for a fleet of B–52's based in the United States. "It would have complete autonomy; more hardly need be said."

In 1954 as in 1959–1961, the Luce press threw its weight behind the Utopian strategy. The June 1954 issue of *Fortune* spoke of the modification of strategy in light of the H-bomb. There was no historical precedent for the large-scale production of such city-destroying weapons. When one bomber with one bomb could take out one city, "it follows that even airpower doctrine, as it is popularly understood, is outmoded." The Soviets were "beginning to crowd U.S. ascendancy in this category of military power, the West's most important element of offensive strength vis-à-vis the U.S.S.R." And *Fortune* warned that United States air-atomic retaliatory power was effective only as long as SAC "can survive a surprise attack." One sure way to insure survivability was through the number of weapons built. According to *Fortune,* the Air Force buildup was not proceeding as fast as advertised, and the three airpower "pros," Symington, Finletter, and Gilpatric, were out to increase the American capability.

The Liberal Utopian Alsops, thoroughly committed to the Republican emphasis on SAC, were also disturbed by the H-bomb. Unlike Conservative Utopians their answer was more defense spending. In late July the Alsops wrote: "But this time more SAC is only part of a much greater defense emergency, which simultaneously demands a much more vigorous defense program and a sustained effort to find a more valid world strategy."

The Utopians were vocal, not only in demanding that nuclear

weapons be used as conventional weapons in war, but also in advocating new, bigger, and better nuclear weapons. They seemed hypnotized by the potential power of the new weapons and strongly recommended the development of the nuclear armory, hoping that by some technological miracle the atomic bomb would economically fill all our political-military needs.

The H-bomb, with its lethal fallout, crushing shock waves, and all-consuming fire storms, once again raised the old problems of morality and war, the need for distinguishing between force and violence, and the absolute necessity for limiting war. Once before, in the B–36 hearings of 1949, this issue had been raised by the Traditionalists, and even though they had logic and morality on their side, they lost the battle because of political expediency, military necessity, and a clever Utopian public relations campaign. Realizing that the H-bomb might be used by the Traditionalists once again to attack their strategy and weapons system, the Utopians immediately went on the offensive. Once again it was an intellectual British Military Utopian who was used as the vehicle for American Utopians to present their strategic ideas.

The Utopian moral argument was expressed in the *Air University Quarterly Review* by Air Marshal Sir Robert Saundby. In the first place, only the Communists and their fellow travelers really want to abolish the H-bomb and the A-bomb "because these weapons are the biggest and perhaps the only, deterrent to Russian and Chinese aggression."

We shrink with horror from new methods and new weapons, even though they are demonstrably more humane, simply because they are new.

Can we afford to trust any totalitarian state, especially one whose avowed object is to communize the whole world, if the rulers of that state know that they are the sole possessors of the master weapon of the age?

Air Marshal Saundby, in an obvious reference to Robert Oppenheimer and other Liberal Traditionalists, protested that there are those who advocate that, whatever anyone else may do, the civilized nations of the Western World have a moral duty to bind themselves by a solemn declaration never to use "A" or "H" bombs in war. I believe that, next to stopping the development of these weapons and leaving the field to Russia, this would be the most dangerous course we could take. Even to let our potential enemies believe that we should hesitate to use them if attacked, would be to bring the danger of a [war nearer].

C. J. V. Murphy in *Fortune* (August 1954) surpassed all prior modifications of massive retaliation with an analysis of Dulles's "agonizing reappraisal," occasioned by the French failure to ratify the European Defense Community, the collapse in Southeast Asia, and the Russian H-bomb and jet bomber delivery vehicles. What Murphy proposed was a variety of military isolation. For the B–47 we needed only Thule, Iceland, the Azores, Spain, French Morocco, North African littoral, Turkey, Okinawa, and Japan. "A 'bare bones' atomic strategy . . . could operate without our present bases in Britain. . . . The new refueling technique makes it at least theoretically possible for SAC to carry out its war plan using only United States bases and the island bases in the Atlantic and Pacific."

Western Europe was vulnerable to Russian bombers, which accounted for Churchill's hopeful talk of "peaceful coexistence." Murphy also accused Churchill and Eden at the Bermuda Conference of repeatedly trying to get the United States to agree not to be the first to use nuclear weapons. According to Murphy, "the U.S. took the position that if the Korean armistice were broken, the war would be widened and the United States would introduce nuclear weapons. Reluctantly, Churchill agreed to go along."

The point Murphy was trying to make was that the Administration did not want to be crippled strategically by its allies. As long as we were dependent upon Britain and France for bases, they had a veto over whether we could use them as a launching place for massive retaliation or pre-emptive war. As John McCone warned the Pentagon in 1951, "The simple fact is that in the first hour of emergency these bases could be taken from us with a telephone call." Thus to the Utopians the truly inter-continental bomber became more and more important, for then and only then could the United States carry out an all-American strategy. No pussyfooting allies could stop the blow that had to be launched.

When the Air Force Association meeting rolled around in late August 1954, demands for more bombers and a "vastly superior" bomber force to match the Soviet Bison were rampant. "The Soviets must be deterred primarily by the certain knowl-edge that we can hurt them more than they can hurt us. It [our force] must be sufficiently superior to enable us to absorb the first heavy blow and still have enough left to win." We must maintain "our lead in the decisive arms" at whatever the cost. General Twining told the assembled delegates:

We stand firm in the defense of the Free World. In our hands we hold the most powerful gun ever designed. The gun we hold can penetrate directly to the heart of the giant whose shadow falls across half of the world.

As long as we hold that gun firmly and steadily he will not deliberately cause us to fire it. Only if we weaken in our relative strength or if we seem to waver in our determination, are we likely to be hit.

Our fingers are not heavy on the trigger and we hope for peace. We seek to avoid incidents rather than to provoke incidents. There is already sufficient reason for war if we want to go to war.

We have an advantage today and we can keep that advantage if we try.

It soon became apparent to the Military Utopians that the air-atomic doctrine was in for some tough sledding. Massive retaliation was under attack by some Liberal Traditionalists for being unsuitable for limited wars. Worldwide alarm over the radioactive dusting of the Japanese fishermen and the Marshall Island natives increased. Atomic weapons were not used in Indochina, for Eisenhower had modified Dulles's doctrine. Eisenhower said the words "massive retaliation" should be dropped. There seemed to be a good chance that nuclear weapons, like poison gas, might even be outlawed.

In the midst of this changing climate of opinion, Twining tried to head off any change of policy. He reminded his listeners that the "Communist propaganda machine has repeatedly called on us for a pledge that we will never again use our superior new weapons." But even worse, he hinted that "other sources" were making the suggestion that "if we promise our enemy we will use only the weapons of his choice, he might not hit us quite so hard." If we did that his "huge land army" and "big air force" would overrun our overseas bases. "He would no longer be restrained by the fear of bringing sudden and heavy retribution down upon his head." The only way to do this was by "weapons of concentrated power." "To fail to use our most powerful weapons if an enemy moves against us might well insure defeat. To fail to make it clear that we are always ready to fight back with every type of weapon we have ever used would tempt an alert and aggressive enemy to gamble on our indecision and to make his first move." The general saw no objection to public debate and discussion over the types of weapons, but slightly annoyed by the criticism of the new strategy, he warned: "We should take care, however, that no enemy is deceived into the belief that the United States lacks the courage to resist any attack with the full measure of its power."

It has always been difficult to bring about any strategy on top of an old strategy. To impose now the old strategy on top of the new is out of the question. . . .
    Even if it were possible to have two complete systems of waging war, how could we know which to use? Would we allow our limited forces, including our Air Force, to be used up in indecisive non-atomic combat, only to have the enemy switch to nuclear weapons at his pleasure?

This defense of massive retaliation by Military Utopians continued throughout 1954. The Air Force Association was critical of the lack of full utilization of the theory behind the Dulles doctrine. "Our big failure to date is to exploit fully our airpower capability by actions short of war." This could be done if the full implications of "control of the air" were understood.

As if straining at the leash, *Air Force* hinted at the need for the immediate initiative, "for we have great power within our grasp. And if we use this power correctly, *before the last chances are gone* and a war of violence is inevitable, who can say the war of persuasion cannot be won in honor and justice? That would be the supreme victory that all of us want." (Italics mine.)

As 1954 came to an end the great doctrinal debate was really just beginning. The Utopians knew that although they had temporary control of the fortress where national security was made, the forces of the old conventional strategy were only temporarily routed. Accelerating technology was forcing a revision of the pure Douhet-Mitchell doctrine. *Aviation Week* wrote that the Air Force "now is convinced of the necessity for improved air defense system." The possibility of having to fight a "broken back" war was being seriously considered. The tactical use of atomic weapons had long since been accepted.

Roswell Gilpatric, ex–Assistant Secretary of the Air Force, attempted to stop the erosion of the air-atomic doctrine. In a letter to the *New York Times* he discussed the problem of limited war:

In United States' experience to date "local wars" — meaning small peripheral wars waged without resort to air-atomic weapons — have not paid off in a military sense. North Korea and North Vietnam are still under Communist control, and there is no reason to believe that, if the United States became militarily involved in the current struggle between Nationalist and Communist China over Quemoy and the Tachen Islands, the result would be any different. The lesson taught by that experience can only be that, regardless of the amount of United States or United Nations military forces committed to a local war in the Far East, the odds are against the free world's winning it by conventional arms.

A foreign policy based on a willingness and ability on the part of the United States to engage in local wars, therefore, does not make much sense.

The real significance of this letter was that a "new new look" was aborning. The revised strategy, a Utopian version of graduated deterrence, called for the possibility of a limited atomic war or making the punishment fit the crime. Henry Kissinger's *Nuclear Weapons and Foreign Policy* was the monument to this innovation, which completely rejected the hopes of using the H-bomb in tactical situations but instead concentrated on "clean bombs" and *smaller,* not larger, atomic weapons for tactical situations.

Writing in the June 1954 *Fortune,* C. J. V. Murphy second-guessed the Joint Chiefs of Staff and the President on the tactical uses of atomic weapons in Korea and Indochina. His source was probably an Air Force staff study. Murphy stated:

It has been conservatively estimated by U.S. tactical planners that an outlay of less than 100 tactical atomic weapons used against Manchurian and North Korean rail and air-base targets would have broken the Korean stalemate; and that an investment in Indo-China of no more than half a dozen, possibly fewer, at the beginning of the siege of Dienbienphu, would have paralyzed the Viet-Minh forces.

The fact that these weapons were not used . . . does not mean they would not be employed effectively. . . . So long as the Strategic Air Command is held in reserve, the U.S. superiority in atomic weapons in their wide variety could in all probability be brought to bear decisively in "little wars" without precipitating a "thermonuclear holocaust."

Not many enthusiastic supporters of tactical atomic weapons had thought the problem through. Three outstanding questions remained unanswered. What was to prevent the escalation of a limited atomic war into a total thermonuclear war, or, when does a tactical atomic weapon become a strategic one? Even more importantly, what happens when the Russians equip their forces with tactical atomic weapons? Walter Millis saw the problem clearly in his review of a book by Colonel George C. Reinhardt and Colonel William R. Kintner, *Atomic Weapons in Land Combat.* "If the great war is deferred for another ten years, as well it may be, the sheer numbers of weapons available on both sides will drastically alter the whole problem and may well make Reinhardt and Kintner as outmoded as Douhet."

Yet, the *New York Times* reported in July that future war-

fare would inevitably be atomic and that the peak of destruction
would be at the outset. It quoted General Gruenther to the effect that NATO planners visualized use of atomic weapons both
in support of ground troops and on targets in enemy territory.

By the end of 1954 it was apparent from official spokesmen
that tactical atomic arms were to be used to bolster NATO's
defenses. General Montgomery was quoted during his anti-
carrier tour of the United States in early December:

I want to make it absolutely clear that we at SHAPE are basing
all our operational planning on using atomic and thermonuclear
weapons in our defense. With us it is no longer: "This may possibly
be used." It is very definitely: "They will be used, if we are
attacked!"

The reason for this action is that we cannot match the
strength that could be brought against us unless we use nuclear
weapons . . .

On December 18, 1954, the *New York Times* reported that
"NATO tells commanders to plan nuclear arms' use." Robert B.
Anderson, Secretary of the Navy, said that "the atomic deterrent
adds substantially to the defensive capacity" of NATO. Hanson
Baldwin remarked the next day that "NATO has no immediate
hope of raising the conventional forces considered necessary for
adequate European security; ergo, we will use our superiority in
atomic arms to compensate for inferiority in manpower."

Finally, on December 22, 1954, John Foster Dulles outlined
in detail the new new look for 1955. He said that aggression in
western Europe would be met with tactical atomic weapons and
wanted to draw the clear distinction between tactical atomic
weapons and strategic weapons. Reiterating a phrase from
President Eisenhower's 1954 State of the Union message, the
Secretary said that tactical atomic weapons, such as atomic
cannon, were fast becoming conventional. Dulles mentioned a
report by the NATO military committee, "which assumes a
unity that includes Western Germany, shows for the first time the
means of developing a forward strategy which could be relied
on to protect Western Europe from invasion. As that capability

is developed, it will surely constitute the strongest deterrent against military aggression. . . . The aggressor would be thrown back at the threshold."

Dulles felt it was not logical to measure military strength in terms of conventional ground forces. Evolutions in strategy and weapons, he declared, have to be reflected in manpower readjustments. "It is in the Far East, where subversion is the main danger, that conventional forces are being reduced in favor of mobile air and sea forces. . . . It was impossible to maintain enough forces to withstand assault at every point on the tremendously long Communist perimeter. The result of such a policy, he said, would be real strength nowhere and bankruptcy everywhere."

Colonel Robert C. Richardson, III, in the winter 1954–1955 issue of the *Air University Quarterly Review,* summed up the Utopian position on tactical nuclear weapons. "The eventual use of nuclear weapons in wars—even local conflicts—is inevitable under present conditions." Atomic plenty means that "a major war must now be atomic in nature." Stefan T. Possony, a consistent Utopian, writing in the same issue said:

As time passes and nuclear technology develops . . . the odds will become increasingly greater that nuclear weapons will have been integrated into, or actually have replaced, "conventional" weapons systems. This process of nuclear substitution seems irresistible if only for reasons of budgetary tightness. Nations would still find it necessary to maintain a conventional combat capability *in addition to the nuclear capability*. Thus, you would create a *double* military establishment, with the second system being the more costly and the less effective. The odds are that no such development will take place and that nations will restrict their military budgets to the acquisition of just one military establishment which by necessity must be based on the atom.

4

1955—Coexistence Blooms

ON THE ORIENTAL CALENDAR OF BEASTS 1955 WAS THE YEAR of the Sheep, signifying, according to tradition, a "quiet, peaceful and pastoral" year. As far as East-West relations went, 1955 saw a definite drift toward peaceful coexistence. The old belligerency of Dulles and Radford faded under the Eisenhower smile and the spirit of Geneva. Three of the most important events of that year were intimately connected with President Eisenhower: the evacuation of the Tachens, the Big Four conference at Geneva, and the President's heart attack.

A newfound equilibrium seemed to permeate the nation and the world. McCarthy had been censured and extreme Conservative Utopian protests were reduced to low whimpers as three of their most sacred illusions were dispelled: an ultimatum was *not* given to Red China; Nationalist China *was* forced to give up territory; and a Republican President *did* sit down with the reddest of Bolshevists. With the advent of the H-bomb the days of "violence and threats of violence" in major state relations had fallen away. This spirit of sweet reasonableness generally has been ascribed to a tacit agreement between the U.S.S.R. and the United States that total thermonuclear war had abolished itself. The words "nuclear stalemate" became common currency among the world's statesmen. The May Day flyover in Moscow produced more long-range jet bombers, making Eisenhower's deci-

sion to go to Geneva that much easier. His spectacular Open
Skies proposal was a first halting step toward preventing accidental war in the Thermonuclear Age.

And for service doctrine 1955, like 1953, was another transitional year. The spate of policy generated by the new look and
massive retaliation had to be digested. Both Utopians and Traditionalists made adjustments to the new technology on either side
of the Iron Curtain. The Traditionalist approach took two complementary forms. The first, continued development of the
mobile, sea-based deterrent, was basically the function of the
Navy with Army support. Second was the continued stress on
conventional limited war and the foot soldier, which was obviously the function of Army theoreticians. Both the Navy and
Army showed an interest in tactical atomic weapons for battlefield use. If this strategic doctrine could have been given a name,
probably it would have been labeled graduated deterrence.

The Utopian approach also had two different types of response
within an over-all strategy beginning to be called counterforce.
The great deterrent preventing general war was still the Strategic
Air Command, but a SAC which had changed its targeting (at
least in theory) from the enemy's cities to its long-range air
forces.

As to the lesser Communist challenges, the Utopians and the
Administration seized on the concept of a limited atomic war
fought to our advantage because we were vastly superior in
quality and quantity of atomic weapons. There were three "ob-
stacles" to hinder the Utopians in creating the superior force
their doctrine claimed they needed. The first was the Russian
air force itself. The more bombers it had, the more problems it
gave to the Military Utopians. A felicitous solution was reached:
engage in a bomber race and tell the American people that if the
Russians ever built more bombers than we did, the game was up.
The object was to frighten the American people and Congress
into building a first strike force under cover of maintaining defensive superiority. This campaign was kicked off in the fall of
1955 with Arthur Godfrey playing a major part, as we shall see.

The Great Debate of 1956, unlike the Great Debate of 1949, was not over whether to build an intercontinental bomber force but over *how many* bombers to build. This led the Utopians to attack their second adversary, the Traditionalists in the Army and Navy, who were siphoning off good American dollars at a time of decreasing world tensions. If the defense pie should become smaller, Utopians would have to receive a bigger slice to keep up with their ever increasing commitments (air defense, tactical air, strategic air, and new missiles).

A third enemy was the Eisenhower Administration itself, including the President and some Air Force leaders, principally Secretary Quarles, who were peddling the doctrine of "adequacy" or "sufficiency." This was to cause the Utopians great grief and ultimate disaster, for out of it would grow and flourish the concept of finite deterrence, *Polaris,* invulnerable deterrents, and eventually the Kennedy shift of 1961–1963. The Military Utopians, never to be underestimated, gave the Traditionalists a run for their money and probably would have won but for an unlucky break in October 1957.

The Russian Sputnik launched at that time did to the B–52 buildup toward counterforce what the Korean War did for the B–36 buildup. Korea introduced the troublesome concept of limited war into the nuclear age. Sputnik, by proving the existence of Russian ICBM's, forced the Eisenhower Administration to accelerate an entirely new weapons concept — the Polaris. In this sense Sputnik made the concept of an invulnerable deterrent an absolute necessity for an oceanic power with only four per cent of the world's area.

Before examining Traditionalist doctrine during 1955, let us look at the perennial problem of preventive war, or pre-emptive war, as it was becoming known. When the argument for initiating a war against the Soviet Union shifted from crude, preventive war-mongering to the more refined terminology of pre-emptive attack, the whole exercise became something of an intellectual game. From Rand Headquarters at Santa Monica, Cambridge, and Princeton, mathematicians, physicists, and economists began to pump a flood of game theory into the strategic marketplace. Thermonuclear war had become a game, and a two-player "zero sum" game at that. Rand served as the "idea factory" for the Military Utopians. Thus it was no accident that the broad strategic Rand view was in sympathy with the Military Utopians and vice versa. This is not to accuse the Rand Corporation of prostituting itself to the Military Utopians, for service doctrine is similar to religious belief. There are many mansions in the Utopian and Traditionalist theologies. Men of good will disagree on the nature of God, and honorable men disagree on the proper means and path to national security. Nevertheless, the process of natural selection has worked amazingly well, for Rand and the Air Staff have rarely had a major disagreement over service doctrine. Indeed, William V. Kennedy, writing in *America*, February 1961, after reviewing a number of Rand publications, recommended that the corporation either be dissolved or made to serve all the services because taxpayers' money was being used for highly "parochial" purposes. The other alternative would be to set up competing "think factories" and rely on the theory of countervailing brain power.

Colonel Robert C. Richardson, III, USAF; Dr. Stefan T. Possony; Colonel George C. Reinhardt, USA; and Captain W. D. Puleston, USN (Ret.) helped intellectualize and refine the doctrine of pre-emptive war during 1955. They were assisted by a Senate outburst at the beginning of the year. Late in 1954 the Chinese Communists had announced they would continue to hold the eleven American airmen captured during the Korean War. This led some in the Senate to demand a Teddy Roosevelt–like rescue of the Americans behind the Bamboo Curtain; others suggested a naval blockade. In September 1954 President Eisenhower had overriden Dulles and three-fourths of the Joint Chiefs of Staff, when he refused to authorize atomic bombing of the artillery positions around Quemoy. In December 1954 the Red Chinese shelled the Chinese Nationalist Tachen Islands, forcing their evacuation by the United States Navy, but not before a bitter Senate debate and the development of some hard feeling between Taipei and Washington. It was during this Senate debate that the preventive war agitation recurred.

The Chinese Communists continued to twist the paper tiger's tail despite the threat of massive retaliation or, possibly, because of it. Senator Knowland gravely warned that the time was coming "in the not too distant future" when the United States and the Free World would stand up to Communist aggression in Asia. This could be done by rejecting talk of "peaceful coexistence." A high Chinese Nationalist official gloomily predicted that the "Communists are going to take our islands one by one and the United States Seventh Fleet is not going to do a damn thing about it. And there is not much we can do about it without American naval and air support." George Yeh, the Chinese ambassador, in a somewhat angry mood announced that he was returning home "where I belong."

Congress responded to President Eisenhower's request for a grant of broad authority with its famous "blank check" to use American armed forces to repel any Communist assault on Formosa. A few senators raised questions implicit in this authority, fearing it might be used as a pretext to launch a preventive war against the Mainland as had been proposed twice in 1954. An incensed Senator Knowland reassured the Senate that "there is not the slightest intent — there is not one iota of desire or intent — for a preventive war or aggression. I only hope and pray that the misinterpretation has not already done great damage to our national security and the security of the men of our Seventh Fleet."

Senator Morse responded to Knowland's attack by saying that he was "aware what a man lets himself in for" by suggesting that even the evil Chinese Communists had the right of sovereignty. He further stated that the Administration's approach could not be reconciled with America's traditional Christian unwillingness to strike first in any way. According to Morse, the resolution said: "We threaten you with aggression if you follow one course of action on your mainland that we think — and are satisfied as far as we are concerned — may result in your making an attack on us." Senator Humphrey wanted to strike out the phrase, possibly referring to Matsu and Quemoy, "to include the securing and protection of such related positions and territories of that area now in friendly hands." Knowland angrily retorted that this would be like giving the Reds a green light on Quemoy and Matsu, "telling the Communists just to come and get them." Bricker described the resolution as an ultimatum involving the calculated risk of war, but was strongly for it because "the policy of firmness is far more likely to prevent war than a vague policy of waiting for the dust to settle."[1] The maverick Ralph E. Flanders said he would vote against the resolution because "put in plain English this is preventive war." Senator George was particularly bellicose: "God keep us out of war, but if war must come let us not draw a line and say that beyond that line is a sanctuary which the enemy may occupy and behind which he may retreat. Let us say that wherever the enemy is we will strike."

Eisenhower stepped in to quell the preventive war storm, saying he alone would make the decision on Formosa, and pledging to keep a tight personal rein on the use of air and naval forces in the Formosa Strait. The President alone, he emphasized, had the responsibility to decide whether they should be used for purposes "other than immediate self-defense or in direct defense of Formosa and the Pescadores." This statement was an important factor in the large majorities the resolution rolled up, for it reassured Congress that its blank check would not be used to carry on a preventive war aimed at Red China or Russia and that the United States would not help Chiang reconquer the mainland.

But Robert Trumbull, reporting for the *New York Times* from Tokyo, said it was "apparent that the United States Air Force has gone onto a full war basis in this area. It is ready to strike anywhere with all the weapons at its command if the Communists attack." Trumbull reported that the "atomic bomb figures prominently in their thinking. It is a popular opinion here that if the United States really wants to stop an enemy's air force, the way to do it is to lay an atomic bomb on each of his bases." Air Force pilots were "frustrated" over the political decision to release the Tachens. They were equally sure that if war came there would be "no privileged sanctuary for the Red planes," for if we were going to defend Quemoy, it would not do much good unless "there is a plan to hit the mainland."

A liberal Democratic "sense of the Senate" resolution was introduced urging the United Nations to take prompt action "to bring about a ceasefire" in the Formosan Strait and requesting the President to take "appropriate steps to achieve that objective." Senator Morse stated there were "powerful forces in America who at this hour want to go to war. Representatives of those forces sit in high places." The Senator added that he was "greatly disturbed and frightened by the attitude that you can't even talk about living up to your responsibilities under the United Nations without running into the argument of the preventive war crowd that unless we can have our own way in the United Nations, we will go it alone."

Walter M. Marseille in the *Bulletin of the Atomic Scientists* (January 1955) gave an excellent analysis of the psychology behind the preventive warriors:

The call for preventive war is the desperate reaction of those who have grown disillusioned about the chances of negotiations but still cling to the illusion of our strength. When we lost our atomic monopoly, we lost the overwhelming military superiority without which the concept of preventive war becomes a mere pretense. . . . Even the more sophisticated advocates of preventive war usually miss the point that the question is not whether preventive action can be morally defended, but whether the non-Communist people can be thus convinced.

Although the spirit of coexistence bloomed in the heavy spring air, a few strident voices called for preventive war. Brigadier General Frank L. Howley, USA (Ret.), criticized Eisenhower for his "friendly correspondence" with Marshal Zhukov. Testifying before the Senate Internal Subcommittee, the former commandant of West Berlin urged preventive war against the

Communist world because it is dedicated to our destruction. "The longer we wait, the more awful the war will be." His reasoning was also based on our fading technological lead. "Now with the big bombs they could paralyze us, make it impossible for us even to retaliate — if we wait long enough."

Vice Air Marshal John L. Plant of the Royal Canadian Air Force was demoted for remarking at an Aviation Writers Association dinner that the Canadian Army be abolished and the funds spent on the RCAF. War, he thought, was inevitable, and the West was "keen, anxious and willing" to take on the Russians and could "knock the hell out of them."

By August the Air Force Association was ready to take a stronger stand than its 1954 declaration of principle, which asked, "At what point are men of good will justified in reaching for their guns?" The new Russian jet bombers were having their effect on doctrine, and the Air Force Association's 1955 statement of policy reflected it:

Given modern weapons and the advantage of initiating surprise attack, one nation can paralyze and conquer other nations without undue risk to itself.

Massive retaliation, as a deterrent to war, as a hope for survival, is steadily becoming obsolete. There can be no practical retaliation, after an all-out surprise attack with thermonuclear weapons, which destroys military bases simultaneously with centers of industry and population.

The Air Force Association then began a line of reasoning that the Rand Corporation, especially Herbert Dinerstein in *War and the Soviet Union; Nuclear Weapons and the Revolution in Soviet Military and Political Thinking,* would pursue with great tenacity: the Soviets have adopted the doctrine of pre-emptive war, thus we have no choice but to do the same.

"History shows," the Air Force Association wrote, "that Communists have no compunction against striking first and without warning. The Korean war once again proved the point. During the past year the advantages of surprise attack have been repeatedly discussed in Soviet publications." Because of the appearance of the doctrine of pre-emptive war in Communist Russia, she

cannot be permitted to make a surprise attack upon us. We must have the ability and the determination to apply our airpower *the instant active aggression becomes evident* on the part of the Soviet Union.

Nor can we permit Soviet Russia to continue to hold the military initiative. . . .

We must exploit whatever temporary advantage we may presume to have in the weapons race by assuming the diplomatic initiative. (Italics mine.)

One of 1955's leading formulators of the pre-emptive doctrine was Captain W. D. Puleston, USN (Ret.), whose book, *The Influence of Force in Foreign Relations,* blamed Franklin D. Roosevelt for the American "new theory" of waiting for the enemy to "strike the first overt blow."

Such an attitude invites Russia to follow the Japanese methods and deliver a surprise attack on United States defense installations, on its concentrated and vulnerable industry, and on its populous cities. . . .

In order to make atomic retaliation effective as a deterrent to aggression, we must decide now and prepare to strike first whenever we have positive evidence that an attack is being mounted against the United States. Such a policy does not contemplate a preventive war or a sneak attack. We would only strike if the prospective enemy did not cease preparing to attack us or our allies by a certain time. . . .

If the government had positive evidence that a nation was deploying its planes or ships in such a way that they could launch a heavy nuclear attack [we should alert our aircraft and ships] . . . and then give the potential enemy notice that if he did not dismount his attack within twelve or twenty-four hours we would feel free to attack at once.

To launch such a first strike the government would have to have "positive evidence" that the enemy was about to attack. If your intelligence services gave you this information, unlike the marshal in the old West, you would draw first because you had read your opponent's mind and would know that in so many seconds he was going to draw on you; therefore, you would beat him to the draw. Puleston then advised our military leaders and the Senate:

Military members of our Joint Chiefs of Staff should reconsider their policy of attempted "retaliation" upon an enemy privileged to deliver the first blow. If they do not, some future historian will record how citizens of the United States, when the country was in the prime of life, misled by some scientists and deluded by their political and military leaders, committed national suicide.

It is not too soon for the United States Senate to resolve that never again shall American armed forces be ordered to allow an enemy the first blow.

Arthur Krock dignified these aggressive theories with a sympathetic column in the *New York Times* (November 3, 1955). Excerpts of Puleston's theory were widely reprinted and the Utopians were quite pleased, for it seemed to give massive retaliation a logical basis and a longer lease on life.

Ansel E. Talbert, writing in the *New York Herald Tribune* in early January 1955, sensed that a debate was underway over the role of the services in the H-bomb era but predicted that it would not be as bitter as the B–36 controversy of pre-Korean days.

According to Talbert, the Navy was willing to go along with the general deterrent concept of the Air Force,

at least for the time being, but its leaders believe that since the advent of the hydrogen bomb the pendulum is swinging strongly to indicate a greatly broadened concept of strategic air power favoring mobile water-borne bases more than ever before. It wants full range in the future to develop guided missile launching ships and submarines, streamlined task forces of fast super aircraft carriers and ever more advanced units of jet-powered attack sea planes and flying boats, all capable of delivering nuclear explosives.

By 1955 Navy Traditionalists were receiving intellectual and political support from new allies — the Army, many physicists, and some scholars. Six years later a change in Administration would solidify these various groups into a new consensus and a new strategy. Massive retaliation and the air-atomic theory it represented was already dying; however, this was not apparent in 1955, and indeed, it was not apparent to many Utopians even as late as the fall of 1963. Traditionalists used 1955 to build for the long pull. Utopians prepared for a full-scale assault on the defense dollar and the Eisenhower Administration in 1956. Time was on the side of the Traditionalists, and the Utopians knew it.

To Traditionalists like Commander Ralph Williams the results of the new power factors were clear. In his article in the *U.S. Naval Institute Proceedings,* "America's Moment of Truth," Commander Williams brilliantly dissected reality from propaganda:

The overwhelming military fact of this era which we may have already entered is the capacity of two powerful nations to destroy each other utterly. There may be some basis for belief that this moment has not yet arrived, but there is no basis whatever for the belief that it will not some day arrive, rather sooner than later, or that there is really very much we can do to forestall its coming. Its advance is paced by Soviet weapons technology and production rather than by our own, and it appears that nothing we shall be able to achieve in the way of defense meantime will in and of itself be sufficient to prevent, in the words of President Eisenhower, the "most hideous kind of damage" in the event we are attacked.

The controlling factor in today's atomic power balance is not superiority, but mere sufficiency. In wars of times gone by there still existed a tolerable relationship between the capability of a weapon to inflict damage and the capacity of its target to absorb punishment, so that it was usually not possible for a belligerent to annihilate an enemy's fighting potential and end a war in one or two massive strokes. . . . But we must now face a situation in which it is possible even for the weaker side to deny victory to the stronger simply by delivering *a sufficient number* of nuclear weapons. . . . *A nation need not have "superiority" in atomic air power. It needs only to have enough* . . . (Italics mine.)

Williams correctly visualized that a "military stalemate" would develop, in which the power dynamics would turn to co-existence. He cautioned that such a state of affairs would not be peaceful in the accepted meaning of the term.

Victory is out. Real peace in the foreseeable future is a remote possibility. At present the best that can reasonably be hoped for from our military efforts will be a tolerable assurance against the outbreak of total war and the stabilization of the existing frontiers which now divide the world in the general vicinity where they now are. These conditions will be extraordinarily hard for many of us to accept. Americans are constitutionally adverse to messing around . . . Yet in the prosecution of a nation's foreign and military policy there are no quick and easy answers, no courses of action which promise decisive results . . .

Commander Williams thus wrote in 1955 one of the clearest and most farseeing analyses of the Age of Deterrence, an age in which total victory is not possible, where limited wars and decades of fierce competition are the order of the day, where there are no shortcuts, no quick and easy, glamorous, magic solutions, a struggle in which the very fiber of Americans will be strained and tested.

At a press conference in mid-January 1955 Eisenhower dispelled fears that we would automatically and indiscriminately use atomic weapons in case of renewed hostilities. He also gave more substance to his earlier statement that we would not rely on a single weapons system for our defense posture.

The alternative strategy also received some unexpected help from Admiral Radford. From one point of view, that of preparing for the "long pull," Radford's position was compatible with the new look of 1953 and its stress on economy so that America would not bankrupt itself while competing in the arms race with Russia. In the middle of September the chairman of the Joint Chiefs of Staff, probably reflecting the President's viewpoint, said:

This is not a "quantity arms race." We have long since leveled off our military strengths for the long pull. We are not attempting to match any nation plane for plane, gun for gun, bomb for bomb, or man for man.

But we are attempting to maintain a qualitative superiority in men, weapons and equipment so as to discourage, and if need be, destroy an aggression with convincing force. The Free World must be certain of the effectiveness of its deterrent to war.[2]

It was evident that the Eisenhower Administration had made the decision not to match the Communists "plane for plane." This ruled out a first strike strategy based on a counterforce. It was this decision that forced the Military Utopians to trigger the 1956 debate over airpower and the bomber gap. Liberal Democratic Utopians were quick to see the political advantage, and the airpower hearings became a reality. In one sense the hearings could be considered the Utopians' revenge for the Geneva Conference and Open Skies.

Much of the scientific community was aroused by the Utopian campaign. As discussed previously the original massive retaliation strategy required the use of hydrogen bombs in tactical situations. Here at last was a bomb so powerful that it could replace whole divisions! The unlooked for side effect or "bonus" was radioactive fallout, which made it a new order of power and prevented its use in thickly populated Europe. The scientist who played the vital part in scaring Utopians in the Atomic Energy Commission and the Pentagon into flight toward the so-called "clean bomb" was Dr. Ralph E. Lapp. In 1954–1955, he wrote a series of expert articles on "fallout" for the *Bulletin of the Atomic Scientists* in the muckracking tradition of Ida Tarbell or Upton Sinclair. He thus forced the establishment to tell the American people the truth concerning the H-bomb. This angered some Liberal Utopians, including Senator Stuart Symington, who intimated that Dr. Lapp did the country a disservice by publishing the facts about fallout and hinted that he had probably violated security by giving away classified data. Military Utopians had already silenced one strategic critic (Oppenheimer) by similar tactics, and the stakes were extremely high.

In the *Bulletin of the Atomic Scientists,* June 1955, Dr. Lapp stated that *"the persistence of fallout for weeks and months is as radical a departure in weapons effect as is the vast area of fallout itself."*

In September 1955 the *Bulletin of the Atomic Scientists* discussed the difference between the Atomic Energy Commission release of February 15, 1955, which claimed that the lethal fallout covered seven thousand square miles, and Atomic Energy Commissioner Dr. Libby's "Operation Candor" address at the University of Chicago on June 3, in which he gave the figure of one hundred thousand square miles. The *Bulletin of the Atomic Scientists* said that Dr. Libby's figures confirmed the fact *"that radioactive fallout has become an immensely important new aspect of nuclear warfare."* It is one thousand times the radio-activity of the 1945 bomb. *"This is new, and it is unexpected."*

There is no doubt that the mutual existence of H-bombs was one of the key factors in bringing about the Geneva Conference. The thermonuclear stalemate had begun to set in, much to the Utopians' unhappiness, for once this concept was accepted by the American people, two things could not happen: the construction of counterforce and total victory over world Communism.

Dr. Leo Szilard discussed these implications and helped advance the alternative strategy.

The Atomic Stalemate between the Soviet Union and America toward which we are now rapidly moving presents a new problem to the world . . . But today it is not enough to *postpone* the war; instead we must somehow create a world that may remain perennially at peace. . . .

Such a stalemate will arise . . . when [the strategic air forces of] America and the Soviet Union will be able to devastate each other with hydrogen bombs to the point where organized government may cease to exist. In this stalemate neither could knock out, by a surprise attack, the capacity of the other to retaliate, for, in the near future, America will be able to rely on intercontinental bombers which can refuel in air; and so will the Soviet Union; and both with have a large number of airstrips dispersed throughout their own country. Thus there will be no real incentive for either nation to strike the first blow even if war were regarded as probably imminent. *And with no reason left to fear an attack, the Atomic Stalemate may acquire a certain degree of stability.*

Dr. Szilard reasoned that the cost of creating an invulnerable deterrent is so great that only the United States and Russia will be able to afford it. Thus there will be created a wholly new situation, at least for the modern age: two invincible, antagonistic super powers. Szilard added: *"As will be seen once the stalemate has been reached, both America and the Soviet Union will be unconquerable, and from then on they may remain unconquerable forever."*

The approaching atomic stalemate was clearly influencing President Eisenhower's thinking. At a press conference in January 1955 he said the United States would not normally use nuclear weapons in a "brushfire" war. He warned, however, that once the nations of the world resorted to force, the use of no weapon could be precluded. What his Administration tried to do was to build up "local forces capable of putting down rebellion and subversion where there is no outright intervention by a major power. . . . As a nation becomes ever more deeply involved in a combat situation, there is just no practical limits you can impose." Eisenhower said it was impossible to draw a sharp line between the use of nuclear weapons for strategic and tactical purposes or to clearly distinguish strategy from tactics. The President also said that "he couldn't conceive of an atomic weapon as being a police weapon."

James Reston on February 6, 1955, made the observation that massive retaliation had faded by its first birthday: "Nobody has mentioned 'massive retaliation' around this city for weeks. All the bold criticism about the stupidity of 'limited war' and all the talk about 'blockading Communist China' and 'liberating the satellites' and 'unleashing Chiang Kai-Shek' have been silenced by the White House."

On February 8 he reported that "the United States is in the process of retreating from its old position of 'unleashing Chiang Kai-Shek' to its new policy of a sterner but much more limited defense of Formosa and the Pescadores." Thus the Eisenhower Administration, despite its dislike of limited war in Korea, was in fact adopting the more traditional use of force as a tool of Cold War policy.

The Traditionalists received unexpected help from General Douglas MacArthur on the folly of total war: "War has become a Frankenstein to destroy both sides. . . . If you lose, you are annihilated. If you win, you stand only to lose. No longer does it possess the chance of a winner of a duel — it contains rather the germs of double suicide."

The stalemate concept was stimulating the Army Traditionalists toward the search for a doctrinal home. First, under the leadership of General Ridgway and then General Taylor, Army theorists carved out their own new strategic look. Their major contribution, with help from civilian scholars, was the formulation of the limited war concept. Being realistic, they understood that the United States defense dollar was finite and that the most glamorous missions performed with the most modern equipment and gadgets received a proportionately larger share of appropriations than the prosaic, old-fashioned foot soldier. H-bombs and atomic weapons had their effect on the Army. One response was the same as the Navy's — turn to mobility. Army leaders realized that an inordinate amount of United States treasure was going into a single mission — the thermonuclear deterrent. Like Navy Traditionalists, they thought this attempt to build a counterforce was unrealistic for a nation that is pledged never to strike first. Why build an "overkill" and attempt to construct a counterforce if the nation will never provide the funds really needed to build it or ever give the decision to launch the preemptive strike? Thus Army thinkers came to the same conclusion as their Navy counterparts: There must be a finite limit to the amount of thermonuclear explosive needed to destroy Russian targets. Slowly Army leaders, under General Taylor, adopted Navy views on deterrence, and Navy leaders, under Admiral Burke, adopted Army views on limited war. In a sense, the services became aware that their doctrines complemented each other.

Ansel E. Talbert, correspondent for the *New York Herald Tribune,* in his review of the 1955 defense issues, accurately summarized the Army-Navy views on limited wars: "Both the Navy and the Army stress a view that there may be many future 'little wars' and that these will not necessarily turn into big ones."

Colonel George C. Reinhardt in November 1955 saw the reason for the West's reverses in Indochina as part of the same post-World War II disease:

. . . the United States and the rest of the free world have consistently underemphasized their armies since the end of World War II. The West has refused to realize that the vast technological advances in warfare did not eliminate, but actually increased, the need for trained soldiers. It has been trying to hold the communist bloc at bay with huckster phrases about miracle weapons, flaunted but never used. The free world has supported its diplomats with press releases about atomic and hydrogen bombs, guided missiles, push-button forces, and strategic bombers. It has tried everything except having enough trained, equipped fighting men. . . .

By far the most eloquent summation of Traditionalist doctrine was the letter General Ridgway sent to Secretary Wilson when the Army Chief of Staff retired. General Ridgway hypothesized that Soviet strategists were giving serious consideration to putting the "onus of initiating the use of military nuclear fire power" on the United States: "Under these conditions, since national objectives could not be realized solely by the possession of nuclear capabilities, no nation would regard nuclear capabilities alone as sufficient, either to prevent, or to win a war."

When nuclear parity actually exists (the Soviet ability to deliver critical damage with fusion weapons), "Soviet strategy will be directed toward the creation of situations which will preclude the use of nuclear weapons on a world-wide basis." Once General Ridgway established this parity base he was ready for his major thesis:

The variable character which general war may assume over the next ten years, then, makes the best Soviet strategy in each different circumstance the employment in their normal role of conventional Soviet ground forces, supported by the Soviet air force and the Soviet navy. Such a strategy is completely consistent with Soviet war objectives, with Soviet strategic doctrine, with Soviet military potentialities, and with the physical nature of the great land mass it occupies. There's no reasonable basis for expecting Soviet strategy necessarily to duplicate United States–Allied strategy, and thus to gamble on a capability of accomplishing, by a single means, an extremely formidable task. This task, even if successful in accom-

*plishing the reduction of United States war-making power, would
attain only one of the major Soviet war objectives. Again it seems
logical to expect that all Soviet war objectives would be combined
to form an integrated Soviet war aim.*

Certainly this was a direct assault on massive retaliation and
current administration policy, and the general calmly acknowledged that it was by adding: "I recognize that the foregoing
position is not reflected in current United States strategy with
respect to air power."

Sounding much like the present Secretary of Defense Mc-
Namara, Ridgway then stated a truth often overlooked in our
affluent society with its penchant for gimmicks and gadgets:

In view of the Free World's appreciable manpower superiority
over the Communist Bloc and of the economic potential of the
United States, it is my view that the Free World has ample resources
to confront the Soviet Bloc enemy in whatever form of aggression
the Soviets choose. The advantage of interior lines on the Communist side can and must be countered by the advantage of strategic
mobility on the Free World side.

*It is my view that the commitments which the United States has
pledged create a positive requirement for an immediate available
mobile joint military force of hard hitting character in which the
versatility of the whole is emphasized and the preponderance of
any one part is de-emphasized.*

Warming to specifics in the discussion of usable military force,
General Ridgway called for a "wide choice of military means
. . . to fill the present large gap in effective deterrence resulting
from United States' preoccupation with long-range bombers as
the principal deterrent."

The new Chief of Staff, General Maxwell Taylor, spent the
next four years in the Army fighting for the implications of
General Ridgway's statement of belief. Upon his retirement, his
book, *The Uncertain Trumpet,* helped ignite the great strategic
debate of 1960–1963. General Taylor's return to active duty as
the President's military adviser and then as chairman of the
Joint Chiefs was a symbolic acceptance of the concept of limited

war and a more flexible strategy for which Army leaders have campaigned so long and doggedly.

In the summer of 1955 General Taylor said that the Army "can proportion its blows to fit the case — from the force of the M. P.'s truncheon to the kilotons of atomic weapons. It can temper its destructive power to the aims and needs of the post-war peace."[3] Later in the fall General Taylor, in an address at Ft. Benning, Georgia, discussed the deterrent role of the Army. He felt that it was absolutely essential to have a whole stable of military weapons capable of meting out the proper amount of military force the situation demanded. Only in this way can we prevent the Communists from nibbling us to death by a thousand cuts, none of which seems justified to launch SAC on Moscow or Peiping, and by quickly checking these local wars prevent the general war which we seek to avoid.

Secretary Wilson, when asked by the press to comment on General Ridgway's and General Taylor's statements that air-power is being overemphasized at the expense of ground troops and ground forces, replied: "Well, obviously I think that the program is about right or I would be advocating a different one." He added a defense of the administration policy, which stressed limited atomic war: "Atomic weapons are new military developments and you could think of your atomic weapons in terms of high-powered artillery rather than terms of megaton bombs. So perhaps that is another point that should be clarified in the military thinking."

The Traditionalist position of war as an institution of society differs markedly from the Utopian view that since war is evil and unnatural, it must be exorcised from the body politic using any manner of means that guarantees victory to your side. The Traditionalist agrees with Lieutenant Colonel M. L. Crosthwait, who in an article, "The True Deterrent," in *Army Combat Forces Journal*, August 1955, tried to walk the narrow path between total war and surrender:

War, it is said, is only lawful in defense of justice. It is not lawful for mere survival, if survival depends on the mass slaughter of noncombatants. We cannot surrender to injustice and tyranny, but neither can we consider the wholesale destruction of innocent human beings along with the aggressors. From the religious point of view, such a policy becomes all the more reprehensible if it comes about because we have denied ourselves any alternative means.

Therefore, as time goes on, the wisdom of reliance on nuclear war is questioned. And when we are faced with the ultimate decision, we may change our minds at the last moment, whatever our previous attitude, and call off nuclear war.

The colonel pointed out that the Communists want to keep a strong and secure base for "world socialism" and are unlikely to tempt us by a direct attack to destroy their industrial-political base. "Thus nuclear deterrents may not be enough. If our basic aim is the prevention of war, Russia may be persuaded that she can win neither a conventional nor a nonconventional conflict." Therefore, the colonel recommended serious consideration be given to warfare without nuclear weapons and warned against the halfway house of limited atomic war. "Thus we must think deeply before discarding the capability of fighting a successful war without nuclear weapons. To compromise on using nuclear weapons tactically but not strategically is no answer. The dividing line in a major war will be too thin."

General Taylor continued his campaign to build morale and pride in the Army and to create a new military doctrine for the Army and ultimately for the Western world. In a speech in October 1955 he said:

. . . the Army exists to prevent the greatest of human tragedies: the occurence of general war. If that deterrence of war is unsuccessful, then the Army is ready to fight and win the war, upon the outcome of which the survival of our nation depends. Furthermore, it is ready to fight it with a view to establishing a better world, as the objective of the post-war peace. . . . In common with its sister services, the Army is bending every effort to emphasize its deterrent strength. By deterrent strength I mean visible, tangible evidence of military effectiveness, which will remind a political aggressor that any attack on the free world will be resisted, and will fail. This strength must be real. It cannot be phony. It cannot be a bluff.

There must be real muscle and not merely shoulder padding. It is the obvious big stick and not the resounding threat which produces true deterrent effect.

It is apparent that General Taylor and other Army theorists were bent on adapting and broadening the deterrent concept to cover a great many contingencies other than total thermonuclear war. The London *Observer,* October 16, 1955, called for the adoption of "graduated deterrence" to increase the flexibility in Western rearming, a strategy which Kissinger had discussed in *Foreign Affairs,* April 1955.

According to the *Observer:* "In a given situation the West should have the possibility to declare that it would use atomic weapons only against enemy forces and their supply lines within the battle zone, and would use them for that purpose ruthlessly and immediately but would not be the first to use them against cities and non-military targets."

The crises in the Formosan Straits lent great emphasis to Traditionalist arguments when the Eisenhower Administration accepted limited war as a possibility. Conventional forces carried out the evacuation of the Tachens in an amphibious operation in reverse.

Senator Humphrey said he opposed an outright United States commitment to defend Quemoy and Matsu because General Ridgway "had made it plain in secret testimony that he thought the Army already too reduced and did not want it to become involved in the Formosan theatre."

Chairman Vinson was unhappy about the Administration's cut in conventional forces. He felt that the Administration had no right to cut below the troop strength Congress had authorized in appropriating funds for the new fiscal year. The chairman wondered, "Who regulates what should be the strength of the Army? The Joint Chiefs of Staff, the Secretary of Defense, the Secretary of the Army, or Congress? At least you [Secretary Stevens] should have consulted the Appropriations Committee and this committee and the committees of similar standing over in the Senate."

Eisenhower let it be known that it was his decision to reduce the size of the Army, and it "was not reached lightly" but it was the correct decision. It was the result of long study "in consultation with every single individual in this Government that I know of that bears any responsibility whatsoever about it."

Eisenhower was obviously not very sympathetic to the premise on which the Army based its case: another limited, conventional war like Korea or Indochina or, rather, the Traditionalist distinction between total war and limited war. At his press conference of December 15, 1954, the President had suggested that the distinction between big wars and little wars was artificial. If the United States could win a big war, it certainly could win a little war. However, the President seemed to contradict himself in his State of the Union message: ". . . we must stay alert to the fact that undue reliance on one weapon or preparation for only one kind of warfare simply invites an enemy to resort to another. We must, therefore, keep in our Armed Forces balance and flexibility adequate to our needs."

This was not lost on General Ridgway, who continued on his own lonely, dissenting way, in testimony to the House Armed Services Committee: "It appears to be obvious, therefore, that a primary means of halting Communist armed encroachment is to maintain combat-ready U.S. Army forces in sufficient strength, suitably deployed, with adequate air and surface transportation and support, for commitment at any threatened point."

The Strategic Army Corps (STRAC) was one of the new forms devised to handle the "brushfire" wars. In these early years it was handicapped by lack of strategic air lift — a deficiency that would not begin to be corrected until spring 1961. An editorial in *Army* in April 1955 pleaded for the "seed corn" of a future army: "The great need today is for a corps or more of organized, trained, and equipped fighting men — a Strategic Army Command, if you will. A deterrent force as potent in brush fires as in global holocaust. A force that will give this nation's leaders the strategic flexibility they must have in a world of peril."

The technical problems the Army had to solve to make the alternative strategy a reality were not as spectacular as the Navy's but were more expensive. The entire strategy — outside the concept of limited war — had to be built around the foot soldier and enough foot soldiers in the proper location at the proper moment to prevent the sudden "pounce" or *fait accompli*. General Ridgway and General Taylor, by their constant references to man, the ultimate weapon, were succeeding in their attempt to increase Army esprit de corps after the dog days following the new look, massive retaliation, and the McCarthy hearings of 1953–1954.

The Army under the dynamic Chief of Research and Development, General James Gavin, created concepts and innovations clustering around the idea of land mobility. "Our Army must be mobile, not only on the ground but in the air," and basic reliance must be placed upon versatile aircraft and mobile naval vessels. General Gavin saw the nation's problem of war in two distinct phases: large-scale war and small-scale threats. "The Army believes that in a long period of Cold War, such as the world has experienced in the last decade, one of our most important tasks is to have a respectable military posture that will discourage the continued creeping aggression through which many peoples have lost their freedom." Only by having truly mobile forces can we defeat local aggression. The general cautioned against overemphasis on machines: "The ultimate *extent to which machines can successfully replace men is one of the great unknowns* in the modern world. . . . As long as there is a war, much of it will be fought on the ground, and that means men *and* machines."

Ansel E. Talbert correctly summed up the Military Utopian position as it existed in the beginning of 1955:

The Air Force wants to continue depending primarily on long-range strategic air power in the shape of high-speed jet bombers aided by numbers of guided missiles of rapidly increasing range, and there is every evidence that it will get its way. It believes that the best defense is an overwhelming good offense, but is willing to give greater stress in the future to strengthening North America's and the free world's air defense with supersonic jet fighters, anti-aircraft missiles, radar networks and other warning devices.

Air Force chiefs also are giving greater current attention to highly mobile tactical air units for putting out "brushfire wars" quickly.

The Military Utopian doctrine in 1955 stressed two major concepts: an overwhelming counterforce aimed primarily against Soviet bombers and bases, and limited atomic war. The first was a response to the increasing size and importance of the Soviet long-range air force. The second was an attempt to parlay our increasing nuclear stockpile into an economical cold war killing. Both trends represented a repudiation, or toning down, of massive retaliation even in the Utopian camp.

In *U.S. News and World Report,* January 28, 1955, Richard S. Leghorn, an Air Force colonel formerly on active duty in Development Planning, United States Air Force, published an article entitled "No Need to Bomb Cities to Win War." He proposed that the United States renounce unilaterally atomic and hydrogen bomb attacks on enemy cities, unless these weapons were used against us first. At the same time the United States would announce that it intended to inflict "nuclear punishment" in the form of tactical nuclear weapons on military targets. Neither the aggressor's population centers nor his industry would be threatened with nuclear weapons unless he attacked our cities first. The colonel was unhappy because the United States attempted to straddle two military strategies: massive retaliation and a conventional World War II strategy. He regarded massive retaliation as a bluff because of our inaction in Indochina and deplored our attempt to prepare for conventional war. To achieve this kind of parity would mean so much regimentation of our industry and manpower that we would lose the freedom we seek to preserve. Colonel Leghorn wanted America to use atomic weapons for limited war by isolating the battlefield and "sealing the borders" to about one hundred miles of the aggressor's territory. Thus sealed off, his invading armies would die on the vine. This nuclear punishment would prevent brushfires from spreading and our present quantitative superiority would give us the advantage. In a total war with Russia our targets should be "counter force," not "counter city." In other words, our targets should be Soviet nuclear forces, which would mean accurate bombing with small atomic weapons, penetration rather than air bursts. Our vulnerable land and sea bases must be eliminated. Our bomber fleet must be "essentially baseless and operated from a large number of small, dispersed, mobile or sub-surface sites close to the Soviet periphery."

Colonel Theodore F. Walkowicz, USAF (Ret.), member of the board of directors of the Air Force Association and good friend of Leghorn, continued this modification of massive retaliation in his article, "Counterforce Strategy" subtitled, "How We Can Exploit America's Atomic Advantage." Like Colonel Leghorn he deplored the concept of a mobilization base. Walkowicz reasoned: "A counter-economy strategy, in the sense of bombing cities and factories, will not do the job now that the United States and the Soviet Union have the mutual ability to destroy each other."

Colonel Walkowicz further stated that United States Air Force strategy "already leans toward destruction of Soviet forces-in-being in the event of war, e.g., SAC's first priority mission is now the elimination of its Red counterpart."

The March 1955 *Bulletin of the Atomic Scientists* shrewdly analyzed Colonel Leghorn's and Colonel Walkowicz's essays:

Both these articles leave the reviewer with the feeling that the Air Force is maneuvering to free its hand to use tactical nuclear weapons without incurring world hatred or the censure of our own people. If our strategy is defined as an attack against the enemy's war machine and not his population, nuclear war, in contemplation, will excite less horror. We would feel fewer misgivings about these plans if we shared their author's convictions about the possibility of confining tactical weapons to military targets.

The *Bulletin* went on to approve of the Truman and Eisenhower decisions not to use atomic weapons in Korea and Indo-

china as an example of the "better part of valor." It also recalled
ironically that "returning the war to the battlefield" was a
strategic view that Dr. Oppenheimer had long ago championed
and for which he was crucified.

A third and more important article supporting the new counterforce strategy appeared in *Fortune* (June 1955) by C. J. V.
Murphy. Murphy, in defending Eisenhower's trip to Geneva,
said it was made possible by "U.S. military superiority, resting
upon an undoubtedly massive air-atomic advantage." Thus the
"fear of a general war with Soviet Russia in the next three to
four years has just about evaporated." Massive retaliation had
done its job well.

In the pragmatic sense, President Eisenhower's bold redressing of
U.S. strategy around the fact of the air-atomic advantage has certainly worked . . . except for the margins around Red China . . .
The primary aim of that strategy continues to be met. . . . Many,
too many, have jibed at the doctrine of massive retaliation. The
fact is that it has saved the balance of power for the West and held
Soviet ambitions in abeyance.

Yet Murphy was slightly peeved that "it was the President
who decided to forbear using atomic weapons" at Matsu and
Quemoy. If massive retaliation was not used to save Indochina
and limited tactical atomic weapons were not used to save the
offshore islands, what would become of the new look grand
strategy, which implied the use of tactical nuclear weapons?
Could it be that this too was a bluff and dead before the strategy
was even initiated? Murphy was plainly worried and rather irri-
tated: "Still unresolved, however, and evaded by the President's
decision, is the overshadowing question of whether the U.S. reluctance to use atomic tactical weapons means the gradual erosion of U.S. positions along the border lands."

By September 1955 a basic Military Utopian decision had
been made, based on the growing number of Russian long-range
jets shown at the 1955 May Day flyover and on the fearful consequences of Eisenhower's Open Skies and the Spirit of Geneva.
Thus in September C. J. V. Murphy published in *Fortune* "The
New Air Situation" as a kickoff for the 1956 campaign to build

a counterforce bomber fleet. He quoted Democratic Senators Symington and Jackson on the passing of United States air superiority in order to get another dig at the Eisenhower Administration theory of "adequacy." "Implicit in the assertion is an imputation that the Eisenhower Administration, by slowing down the U.S. air buildup, has frittered away, or at least dangerously compromised, the air-nuclear advantage that has been the primary American military resource of the past decade."

Murphy then prepared the groundwork for the airpower hearings of 1956 by creating a backfire for the counterforce concept. The key feature in any counterforce strategy is a very large number of delivery vehicles. One way to get the thousands of vehicles needed was to scare the American people and their congressional representatives into forcing the executive branch to modify its strategy.

Therefore, Murphy dramatically related that on August 3, the Air Force abruptly announced a drastic speedup of new "supersonic aircraft." In May the Air Force with the "same abruptness broke open its B–52 production schedule." To the "intelligence community" Soviet progress necessitated a United States speedup. It would be a much tougher task to keep the United States lead after 1958 "than was assumed only a few months ago." Two reasons were given for this: (1) the April-May Moscow flyovers, which showed Bison, Badger, Bear, Farmer, and Flashlight (Russian bombers and fighters); and (2) "a sharp upward revision of Washington estimates of Soviet productive capacity, in consequence of an extraordinary test problem submitted to a group of U.S. aircraft manufacturers after the Moscow displays."

John F. Loosbrock, one of the editors of *Air Force* (September 1955), was incensed at the Eisenhower Administration decision to build "a second-best air force."

What it boils down to, from this corner, is that we are not going to even try to build an Air Force capable of whipping Russia's one, two or five years from now. The Air Force used to be criticized because it made a sacred cow of the 143-wing force. Now no one dares to suggest that 135 wings in 1957 might not be enough. How sacred can you get? The die has been cast. We are planning on a second-best Air Force and gambling that it will never have to be used. If the gamble pays off we will have saved a great deal of money. If it fails we will have lost everything.

Lord Montgomery, on a 1955 repeat American appearance sponsored and escorted by the Air Force, resumed his attacks on the Traditionalists. To help celebrate his grand tour, *Air Force* magazine in November 1955 reprinted the general's recent speech called "Tradition versus Progress." It might well have been entitled "The Traditionalist versus the Utopian in the Outlook Toward War and Defense Policy." The hero of El Alamein called for a release of the "air forces from bondage" so that they could be forged into one mighty weapon.

The keyword of the old world is tradition; the keyword of the modern world is progress. . . . I hold the view that when the two meet, if a compromise cannot be found it is tradition that must give way. . . .

Looking into the distant future, we must take as our objective bringing the three services more closely together — even to the extent of combining them into one. Until this is done, we limit ourselves to approaching, but not achieving, an ultimate economy of force in the real sense of the word.

Late in 1955 the Military Utopians received expected help from Arthur Godfrey. The TV strategist and great friend of General LeMay called for thousands of B–52's and suggested that Secretary Wilson "should have been patted affectionately on the fanny long ago and retired."

By the close of 1955 Utopian strategists, spokesmen, and statesmen had set the stage for the great airpower debate of 1956 between the Military and Liberal Utopians versus the Eisenhower Administration and some Traditionalists. Unfortunately for the Utopians' ultimate hopes for counterforce, 1956 was also an election year. In many Republican minds bombers and airpower were associated with the Democratic party, but aircraft carriers and submarines escaped such partisan identification.

5

1956—The Great Airpower Debate

MODERN SCIENTIFIC WEAPONS SYSTEMS INFLUENCE AND cast their shadows over world events long before they become operational. In 1956 a light but persistent cloud on the military horizon was the threat of the ballistic missile. The initials ICBM and IRBM were becoming familiar to the American public. The ancient gods — Jupiter, Atlas, and Thor — once again waged their titanic battles, not around the clouds of Mount Olympus, but within the halls of the Pentagon, government arsenals in Alabama, and aircraft plants in California. The bitter Army and Air Force struggle over control of the intermediate-range ballistic missile, Jupiter, was resolved by the end of the year against the Army. The Navy-Air Force feud over the strategic bombing potential of the new Forrestal class aircraft carrier was revived, and partisan politics became thoroughly entangled in the defense issue.

The Democrats controlled Congress in the election year 1956. As a result of a cluster of factors, an Armed Services subcommittee began its airpower hearings in April. Although originally set up to investigate the relative strength of the United States Air Force and the Soviet Air Force, the Committee was persuaded by Republican Senators Saltonstall and Duff to broaden the hearings to cover all American airpower. This resulted in one of the sharpest political-military splits in recent history. The Democratic majority tended to back the Air Force position, which was critical of the Eisenhower Administration's refusal to buy a counterforce. The Republican minority, by broadening the scope of the investigations to include naval air and army missile power, vented pressure and presented a balanced view of America's defenses. Symington wanted to accomplish in 1956 with the airpower hearings what Finletter had achieved in 1948 with his report, "Survival in the Air Age," and what the B–36 hearings had accomplished in 1949. He wanted to dramatize the H-bomb-carrying B–52 jet bomber fleet and force the American people to repudiate an Administration and political party that refused to build the "superior" force needed to regain our 1947–1952 position of overwhelming strength. Unfortunately for the Liberal Utopians an unfriendly Administration was in power, and it showed every sign of remaining so for another four years. Eisenhower, after a brief flirtation with pure air-atomic strategy, had slowly begun to reject it and put much greater stress on the traditional concept of balanced forces. The move away from massive retaliation was aided by the four factors that made it possible in the first place: (1) economy, (2) unpredictable international events, (3) Eisenhower's fear of a garrison state and, (4) the increasing technological obsolescence of new weapons. It was soon realized that the counterforce implications of massive retaliation entailed a fantastic budgetary expenditure: air defense, early warning systems, offensive bomber fleet, bases, stockpiling, adding up to nearly 75 per cent of the defense budget. There was no assurance that even this amount would have reversed events in Indochina, Korea or the Tachens or, in 1956, Hungary and Suez.

Thomas K. Finletter, one of Stevenson's advisers, recommended that the Democratic candidate, if elected, institute a single military service. It was apparent to the Utopians that the only way the air-atomic doctrine of counterforce would ever be carried out would be to have a single service and a single Chief of Staff, for only then would it be possible to "ruthlessly purge" old-fashioned Traditionalists and give air-atomic forces their proper priority. On this point President Eisenhower had some very definite ideas.

One of the basic reasons for the new look of 1953 was President Eisenhower's passionately held belief that the United States could not stand huge defense expenditures for a long period of time without losing its liberties and bankrupting the nation. The President had been afraid of the garrison state in 1953, and in one of his last official acts in 1961 issued his famous warning concerning the military-industrial complex.

Throughout the airpower hearings the ballistic missile challenged the B–52 for top billing. Evidently as a result of Russian ICBM and IRBM tests in 1955 the National Security Council recommended a thorough re-examination of United States strategic weapons systems. The Killian Committee, set up to carry out this study, recommended that the United States develop a sea-based intermediate range ballistic missile under Army-Navy sponsorship. Thus the United States would have under development Atlas and Titan ICBM's and two IRBM's, Thor and Jupiter. Because of its mobility and concealment the sea-based weapon would be truly revolutionary, and throughout the hearings and speeches of 1956 Traditionalists continually emphasized these two aspects of ballistic protection.

The outstanding international events of 1956 were the Hungarian uprising and the Suez War. The United States did not invoke massive retaliation to stop the Budapest blood bath any more than it did in the 1953 East German riots. Instead, Bulganin brandished his rocket version of massive retaliation at Paris and London to help persuade France and Britain to call off the Suez invasion. It is a debatable point which was more successful in ending the Suez adventure: United States and United Nations "moral and financial persuasion" or U.S.S.R. rocket and "volunteer" threats. Be that as it may, the Hungarian issue was blurred, and Soviet Russia became the temporary hero of the Arab world as she stood poised to place herself astride the sources of the western European oil. Russian-made MIG's and submarines became commonplace in the eastern Mediterranean.

The centuries-old dream of the Czars was about to be realized — if only by proxy.

The Western rollback was accelerating. How could this deteriorating situation be explained with the Baghdad Pact in operation and the Radford-Dulles Line ostensibly "sealing off" the Sino-Soviet Bloc. What part did the coming Russian parity in jet bombers, H-bombs, and the soon-to-be operational ICBM's play? Were they more important than Western weakness in conventional forces, which Suez had so vividly demonstrated?

The Eisenhower Administration rolled to a smashing election victory on the rather innocuous battle cry "Peace, Progress, and Prosperity." President Eisenhower's second inaugural address was devoted largely to the quest for peace.

Yet Utopians were advocating the "exercise of the initiative," the 1956 euphemism for aggressive war.

In the course of the airpower hearings Senator Symington questioned General LeMay: "In what year, at what time, if the present programs go along, ours, vis-à-vis the Communists', in what year do you think they will be in a position, if they hit us, to destroy us? We will accept it as a guess from the man who has the most right to guess."

General LeMay replied: "I don't like to guess on those things, but if you insist, I will come up with a guess. You noticed on the wargaming, the staff exercise, we gave you what happened in 1960 with a surprise attack; we lost definitely with that number. So that is definite; 1960, he can do it with a complete surprise attack."

Since the Utopian theory advocated by LeMay was founded on fixed-based bombers, thousands of them were required to survive a surprise attack and to retaliate with overwhelming force.

The key to counterforce was and is large numbers of bombers and missile delivery systems that can be used for either first or second strike. The only way to *guarantee* the future adoption of a first strike philosophy by an Administration that would allow an exercise of initiative and a pre-emptive strike was to build the force and have it "in being." This was the real significance of the airpower hearings of 1956.

One of the bluntest examples of the Utopian link between numbers and aggressive war was found in Arthur Godfrey's article in the *Saturday Evening Post,* December 4, 1955. The television star and ex-naval commander had resigned his commission in early 1955 so that he could "inform the people of this country about America's desperate need for air power — now!" Godfrey claimed that the only man the Russians were afraid of was General LeMay. He "will go down in history as the one man who had the vision and the understanding and the know-how and the sheer guts to whip SAC into shape at the crucial time when it was so desperately needed." After deifying LeMay, Godfrey built up the bomber, that "remarkably fast, long-range nuclear B–52." Preparing the way for the airpower hearings, Godfrey said: "The number in actual service is so small as to be pathetic, and at the rate they are being produced today it will be twenty-four years before we have the number required to provide the minimum protection this country must have. Are you shocked? I hope so. . . . We don't want war. We want a striking force so awesome that there won't be any war."

Godfrey then warned of a Russian air attack so crippling and devastating that we might never recover, *"and we couldn't stop the attack once it was launched!"* Our course was simple; since SAC's main targets were the Russian atomic forces, it must smash "their whole capacity to make air war upon America." One of the ways to do this was to "prevent as much of their bomber force from leaving the ground as is possible. . . . We can't afford to allow even one plane to arrive over target. So . . . we must never let the enemy get off the ground!" The television star turned military strategist did not spell this out, but his recommendations, if they meant anything, called for pre-emptive or preventive war.

The *Air University Quarterly Review,* Summer 1956, added to the great airpower debate by registering its approval of Dulles's famous brinkmanship interview in *Life,* January 16,

1956. Brigadier General Lloyd P. Hopwood wrote that Dulles showed how

the threat of retaliation can assume the characteristics of initiative. The technique displays simplicity of a high order. If we take the political initiative to advise the enemy of our terms of engagement should he elect to exercise military initiative, we enable him to calculate his risk. So far the Communists have found the calculable risk too great, because the nature of our announced retaliatory program extends to them the risky alternatives of losing their initiative or accepting an expanded war, neither of which they have cared to accept.

In the same issue in an article, "The Element of Surprise in Modern Warfare," Colonel Jack D. Nicholas maintained that "conceding the initiative in the thermonuclear age is an enormous concession. At best it could produce a critical military situation for us. At worst it carries the seeds of a national disaster."

Besides bearing the connotation of receiving the first blow, to rely solely on the single principle of "massive retaliation" leaves a large gap in a meaningful policy of deterrence which should cover the widest possible scope of contingencies. (For example, the principle of "massive retaliation" does not abolish Communist freedom of maneuver, as both Korea and Indo-China have shown. It leaves open other courses of action — political infiltration, subversion and Communist inspired civil wars.)

More "initiative" talk came from Lieutenant Colonel Warren E. Ferguson, USAF, a Southern Baptist chaplain, whose article, "How to Use Airpower Morally," was published in *Air Force,* August 1956. He set out to help the flyers "be sure of their moral right to hit targets with weapons of mass destruction." Our duty is clear: "Citizens of the United States should accept the fact that our government must take the lead in blocking international unrighteousness." In face of this threat we must take the initiative by applying pressure. The chaplain attacked "passive containment" as wrong because it caused "us to react to other pressures rather than take the initiative ourselves and use our pressures for moral purposes." The chaplain also attacked limited war and weapons restriction: ". . . we are morally bound to refuse any limits that will deny victory *with a minimum sacrifice of American lives.* We must never let limited war cause us to sacrifice lives needlessly." The chaplain's answer to general war is that "we would be morally required to win as easily, as quickly, as decisively as possible. The only way to win such a war is to inflict staggering blows on the enemy's power to wage war. If we fail to do this in the swiftest and most thorough manner, we would invite the destruction of morally responsible civilization." Only airpower with its most modern weapons can apply this "total war punishment." However, if war is required, he continued: "I believe that our most humane course would be to aim a stunning blow at the most appropriate enemy targets even though the toll in lives might be great. Full application of airpower with its best weapons is less brutal than alternative ways of fighting modern wars because it is decisive, sure, and swift. Prolonged torture is immoral when swift victory is possible." Obviously the chaplain felt that we would be the victors by a "decisive, sure, and swift 'exercise of the initiative.' "

A *Fortune* editorial, in December 1956, contained a rather cryptic note that could be interpreted as a veiled plea for exercising the initiative before it was too late: "We would do better to assume that sometime in the next eight or ten years, preferably soon, some of the world's urgent business is going to be resolved. To say this is not to prophesy, much less advocate World War III." So stated it came pretty close to some form of aggressive war while our technical superiority still stood.

The greatest boost to the Traditionalist concept of balanced deterrence took place in 1956 when the Eisenhower Administration discovered the United States Navy was a perfect bulwark, not only against creeping Communist limited aggression, but also against politically inspired attacks by the Military Utopians and their Democratic allies.

President Eisenhower at his press conference, May 5, 1956, generously praised the United States Navy:

We have the most powerful Navy in the world. There is no Navy that even approaches it in power, and it features one thing, air power.

No one has talked about that. We have bases around the world, established for the particular purpose of using the medium bomber, and not being forced to make all our bases in the United States and, therefore, depend on intercontinental machines. . . . But what I do want to say is that the whole question of air power is not confined to one simple type of airplane. . . . We are not trying to match the Russians in ground forces. And in the years gone by, some of you are old enough to remember when we made no attempt to match Britain in sea forces. . . . We need what our requirements demand, and that doesn't necessarily mean that we have the same as anybody else. . . . Now we have got a tremendous air power, a mobile air power in the sea forces. It hasn't even been mentioned yet.

Thus President Eisenhower set forth the Administration line that Secretary Quarles, Admiral Burke, Secretary Thomas, Admiral Radford, and Charles Wilson were to follow: "adequacy" of deterrent power, a "visible deterrent," and increasing emphasis on mobile carrier air bases with their "medium bombers." The other part of balanced deterrence, mobile, conventional forces for limited war, unfortunately received very little attention at this time.

The formulation of the Traditionalist deterrent doctrine during 1956 was aided by outside scientific and scholarly thinkers. In retrospect, the most unexpected help for the new, or alternative, deterrent doctrine came from General LeMay himself. The counsel, Mr. Fowler Hamilton, commented in questioning LeMay during the airpower hearings:

The view is sometimes expressed by non-military people [civilian scholars, scientists, and other civilians] that even if our long-range Air Force becomes weaker than the Russians, our country would not be imperiled because modern weapons are so devastating not even the Russians would dare to start a war because of the damage our weaker Air Force could impose upon them before the Russians won the war. What is your opinion on this view?

GENERAL LEMAY: It is true in theory that a smaller force could still present a deterrent effect, but I do not believe the theory holds for force levels which are obtainable in the time period under discussion. Certainly there is a number of high-yield weapons which the Soviets would not be willing to accept even in exchange for so-called victory. What this unacceptable number is I am not in a position to say. *If this unacceptable number could be delivered by a weaker force after a surprise attack and the Soviets knew it could and would be delivered, such a force even though weaker could deter him from starting a war.* (Italics mine.)

It was exactly this theory that the Traditionalists adopted and modified. General LeMay's words were at the heart of the concept, called by its friends finite deterrence, and by its enemies, minimum deterrence. Admiral Radford lent his military prestige to the new concept of deterrence, which really was not very new, for Military Traditionalists had been proselytizing this very theory for over a decade.

In the Finletter Report, the B–36 and MacArthur hearings, the main claim of the Utopians was that the global airpower of the United States Air Force deterred, or prevented, war. But as the Russians built up their delivery capability, the Utopians began to change their strategy. First, the targets changed from Russian industry and cities to the Russian air force. Second, the idea of winning a total nuclear war came into vogue especially after the Russian ICBM appeared. This was accompanied by a new outburst of first strike and pre-emptive war talk and by the demand and campaign to build a numerically superior "war-winning" counterforce.

When Radford, testifying at the airpower hearings, came out for a "visible deterrent," he helped advance the finite deterrence concept. "This visible deterrent may be obtained with very small forces. . . . I think that there will be a change [in the years 1957–1960]. We are moving with our atomic weapons capability toward more powerful deterrents with smaller forces. In other words, a very small force can have a very effective deterrent power, and I think we have to explain that to our allies."

The Minority Report of the Subcommittee on the Air Force agreed with Admiral Radford that "we can never engage in a numbers race with Russia. We do not want to do so. What we do want are balanced land, sea and air forces which give us a visible deterrent and such power to retaliate quickly and devastatingly that no enemy would dare to attack us."

The "small forces," which Admiral Radford suggested would serve as a visible deterrent, were spelled out by Admiral Arleigh Burke as existing mainly in the Navy — especially with the growing menace of intercontinental ballistic missiles. In his opening statement to the Senate Committee, the Chief of Naval Operations expressed his views on how the nation's military forces would best be able to survive a surprise nuclear attack, and in doing so, stated the Navy's position on the proper form of deterrent forces:

Our forces must be able to withstand surprise attack and strike immediate, powerful, telling blows in return. Survival under nuclear attack requires a high degree of mobility and dispersion, both of which are basic characteristics of naval forces. If a general war should start with a surprise atomic attack, naval forces operating well dispersed at sea will play an important part in the immediate retaliation. After the first blows on the principal stationary targets are struck by both sides, our mobile, far-ranging Navy alone may remain sufficiently undamaged to carry forward a continuingly powerful attack.

Utopians misunderstood this position as an intention to usurp the Air Force's role of strategic bombing. Admiral Burke took special pains to reassure the committee: "The Navy has no desire to pre-empt responsibility for the strategic targets assigned to the Air Force. That responsibility is properly theirs, but the Navy can, is ready, and of course, willing to contribute to that responsibility when called upon to do so."

Secretary of Defense Wilson, much to Senator Symington's irritation, took a line similar to Burke's. "Engine Charlie's" statement on deterrent airpower included SAC, supported by carrier task forces. "We expect to increase our capability to deliver atomic weapons with supersonic missiles, launched from land, or from our carriers, submarine and other warships . . .

[and] ballistic missiles of intermediate range, which can be launched from our ships or allied bases able to carry nuclear attack to practically any point on the earth's surface."

Symington was so angered that toward the end of the hearings, with Secretary of Defense Wilson on the stand, he read a statement in which he claimed Wilson was unilaterally and unconstitutionally contradicting General Twining and Allen Dulles of CIA on the relative military strength of the United States and the Soviet Union. Symington's statement was one last drastic attempt to dramatize the need for counterforce and to force the Administration to spend the nine hundred million dollars voted by Congress for SAC and B–52's.

Saltonstall defended Wilson and assured Senator Symington and the American people that President Eisenhower would make the final decision in the "best interests of the defense of our country."

How do we explain the disagreement between Symington and Wilson? The Utopians were (and are) still thinking in old-fashioned terms of winning total wars through nuclear bombing. This strategy was never carried out, but it is demonstrably true that if side A has a monopoly of the bomb and means of delivery, it can pound side B into submission, and the recipient would be helpless. But by 1956–1957 it was impossible to achieve the desired devastation of Russia without suffering tremendous destruction to our own country.

The Traditionalists were looking to a future that would be dominated by a relatively invulnerable ballistic missile — the Polaris. Since they did not believe that a total nuclear war could be "won" in the accepted sense, they devoted their energies to preventing a total war. This prevention took two forms: protection of a relatively small retaliatory force by mobility and concealment, and creation of the proper type of conventional forces to prevent local wars from expanding into a worldwide conflagration. The concept of stability, or mutual deterrence, was readily accepted by the Traditionalists.

Evidence of the shift from the possibility of winning total

wars as the *raison d'être* of military forces to the necessity of preventing such wars was seen in the *Bulletin of the Atomic Scientists,* January 1956. Eugene Rabinowitch wrote: "As long as the peace-through-deterrence idea is kept in proper perspective — as a desperate, temporary means to achieve a 'breathing spell' during which mankind can search for a permanent solution, there is not much we can say against it: in fact, the last ten years have left us with little to rely upon, as safeguards of peace, except deterrence."

Dr. Rabinowitch observed that once upon a time the nation state could shield its territory and citizens from enemy attack, but this was no longer true. "The word 'defense' has therefore acquired a hollow sound. Instead of *defense,* we have — or soon will have — only *deterrence;* that is a tremendous change, and it may take more than a generation fully to comprehend it."

Raymond Aron, the distinguished French sociologist and Traditionalist military commentator, noted in the April 1956 *Bulletin of the Atomic Scientists* that throughout history man has sought to meet the threat of new weapons by armor or reprisal. Armor against the new weapons is no longer feasible, thus the only possibility is retaliation. "Multiplication, dispersion and a camouflage of the means of delivering thermonuclear bombs contribute more effectively to the prevention of war than measures which would reduce somewhat the destructive potential" of the attackers' bombs. As atomic forces become more equal, he argued, threats like massive retaliation will be less and less credible, and the need for conventional forces will increase. The classical distinction between limited and total wars will reassert itself, and the movement toward total war, begun at Sarajevo, will usher in a new order of diplomacy.

Other civilian strategists were also moving toward a new concept of deterrence based on stability. Two of the most significant civilian thinkers, C. W. Sherwin and Warren Amster, were convinced that the great war danger was strategic instability. Sherwin felt it was up to science to make stability of the weapons system the first order of business. These weapons systems, to be ideal for deterrence, should be "small, light, cheap nuclear weapons and small, very fast, airborne delivery vehicles." His aim was to make strategic war so dangerous and risky that it would be useless even for oligarchies or dictatorships to use as a tool of national policy. War to Sherwin had become a "non-zero-sum" game, a game which cannot be wargamed. "In the past war has approximated a 'zero-sum' game: what one wins, the other loses, and relatively little is wasted in the playing."

Because of the nature of modern industrial society, he added, counter-economy warfare will be highly efficient, and counter-force warfare will be moderately inefficient. Thus in total nuclear war both sides can expect very heavy losses, and the question of winning becomes academic. Simply stated, weapons can be dispersed, hidden, or protected; any one weapon can take out any city that is, for all practical purposes, defenseless. Thus Sherwin hypothesized that counterforce strategic warfare would be relatively inefficient in spite of the weapons revolution.

Amster, in his revolutionary paper on warfare entitled "The Design of a Deterrent Air Weapon System," listed the reasons for a deterrent system as: "(1) to prevent the start of a strategic war; (2) to stop such a war, should it start; and (3) failing this, to carry out a pre-determined amount of destruction of the attacker's country." In no instance would Amster's strategy allow the attacked country to launch a "counter-force" blow, for "such a blow is not practical if both countries have fully exploited the possibilities for mobility, dispersion, and 'hardening' (protection) of their forces."

Under the Amster strategy "retaliation is not *massive,* but *measured.* Also, only strategic attack invokes the retaliation." The deterrent force only covers one contingency and one type of war: direct thermonuclear attack against the United States, which, of course, would be a total war. Amster argued: "The purpose of the measured response is not to *win,* but to prove to the attacker that his losses are likely to be incredibly large, in the hope that by this demonstration the war will be stopped before both sides are irreparably destroyed. For example, if one side accidentally launched a weapon, the strategy (publicly announced in advance) would call for retaliation by one weapon, not a hail of weapons."

In the summer of 1956 Hanson Baldwin also came out for graduated deterrence. He reviewed Operation Sage Brush, a limited atomic war maneuver held in late 1955, and concluded that such a war was not suited to NATO.

> In a thickly settled area like Western Europe this is a stultifying and self-defeating strategy, for no such large-scale tactical nuclear war in this heavily industrialized, heavily populated region could be limited. . . . A nuclear war in Western Europe would almost certainly spread into a "no-holds-barred" conflict, and Western Europe, in any case, would emerge a desert — a consumation not likely to win friends or influence people. . . .
>
> The objective of "graduated deterrence" or selective force must be, therefore (as in Gilbert and Sullivan where "the punishment fits the crime"), an entire spectrum of military capabilities. We must be capable of fighting all-out nuclear war, a limited nuclear war, a major nonnuclear war, small scale brush wars. But, if we want to survive, we shall avoid, like death, confining our capabilities to any one weapon, one system. We must be able to win without involving atomic weapons; if we cannot, our fate is sealed.[1]

Throughout 1956 Navy Traditionalists continued to stress three other concepts besides the broad deterrent philosophy of "adequacy": (1) belief in the concept of limited war, (2) belief in the virtues of mobility, which often included a defense of the way military operations were handled in Korea, and (3) belief in the capability of naval forces as part of the thermonuclear deterrent.

In 1955 Military Traditionalists had changed leadership, and two powerful spokesmen for the alternative strategy acceded to power; both Admiral Arleigh Burke and General Maxwell Taylor contributed greatly to shaping the new strategy. A few months after Admiral Burke took over as Chief of Naval Operations the *Washington Post* commented: "True, the Air Force has replaced the Navy as the 'first line of defense' and is taking the biggest share of the defense dollar. But after a period of uncertainty, the Navy again is riding high on the waves heading confidently into the future."

Admiral Burke hammered away on two deceptively complex and meaningful words — mobility and flexibility. The concept of mobility, as naval thinkers developed it, offered protection against the ICBM, for moving naval forces offered a poor target for the new war rockets. Hence they were, despite their relatively small numbers, a vital total war deterrent. Mobile naval forces could also speed to global "hot spots" and by their flexibility could handle everything from a diplomatic show of force to limited wars like Korea.

General Taylor stressed the fact that only Army ground troops could prevent limited wars from escalating into total wars. But in order to be effective in backing up our national interests, ground forces had to be "in being" with the mobility to get to crisis spots before a *fait accompli* took place. In General Taylor's mind, the lowly infantryman was as important a deterrent as mighty SAC.

Colonel William Kintner examined the effects of hydrogen weapons on United States strategy in the March 1956 *Naval Institute Proceedings* and concluded that, barring a technological breakthrough, the "turbulent stability" of the hydrogen stalemate will last. The exploding megaton weapons over Siberian tundra led the colonel to expect a period of nuclear parity in the years ahead. "Such an analysis may indicate that we are asking atomic weapons to carry more than their proper share of the U.S. security load." Invulnerable deterrents "cannot be the sole answer." Because of the mutual existence of these suicide weapons, the Free World "needs some more tangible shield than the threat of reprisal." Consequently, Soviet atomic achievements must be regarded as introducing a decisive alteration in the world's military balance. "Unless we also become strong in forces capable of fighting a possible non-nuclear war . . . the USSR's superiority in standard military establishment may be beyond our ability to overcome."

On April 17 Admiral Burke called stationary targets "sitting ducks" for missiles. "If a surprise attack should ever come . . .

our mobile launching sites . . . must be able to strike back instantly. . . . Our security may depend upon our ability to disperse under atomic threat and survive the surprise blows of the aggressor."

At the National Security Industrial Association meeting on September 26, Admiral Burke gave one of the most significant speeches of his six years as Chief of Naval Operations on the topic of deterrents. "The problem of providing effective deterrents against the machinations of the international aggressor leads to an inescapable conclusion. Be prepared for any eventuality." Near the end of his address the Chief of Naval Operations zeroed in on the heart of the finite deterrent concept and began the real formulation of the alternative strategy — even though the exact delivery vehicle was not yet clear:

It is now possible to estimate the number of hydrogen weapons it would take to assure a sufficient nuclear deterrent. Many of the required number of weapons can be mounted in ships and submarines for missile and aircraft delivery anywhere in the world. When so mounted they could cruise well-dispersed over the 100 million square miles of the world oceans ready for any eventuality, ready to attack from the sea, and to draw enemy counterattacks which might otherwise be launched against population centers. . . .

We can be quite sure that the side which develops this kind of force first will have the cards stacked heavily in his favor at every council table in the world. . . . Take a long, careful look at the globe, at the huge expanse of ocean that surrounds our continent and all other continents. What goes on out there on the oceans in the years ahead will have a greater effect on the survival of the United States and the entire Free World than it has ever had before.

In late October in one of his finest speeches, Under Secretary of the Navy Thomas S. Gates developed the new deterrent concept that Admiral Burke had begun to outline.

When the capability exists to render entire continents blasted and radioactive, maximum dispersal is mandatory to survival — not only to military forces but to all Americans. On land, on the pigmy scale of atomic might and radioactive contamination, the continent of North America becomes an island on the oceans of the world. There is simply not space in the U.S. for us to adequately disperse.

Only on the sea can complete dispersal be achieved and an adequate buffer zone found to dissipate harmlessly the mightiest bomb which can be built.

One of the ways the Navy could contribute to the deterrent was through sea-based ballistic missiles. During 1956 the Navy and Army cooperated in developing a mobile, ocean-launched IRBM — the Jupiter. The lightweight warhead problem had been solved, but the Jupiter IRBM recommended by the Killian Committee in 1954 and authorized by the Secretary of Defense in the fall of 1955, was liquid-fueled, which made shipboard launching extremely hazardous. The Navy had the responsibility for the solid fuel program and in 1956 achieved a spectacular breakthrough. Admiral Libby in the airpower hearings quite casually acknowledged to Senator Jackson that the Navy had a "solid propellant development program." As a result in December 1956 the Navy withdrew from the Jupiter Program and concentrated on a new project called the Polaris. The next step was obvious: to marry the new solid-fueled rocket to the atomic submarine.

Even Senator Symington remarked that "one of the most desirable launching platforms which we have would be from the sea. Take some of these atomic submarines. I think the record shows . . . they went 36,000 miles." Captain Searcy, USN, replied, "It is approaching 50,000 miles." Symington: "Without refueling?" Captain Searcy: "Yes, sir." Symington: "Certainly at sea you have a wonderful opportunity to launch missiles from submarines or surface vessels."

Admiral Burke, for once in his life, was quick to agree with the senator from Missouri. "The Fleet Ballistic Missile, under development, will add greatly to our deterrent and retaliatory power. Indeed, many authorities are convinced that the ballistic missile will reach its peak of effectiveness when launched from ships cruising on the high seas."

Senator James Duff, who was instrumental in broadening the scope of the hearings to include naval air, queried Admiral Burke on the potentialities of the sea-based IRBM:

SENATOR DUFF: I may be wrong about this, but my recollection of the testimony was that if that missile is perfected as anticipated, that you would be able from your ships to bring in the range of that missile all the Eurasian continent except a small area that did not exceed 10 per cent of the total of the Eurasian area, is that right?

BURKE: Yes, sir. . . .

SENATOR SYMINGTON: Pursuing that, if you get the ICBM 5,500 miles, you can hit any target in the world from the United States, can't you? . . . And you could hit any Russian target from this country, couldn't you?

BURKE: Yes, sir.

Thus the issue was joined, at least in skeleton form, for the great strategic debate of 1960 to 1963 between mobile, sea-based IRBM deterrents with the magic range of 1700 miles or beyond versus the fixed, continental-based bomber and ICBM.

The conventional land forces aspect of balanced deterrence received scanty attention in 1956. The Army continued to emphasize man the land animal, the likelihood of limited war, the need for air lift, organic air, and ballistic missile support. Throughout the airpower hearings General Taylor, General Howze, and General Medaris brilliantly presented the Army's case for limited war, air lift, tactical air, battlefield ballistic missiles, and air defense. General Gavin made the highly un-popular comment — to Utopian circles — that there would be hundreds of millions of casualties in Europe or Asia in a total war — all depending on which way the wind was blowing the radioactivity. Symington, taking the typical Utopian view, at-tempted to minimize the significance of General Gavin's state-ment: "Only this week I saw Dr. Ralph Lapp on the television and he said in effect we could destroy the world with what we were doing now if we were not careful. Then some other scientists with probably just as many degrees behind their names, said what we were doing now was no more dangerous than the radium on a wrist watch."

During the hearings Secretary Wilson mentioned that Curtis LeMay had once wanted two thousand B–52's, and "some eager beaver in the Air Staff or something is always trying to over-promote the Air Force . . . [which] is a very deplorable business."

In the course of the hearings the Military Utopians were given every opportunity to complain that the United States was not building a sufficient number of B–52 long-range jet bombers.

MR. HAMILTON: Is it not vital that SAC's strength be considerably more than the strategic air strength of Russia, because the United States would never make the first all-out nuclear attack, and much of its strength would be destroyed if the enemy made such an attack?

GENERAL LeMAY: If we suffer a surprise attack, it is reasonable to assume that we will suffer losses to our force. The remainder should be strong enough to inflict damage on the enemy that will be unacceptable to him if we are going to succeed in deterring an attack in the first place. It is then reasonable to assume that the original force without losses should certainly be initially stronger than the Soviet force.

MR. HAMILTON: Is it not true that if the present programs of United States and Russia continue, within four years at the latest the strategic air force of Russia will be superior in intercontinental bombers to that of the United States?

GENERAL LeMAY: Yes, if our estimates of Soviet production are correct.

Later in the hearings Senator Symington, after looking at SAC briefing charts comparing Bison and B–52 production figures, made this summary, aimed directly at creating the illusion of a vast bomber gap opening up a few years in the future:

On this chart am I to understand from this that on the basis of the present plans and programs of the United States, the total number of intercontinental bombers by July 1, 1959, will be less than the estimate of total Soviet production of the Bisons and Bears, even after a stepup to 20 per month. . . . So that the total, if we stay at 17 a month peak, if we hit it and stay at it, based on present programming, the Communist intercontinental bomber strength will be just a little over double the strength of the United States, is that correct?

General John P. McConnell, USAF, replied, "That is correct."

The key factor here is not United States production or productive capacity. Military Utopians and their allies have but one solution: build more bombers and missiles than our enemies. Somehow sheer numbers will magically guarantee our salvation by solving all our defense problems. The whole Utopian argument for counterforce was based, on the surface at least, on intelligence estimates of Russian Bison and Bear production. Admiral Radford testified that some groups as a matter of policy inflate their estimates. Secretary Wilson at a press conference on May 1, 1956, told reporters that he could not agree with General LeMay's prediction that the United States would be inferior in long-range bombers in two to four years because of the lack of data and many assumptions that must be made. To this statement Senator Symington directed an all-important question to General LeMay: "Now the information that was given us with respect to the growing discrepancy in favor of the Communists was given us by Mr. Dulles, head of the Central Intelligence Agency, and by you. Presumably your information comes from the Joint Intelligence; does it not?"

General LeMay answered, "Yes, sir." Senator Jackson then moved to have the national intelligence estimates of Bears and Bisons for 1956–1960 placed in the record.

Thus the fabric of the Utopian position was woven; the strategy, doctrine, and weapons were all in being and buttressed with the latest CIA intelligence estimates. Only one thing was lacking: money to keep up with the Russian bombers the intelligence estimates hypothesized the Soviets were likely to build. Senator Symington sought to give the impression the Eisenhower Administration was more interested in balancing the budget than in giving the American people the security it needed.

"It is true, is it not," Symington asked General C. S. Irvine, USAF, "that our failure to produce as many B–52's as the Bison long-range bomber production of their intercontinental bombers was and is a matter of policy and not United States capability? Isn't that a fair statement?" General Irvine replied, "That is correct," and amplified: "We could have accelerated this program any time we chose to spend the money, beginning — and here, again, it is how much of a production gamble you want to take and how much you want to rely on the engineering capability of a great organization like Boeing — we could have accelerated the program in 1951, 1952, or any time since."

The Democratic majority in their report stressed that "testimony is to the effect that, provided adequate funds were expended," the limitations of technical personnel, modern jet tankers, jet bombers, and their supporting bases, "could be removed and our present estimated strategic air superiority maintained over the Russians." The committee concluded that because the administration had not acted on national intelligence information and ignored or underestimated Soviet military progress, the "defenses of the United States have been weakened." The Soviets were closing the qualitative gap, having already attained quantitative superiority in military airpower. The Democratic majority then concluded that

(20) Financial considerations have often been placed ahead of defense requirements, to the serious damage of our airpower strength relative to that of Russia; and hence to our national security.

(21) The United States has the capacity to produce and maintain airpower which is relatively stronger than that of the Soviets; but the Department of Defense has not utilized this capacity.

(22) With proper programing and administration in the Department of Defense, it would be possible to maintain air supremacy over the Soviets without jeopardizing a sound economy and without imposing additional tax burdens upon the people.

(23) Under our form of government, the American people have not only the right, but also the need, to receive all information about our national defense which would not help a possible enemy. Nevertheless the public is neither adequately nor accurately informed about our military strength as against the great and growing military strength of the Communists.

The public has failed to receive from official sources complete, accurate and timely information which it has the right to know.

The extent to which the Military Utopian and the Liberal Utopian politicians complemented and supplemented each other needs no further elaboration. It is sufficient to say that military policy and partisan politics were deeply interwoven in the election year 1956.

Let us now examine how this doctrine and strategy were accepted and furthered by Utopian allies. Their spokesmen and publications mirrored the over-all Military Utopian concept of the need for a counterforce to deter, fight, and win a total atomic war.

Throughout 1956 to 1960 it was the habit of certain high-ranking Military Utopians to deliver ominous speeches in December or January to define their military line as it would develop in the following year. General Power was often the Utopian choice as spokesman. In early 1956 he said that the real and immediate threat that Soviet technological advances held was that they would leave the United States at Russia's mercy, thereby wiping out the advantages of our current deterrent force. This was a major concern of the Air Force because we were in danger of losing both quantitative and qualitative superiority. Fortunately, we still had our "creative superiority" and our "Yankee ingenuity."

Robert Hotz, editor of *Aviation Week* (January 30, 1956), reacted as expected to General Power's and Trevor Gardner's warnings that the Russians were fast closing the gap in the technical race: "The airpower issue poses perhaps the gravest crisis in our history as a nation. . . . The airpower issue should cut across all political ties, dissolve all inter-service rivalries, and occupy the most serious attention from the American people and their leaders."

Major De Seversky's speech in California, November 12, 1955, was the purest of pure Utopian doctrine, second only to the Air Force manuals. "To sum up, the air ocean is one and indivisible and must be controlled by a single, homogenous force — and I mean, of course, the USAF. . . . We have reached the stage of absurdity where the Navy is a self-contained Defense Department in itself. . . . We must remove the curse of the outmoded strategy of balanced forces and free the American creative genius from the confines of this fallacious concept."

The intercontinental bomber concept was sabotaged and suppressed, he charged, and in the place of "fighting long-range bombers" the Air Force had to resort to the "innocuous air tankers." We must be able to achieve "global command of the air directly from this continent." Thus De Seversky returned to his favorite concept of military isolationism and Fortress America.

The political aspects of the airpower battle of 1956 were apparent in an *Aviation Week* article (March 12, 1956) by Claude Witze: "The U.S. Air Force today is deep in a fight for technical survival. Victory is essential if America is to continue to hold the airpower necessary in this age of the Atomic Deadlock. In this battle, USAF faces the dangerous combination of unbelievable progress in Russia and something bordering on complacency at home."

Another *Aviation Week* writer explained the "complacency": "This difference between the USAF B–52 policy imposed by Defense Department limitations on the budget and the program based on military urgency proposed by Gen. LeMay is typical of the widening gulf between the real needs of our modern military airpower and the artificial limits being set by concern over spending."

General White obliquely agreed and warned that the Russians had "almost closed the airpower gap. . . . Of course we can outproduce the Communists. There is no doubt about that. Our production potential is not the reason we are falling behind." Obviously, the reasons were political and financial. Senator Symington, the most vocal of the Liberal Utopians, commented, "It was never more clear . . . that in 1956 this Administration is deliberately risking our national survival in order to balance the federal budget." Trevor Gardner, after resigning his Department of Defense post, went on television and told his audience: "The Fiscal 1957 budget will guarantee the United States the second best Air Force in the world. . . . Responsibility for the lack of sufficient funds in the Fiscal 1957 budget rests squarely on President Eisenhower, Defense Secretary Charles E. Wilson,

. . . Quarles and the Bureau of Budget, all of whom . . . failed to support the USAF program."

Eisenhower's decision to run again was met with little enthusiasm in the columns of *Aviation Week:* "[The decision] will tend to preserve the status quo in airpower policy of a substantial, stable program operating without much regard to the progress made by the Russians. . . . Biggest hope for critics of current airpower policy, who are genuinely worried by Russian progress during the past few years, is to penetrate the Pentagon political curtain of censorship and get the facts directly to the President and the American people."

The possibility that the Russians would have an ICBM before we had was heightened by Khrushchev's boast: "I am quite sure that we will have a guided missile with hydrogen bomb warhead that can fall anywhere in the world. . . . so you think we are behind you?" This gave the long-range bomber advocates additional ammunition because of the possibility that the B–47 bombers would be neutralized by the Russian missile; hence the need for even more B–52 intercontinental bombers.

C. J. V. Murphy took the long view and correctly realized that the real roadblock to counterforce lay in the organization of the Department of Defense, more specifically, the existence of three services competing for the budget dollar and offering alternative strategies and dissenting views to existing ones. Murphy's solution (*Fortune,* May 1956), like Symington's, was to reopen the Key West and Newport agreements of 1948 that set forth American military roles and missions, using the technological argument that missiles were making the agreements "more and more artificial and, indeed, obsolete."

Thus the old 1:1:1 ratio of military budgeting, which gave rise to so much controversy in the late 1940's, has been shattered beyond recognition. Now the big question is not merely whether still more money should be poured into the Air Force; rather it is whether, in light of the increasingly clear logic of the new weapons, the traditional roles and missions of the Army and Navy should not be radically redefined, and the investment in them still further reduced.

General White, before a summer meeting of the Aviation Writers Association in San Francisco, said "free transfer of men among the services" would allow the men in the three services to think more about defense and less about "gaining or keeping weapons, and missions for their own particular branch."

With the passing of time, the roles and missions of all the services seem to overlap more and more. Conceivably, if these trends continue, the day would come when, for practical purposes, all three services would have the same weapons, the same capabilities and limitations, and all attempting to do the same jobs. If that happens, perhaps we certainly would find it advisable to standardize uniforms and streamline the organizations.

Newsweek's General Spaatz agreed that "what is needed is a complete integration of the services — one uniform, a single promotion list, interchangeability of personnel, and a General Staff presided over by a Chief of Staff under a civilian Secretary of Defense."

Secretary of Defense Wilson came out against single service, saying it would force arguments into "other forms" and stifle "intelligent discussions."

By the end of the airpower hearings it was apparent that the Utopians were not going to be successful. The "revolt of the air generals" had been largely dissipated by President Eisenhower's great prestige.

Air Force magazine (August), reflecting the frustration of the Military Utopians, called 1956 the "Year of Indecision."

The Utopians, if they were ever to build a counterforce, had to destroy the concept that a nuclear stalemate could possibly exist. This basic premise of the Eisenhower Administration was challenged in a remarkable article, "The Nuclear Stalemate," in *Air Force*, August 1956, by Colonel, now General, Robert C. Richardson, III.

We hear a lot about "nuclear stalemate" these days, and I think it's time we took a good look at the theory and its implications. Briefly, the nuclear stalemate concept holds that when both the United States and the Soviet Union possess an effective strategic atomic capability, neither side will allow total war to occur on the grounds that it would be tantamount to mutual suicide.

This sounds good if you say it quickly. But I suggest it is largely based on wishful thinking and superficial analysis. . . . At a minimum it has now been repeated so often, and in so many forms, that it already is influencing our current defense policy by channeling resources into limited or conventional war capabilities to the detriment of home defense and of the capacity for total war.

Reliance on, or use of, the stalemate thesis in formulating defense policy is to lean on a very weak reed. I suggest that the so-called atomic "stalemate" or "stand off" is more of a psychological than a real deterrent. At best it is a cliché born of the natural tendency to rationalize away the prospects of total atomic war.

In *Air Force*, October 1956, a new argument was advanced: "Evaluation of the advantages which new weapons bring to surprise aggression has led to repeated warnings that fifty to 100 enemy bombs could bring our nation to its knees. Predictions such as this have not been refuted by the knowledge that we could strike back effectively."

In addition to the stalemate argument, a perennial threat to counterforce was the doctrine of limited war. John F. Loosbrock, taking advantage of the Eisenhower Administration's still unchanged strategy of fighting limited atomic wars, attempted to devastate the argument over conventional limited wars in a November 1956 *Air Force* article. He quoted Secretary of Air Quarles to prove that in any new Korea we will use our "best weapons" quickly in an attempt to get the war over and prevent it from spreading:

The implication of Mr. Quarles' statement is an unexpressed fear of our becoming overly preoccupied with the little war, to the extent that our deterrent capability in terms of all-out conflict is in danger of erosion through increasingly heavy budgetary demands for organization and equipment which contribute little or nothing to our basic deterrent posture. . . .

The argument that local wars can best be won with conventional means (i.e., non-nuclear weapons and surface forces), is a convenient one for those services and individuals who even now are faced with ever-shrinking roles and missions. But is the basis for such thinking militarily sound, or largely a product of emotion and tradition? . . .

If we delude ourselves that little wars call for little weapons, we may well be extending an engraved invitation for aggression. . . . Today's nuclear weapons, coupled with our determination to use them if needed, can take the profit out of aggressive war, big or little. Either our deterrent is powerful enough to deter, or it isn't. And if it isn't, all the "conventional capability" we might muster will not save us from the nuclear fireballs.

C. J. V. Murphy took a similar line in his analysis (*Fortune,* December 1956) of Eisenhower's "most crucial defense budget."

Colonel Murphy, already aware of the preliminary budget percentages, predicted that under the "new New Look" the Air Force would get one-half of the thirty-eight billion defense dollars. But the Air Staff maintained it needed twenty-three billion dollars for the manned aircraft in being, the missiles, and the Dew Line. With the new ballistic missiles it was clear "that a new era of strategy was imminent. . . ."

Little did C. J. V. Murphy and other Utopians realize how new and how revolutionary ballistic missiles would be. The advent of Sputnik in 1957 would presage the beginning of the end of the manned bomber.

6

1957 – The Ballistic Missile
Comes of Age

P RESIDENT EISENHOWER DEVOTED HIS SECOND INAUGURAL
address to the quest for peace. The dangers of World War III,
which had been on everyone's mind in late October and early
November, had subsided. The fleets returned to normal training
exercises, and SAC was no longer on full alert. Slogans like
"Christmas Eve in Tel-Aviv" and "New Year's in Algiers" remained nothing more than memories of the weeks when the
great naval task forces began throwing their supply lines across
the Pacific and Indian Oceans into the Persian Gulf. The
Marines in Okinawa once again settled down to their hybrid
existence — half modern America, half old Japan. The first
Danish and Norwegian contingents of the United Nations police
force moved into the Gaza Strip, flying the blue and white flag
of the United Nations.

The President of the United States had kind, almost patronizing, words for the Russian people: "We honor, no less in this
divided world than in a less tormented time, the people of
Russia. We do not dread, rather do we welcome, their progress
in education and industry." By the end of the year after the
shock of Sputnik, it was *American* "education and industry"
that seemed to need "progress." The orbiting Russian satellite

dramatized and authenticated the Soviet boast in August of an ICBM. What this meant for grand strategy and service doctrine was not yet clear. One senator asked for more B–52's, another demanded a crash missile program complete with a czar, and another called for the inevitable congressional investigation. The Army-Air Force feud over whether a ballistic missile was a guided bullet or a pilotless plane continued unabated. After the failure of Vanguard to place an American satellite in orbit, the Army and Redstone Arsenal were given the job, which they admirably performed. This did not help the Army to regain operational control of the Jupiter IRBM, which was given to the Air Force. Eventually the Army Ballistic Missile Agency was transferred to the National Aeronautics and Space Administration. Many observers felt that the Army program had fallen victim to interservice competition complicated by a private industry–government arsenal conflict.

The Eisenhower Doctrine, passed by a joint resolution of Congress in 1957, was our first major reaction to Soviet penetration of the Middle East. This was an extension of the previous decade's Truman Doctrine, which had been instrumental in "saving" Italy, Greece, and Turkey. The wording of this new doctrine was peculiar, at least in view of the actual Middle East situation. The United States considered the preservation of the independence and integrity of the Middle Eastern nations vital to American security. In addition, the United States was prepared to use armed force to assist any nation "requesting assistance against armed aggression from any country controlled by international Communism."

Almost immediately internal trouble broke out in Jordan, fomented not by Russia but by an apparent Soviet stooge — Gamel Abdel Nasser. The Eisenhower doctrine was modified accordingly, the Sixth Fleet moved into position, and a ten-million-dollar loan was made to Jordan. Once again it was obvious that the old-line-crossing aggression like Korea had been dropped from the Communist bag of international tricks as too provocative. Instead, "indirect aggression," internal subversion, border infiltration, "popular" uprisings became the tools for advancing world revolution. Too often it was difficult to separate true nationalism and the desire for neutrality from Moscow- or Peiping-directed "wars of liberation." The case of Nasser, much to our surprise and gratification, proved to be an example of the former.

As C. J. V. Murphy predicted, the Suez War and the uneasy Middle East situation gave added impetus to the proponents of limited war. There is excellent circumstantial evidence that after his re-election President Eisenhower ordered a new new look. Out of this reappraisal came the full-blown concept of limited atomic war, which represented a compromise between a Korean-type conventional buildup and a sole reliance on massive retalia-tion. Nuclear plenty, which had made the new look possible in 1953–1954, had increased the size, variety, and quantity of atomic weapons to such a degree that by 1957 they could be said to be truly conventional.

Henry Kissinger's study *Nuclear Weapons and Foreign Policy,* published in June 1957, served as a stalking horse for a major change in American military policy. In those balmy days before Sputnik, blithe assumptions could be made about the permanent technological superiority of the American people. Seen in per-spective, this attempt to create a doctrine for limited atomic war was the last unsuccessful attempt to deny the concurrent develop-ment of modern industrial societies. It was the Utopians' final try before even the most skeptical would have to acknowledge that, in some areas at least, Russian technology had outdistanced ours. John Foster Dulles in *Foreign Affairs,* October 1956, had already placed his stamp of approval on the modification of mas-sive retaliation. Kissinger's reasoning, which was only a rationale for refusing to create the large non-nuclear forces that world conditions had demanded since 1945, sounded rather hollow after the Russian technological breakthroughs in the fall of 1957:

In the event of war, which side is likely to gain by fighting a limited nuclear war? Here our superior industrial potential, the broader range of our technology, and the adaptability of our social institutions should give us the advantage. . . . For a nation with a superior industrial capacity and a broader base of technology, it will be strategically most productive to use weapons sufficiently complex to exploit its industrial advantage, sufficiently destructive so that manpower cannot be substituted for technology, yet discriminating enough to permit the establishment of a significant margin of superiority.

Kissinger acknowledged that in a few strategic weapons, the Soviets by great concentration of effort, did remarkably well. "It is much less certain that with its inferior industrial plant it could compete with us in developing the diversified capability for a limited nuclear war — the wide spectrum of weapons, means of transportation, and elaborate systems of communication." China's problem would be even worse, and "when manpower can no longer be substituted for material, the strategic significance of Communist China may be much reduced. . . ." Kissinger, after making these very large assumptions about our technological superiority, then inquired into the situation that would exist if the Russians did produce the equipment for limited nuclear war after all. Dr. Kissinger's case at this point of his strategic development sounded very much like the Utopian Major De Seversky.

The introduction of nuclear weapons on the battlefield will shake the very basis of Soviet tactical doctrine. No longer will the Soviet bloc be able to rely on massed manpower as in World War II and in Korea. In a limited nuclear war, dispersal is the key to survival, and mobility the prerequisite to success. Everything depends on leadership of a high order, personal initiative, and mechanical aptitude, qualities more prevalent in our society than in the Soviet bloc. To be sure the Soviet forces can train and equip units for nuclear war. But self-reliance, spontaneity, and initiative cannot be acquired by training; they grow naturally out of social institutions or they do not come into being. And a society like that of the Soviet Union, in which everything is done according to plan and by government direction, will have extraordinary difficulty inculcating these qualities.

Here was the heart of the new new look of 1957. Kissinger was called in to put in book form a study conducted by the

Council on Foreign Relations. The basic assumptions in his book were: (1) Nuclear war can be limited if we draw up the proper rules. (2) We should take the initiative in this type of warfare because of our superior industrial base and superior democratic institutions. This solution to the dilemma of limited war seemed as American as hot dogs or supermarkets. The limited atomic warfare doctrine of the second Eisenhower Administration had a longer life than that ninety-day wonder, massive retaliation. Limited nuclear war died in the blue eastern Mediterranean in the summer of 1958, about a year after its birth. According to General Taylor: "During the Lebanon landing in 1958, the United States Army had an Honest John rocket afloat off Beirut but was not allowed to land it because it could fire an atomic warhead as well as a conventional one. In this instance, our political leaders felt that it was against the national interest even to suggest by the presence of the weapon that we might use atomic weapons in Lebanon."

In the Quemoy crisis a few weeks later, conventional, albeit unorthodox methods (pre-loaded amphibious supply trucks), not atomic weapons, were used to break the ring of Chinese Communist fire that was effectively blockading the offshore island.

Kissinger's book was based on the wishful thinking that somehow technology would save us from "any more Koreas." The strategy it represented was the concept of graduated deterrence (making the *nuclear* punishment fit the crime), formulated by two English Traditionalist strategists, Admiral Buzzard and Alistair Buchan, which, by their own admission, was not the preferred one but the only one *politically* feasible for the Western democracies. The United States Army and Navy reluctantly joined the Air Force and took Dr. Teller's advice to apply themselves to finding ways to use the new nuclear technology in war. Thus the last three years of the Eisenhower Administration found the West committed to nuclear defense of Europe through NATO's tactical atomic capability. Forces necessary to fight a non-nuclear limited war were progressively cut back. Fortunately, the second Berlin crisis of 1959 faded without war and without testing the new strategy. But from fall 1957 to summer 1961, the West was on the global defensive and it knew not why.

The only solution the Utopians could advance was more and more, bigger and better thermonuclear and atomic weapons. Our atomic stockpiles increased to the equivalent of ten tons of TNT for every person on the globe, and yet our international position deteriorated at an increasing rate.

The last years of Dulles's life were consumed hustling from crisis to crisis. One of the basic reasons for this international treadmill was that our world commitments had grown way out of balance with the *usable* force on hand to deal with Communist action.

Until Sputnik's appearance, 1957 was the Indian summer of the postwar era. America and the world were being crowded by a dynamic social system that had grafted Western technology onto a centralized social order. The Red rockets Bulganin had rattled at London and Paris would soon influence the Eisenhower Administration to try for a new round of peaceful coexistence, ending in a shambles at Paris in 1960.

The conventional land weakness, stemming from both new looks, was instrumental in speeding the loss of Laos and the creation of the third Berlin crisis of 1961. The shock of Sputnik allowed the Eisenhower Administration to accelerate the Polaris weapons system, which measurably reduced the chance of Berlin setting off World War III. Although the Eisenhower Administration did not realize or acknowledge it, 1957 represented a dead end to the doctrine of limited nuclear war, which various Utopians in and out of Washington had sold to Eisenhower but not to the world or even to the American public. Sputnik also destroyed the bomber offensive and the concept that the air battle for the air ocean is essential to victory.

The Age of Deterrence was greatly accelerated on that Saturday in October 1957 when the first man-made object broke free from the earth's gravitational field. United States grand strategy and individual service doctrine would have to be adapted to the new technology. Although it was not clear at the time to many, the means to this end was not through more defense reorganization or even greater dependence on nuclear weapons, but a return to traditional, old-fashioned dependence on men, ships, and rifles. The more modern the weapons became for waging total war, the more primitive and medieval became the techniques for waging limited and unconventional warfare. National self-restraint and patience became increasingly necessary, since no place on the globe was farther than a thirty-minute missile flight from Armageddon.

Early in February Admiral Burke cautioned:

A fundamental change has taken place in warfare and it is imperative that we recognize this. This change is the re-introduction of the element which has been largely absent in modern warfare — the element of restraint.

The present overwhelming disparity between offensive and defensive capabilities, has eliminated any expectation of gain from unrestrained warfare. All-out war has been reduced to an act of desperation — a last resort after hope is abandoned and gain forsaken.

Deterrent power provides one of the essential requirements of our defense posture, by continuing to make big wars unlikely. But deterrent power is not employable power — the value of any deterrent lies in its not being used. Meanwhile, there are other requirements to be met. There is the continuing problem of small wars, how to keep them from starting, but if started, how to keep them small.

Another problem, the Admiral told the English Speaking Union in London, is that

new weapons and new techniques have increased the vulnerability of and types of installations. This is particularly true of fixed bases which can be accurately located well in advance of attack. We in the United States Navy are particularly concerned about the increased vulnerability of stationary bases which support our forces at sea. To us in the Navy this means greater emphasis on moving forces, and less reliance on stationary bases for support.

The American Chief of Naval Operations told his British audience not to underestimate the threat of nuclear-powered, missile-firing submarines because "powerful new weapons invariably add to our strength at sea."

A few months later two speeches — one by an American and the other by a Britisher — spelled out specifically what Admiral Burke had only hinted at. On May 27, 1957, Senator Jackson delivered a memorable speech on "Ballistic Sea Power — Fourth Dimension of Warfare," in which he listed the many advantages of this "supreme deterrent of the ballistic era." This weapons system (1) could move in close, (2) was far less vulnerable, (3) was continually moving, dispersed, and did not need refueling for years, (4) was difficult to locate or destroy, (5) could not be eliminated by one massive attack like land power, (6) would draw missiles away from our homeland, and (7) reduced the possibility or likelihood of surprise attack. The senator wondered if it was just another weapon or the supreme deterrent of the missile age. Because of service rivalries and political and international implications, Senator Jackson thought that Department of Defense could not resolve the question, and he called for a presidentially appointed commission on ballistic seapower to help the President and National Security Council settle this vital question.[1]

Mr. Humphrey Atkins rose in the House of Commons during a debate over British defense policy to make similar comments. Mr. Atkins reminded his colleagues that

one big disadvantage for this country is that, while we may have deterrents, we must also provide places from which to launch them. This is a small island, and such sites might readily be located and charted. We might find them demolished by an enemy at the first onslaught, and then, at one strike, we should be deprived of our power to retaliate.

It seems to me that the Navy provides a possible solution to this problem. I do not say that it can be done immediately, but in the future the Navy could provide mobile platforms from which nuclear weapons of one sort or another could be launched. Such mobile platforms could disappear from the ken of a potential enemy. They might be discovered eventually, but at least it would be possible to move them about, and that is something that could not be done with land sites. Whether such mobile platforms should take the form of an aircraft carrier, . . . or whether they should assume some other form from which ballistic weapons could be fired, I do not know, but I think that is a role which the Navy could perform.[2]

Duncan Sandys, commenting on the British White Paper on Defense that caused such a stir in certain sections of the Western world, said:

It must be frankly recognized that there is at present no means of providing adequate protection for the people of this country against the consequences of an attack with nuclear weapons. Even if it were only a dozen, they could with megaton bombs inflict wide-spread devastation.

This makes it more than ever clear that the overriding consideration in all military planning must be to prevent war rather than to prepare for it.

This White Paper stated that Britain would stress missiles, thermonuclear warheads, and tactical atomic weapons, to which *Army* magazine in June 1957 replied: "The suggestion that the U.S. should follow Great Britain and go on a drastic military diet by reducing the strength of its Army disregards so many fundamental and easily discernible facts and conditions that it is astonishing that anyone would advance it."

It is hard to separate the concept of deterrence from limited war and more difficult still to meaningfully explain those differences to democratic nations on both sides of the Atlantic. However, it is plain that somewhere there is a balance between money spent on forces to prevent total war and money spent on forces to fight limited war. In the last years of Eisenhower's Administration so much money was spent on the big war deterrent that under a finite budget very little was left to prepare for the most likely type of conflict — limited war. Lloyd Norman explored this relationship very thoroughly in *Army,* January 1957. He discussed General Taylor's remarks on deterrence before the airpower hearings and explained what General Taylor meant was that the United States needed enough atomic airpower deterrence to prevent a total atomic war — but not to fight and win that war. Norman made this perceptive observation:

The implication of this profoundly important statement is that the U.S. should not attempt to bankrupt its economy by buying all the atomic bombers, ICBM missiles, and nuclear weapons needed to win the big war. Just enough to convince Soviet Russia that such a war would not be profitable to her and would end in destroying her.

Now, Air Force leaders and their strategists have made it clear that they believe the only effective deterrent to keep Soviet Russia from going to war is atomic airpower in sufficient massive strength to win a total war. This means they believe that Soviet Russia would not be deterred by a token display of atomic airpower or by enough bombers and nuclear bombs to destroy say fifty per cent of Soviet targets, or seventy-five per cent.

The Air Force strategy requires that it have enough weapons of atomic airpower not only to guarantee at all times the complete destruction of 100 per cent of Soviet targets. . . . [One Air Force source was quoted by Norman]: "We now have enough atomic bombs and we can deliver them to knock out Soviet targets at least five times."

Hanson Baldwin also took sharp issue with the Air Force doctrine:

. . . our military policies ought once and for all to renounce the pernicious one-weapon, one-service concept. We must build our armed forces upon a flexible strategic concept. . . . We cannot win the world struggle unless we are capable of multiple responses to multiple threats.

If we build our entire strategy upon massive retaliation, if we have to invoke nuclear weapons to meet any aggression, if we have no answer to the kind of creeping communism that has had such successes in Asia and the Middle East we are undone. We need deterrents to all types of aggression; we should not commit ourselves to rigid and inflexible responses. We should be prepared to fight any kind of war anywhere. Above all, we should retain enough conventional strength to enable us to answer a conventional attack with conventional means. . . .

Even if we built up a tremendous stock of atom bombs and missiles we could still lose the world for lack of a rifle.[3]

Baldwin's plea received scant support from the committee report of the airpower hearings released on February 20, 1957. It called for a vast increase in B-52 production to keep ahead of purportedly booming Russian production of long-range Bison and Bears. However, slowly but surely the news began to "leak" from official sources that a new national intelligence estimate revealed the Russians had mysteriously cut back their bomber production and would not surpass us until after 1959, if then. In 1961 it became known that the Russians had built less than one hundred long-range Bison and Bears, and it was speculated that this knowledge came from the U–2 flights. The Russians had indeed created a Potemkin Village as Charles Wilson had once insisted to the great derision of Utopian spokesmen. All the partisan service carping and political criticism since 1954, when the first bogus *Aviation Week* bomber pictures appeared, up through the Air Force–CIA intelligence estimates in 1956, were not for naught. The American bombers were built.

The danger of a monolithic organization in the intelligence community was never more clearly revealed than in the great bomber and missile gap hoaxes of 1954 to 1961. Democratic liberals used raw intelligence data to embarrass Eisenhower much the same as Herbert Brownell used raw FBI files to embarrass President Truman. During a speech in California in February 1957, Admiral Radford gave the first official hint that there had been a change in the intelligence estimates: "Now it would be great folly *not* to think of the Soviet Union as a first-rate airpower. They definitely are big league. But my assessment of all the information available to me leads me to conclude that they are still number two in the league. Our job is to keep it that way."

Air Force in May 1957 took on an air of outraged innocence in the article, "Hitting the Air Force Below the Belt": "A particularly vicious and unwarranted attack on the integrity of Air Force leaders, apropos the revised intelligence estimates of Soviet heavy-bomber production appeared in the March 9 edition of the *Arizona Daily Star* (Tuscon, Ariz.), in a long editorial entitled 'A 900-Million-Dollar Bobble.'" According to *Air Force,* the paper's editor, William R. Matthews, once special advisor to Secretary of Defense James V. Forrestal, went "out of his way to undermine his readers' confidence in the men who

shape our airpower policies." The *Arizona Daily Star* quoted
a *U.S. News and World Report* story of March 8, 1957, which
laid the facts on the line in relation to U.S.–U.S.S.R. bomber
production. William R. Matthews wrote that the revised estimates

tell a self-evident story of inexcusably mistaken estimates made by
top officers of the Air Force of their own intelligence, and shocking
gullibility of Senator Symington and his Congressional colleagues.
The probabilities are that the so-called intelligence originated in the
minds of some 'armament spenders' who, on the advice of their
well-paid public relations advisers in New York, deliberately planted
the misinformation on the Air Force officials and Senator Symington as a way of frightening the American people and members of
Congress into spending this extra $900 million.

Air Force summarized its views on the revised estimates in
April 1957: "They are temporary in nature, and apply only over
the next two years. They represent only a fraction of over-all
Soviet strength. They have already been reflected in the present
budget. We trust that the Congress will weigh these factors carefully in their current examination of the Air Force budget."

Senator Symington called Allen Dulles to ask for a memo
explaining why the new National Intelligence Estimates differed
from the testimony that Dulles had given the Airpower Committee in April 1956. Dulles's memo, which was inserted into
the *Congressional Record* on April 4, read in part:

DEAR SENATOR SYMINGTON:
    . . . The facts are as follows.
    The intelligence community is continually reviewing its current
and projected estimates of Soviet strength against the best evidence
obtainable. . . .
    The estimate of Soviet heavy-bomber strength as of April 1, 1956,
which was given in my testimony before your subcommittee, was
based largely on an estimated build-up rate which rested upon
earlier evidence.
    Subsequent to my testimony before your subcommittee in April
1956, the intelligence community acquired new and better evidence
on Soviet heavy-bomber production and strength in operational
units, and we undertook a complete review of our estimates on this

subject. Our revised estimate was not completed until after the conclusion of hearings before your subcommittee and after the adjournment of the Congress. It was based on new evidence and not on any extraneous considerations. This new agreed National Estimate revised downward the estimated total production of Bison as of July 1, 1956, but did not change the estimated number of modern bombers which the USSR could and, in the opinion of competent experts, probably would provide in its long-range force in the time period beyond the next two years, as submitted to your subcommittee in April. Obviously, this estimate of future Soviet heavy-bomber strength will be subject to constant review in the light of new intelligence.

Later in the year *Aviation Week* printed security information, probably from military intelligence or CIA, to attempt again to embarrass the Eisenhower Administration. The first leak came in late August as a reaction to the Soviet boast of their successful ICBM. Robert Hotz in *Aviation Week,* September 9, 1957, wrote an article blasting the so-called "Missile Misinformation." "The White House and Pentagon know when the Russians began their ICBM test firing program, they know approximately how many rounds have been fired to date and the general performance of these rounds in altitude and range." Robert Hotz wondered, "So why conceal them [the facts about Russian ICBM's] from the American public?" Symington accused the Eisenhower Administration of "unilateral disarmament" despite the Soviet ICBM threat, but he was not surprised because, in his mind, the Defense Department was geared to fight World War II rather World War III.

After Sputnik *Aviation Week* broke one of its biggest stories: The United States radar bases in Turkey had been spying on Russian missiles for years. Joseph Alsop used similar sources for his column and made the missile gap a political issue from 1958 to 1961. According to *Aviation Week* the "U.S. has been tapping Russia's missile secrets for more than two years by means of extremely powerful long-range radar and *other equipment based in Turkey."* (Italics mine.) The story added that the General Electric radar with a range of 1000 to 3000 miles, located near Samsun, Turkey, had detected long-range firings in early summer 1957. During June, July, and August there had been at least eight firings.[4] *Aviation Week* also hinted by the words "other equipment based in Turkey" that the Lockheed U–2 had also spotted the firings or the launching pads. The close relationship of the Air Force and CIA in the U–2 case became an open and embarrassing secret when Gary Powers was shot down over Sverdlovsk in May 1960.

Hotz addressed a screaming editorial at President Eisenhower entitled, "Why Mr. President?" "It is high time," the angry editor wrote, "the American people asked President Eisenhower why, in view of the overwhelming evidence available to him during the past two years on Soviet technical progress, he is still pursuing a policy that is slowing the pace of our military technology and sapping our future military strength."[5]

The ground was well prepared for exploitation of the defense issue and, more specifically, the missile gap controversy from 1958 to 1961. For the Utopians this meant another chance at selling counterforce based on bombers and missiles.

As usual, it remained for C. J. V. Murphy to give his stamp of approval to the modification of strategy and explain it in *Fortune,* August 1957, to his business audience, which had a special interest in the Eisenhower Administration. "America's Widening Military Margin" proved to be an unfortunate title choice in view of the Russian ICBM and Sputnik.

The basic thesis of the *Fortune* article was that the Russians at the London Disarmament Conference wanted to slow down the arms race because "the U.S. pace is too stiff for their existing technical resources to match." We should continue to push, Murphy advised, all along the atomic weapons spectrum, for without these weapons our world position would be undermined. "The military balance of power would inevitably swing back to the sheer Communist mass. Without nuclear weapons U.S. air power would be relatively ineffectual in a war with either Soviet Russia or Red China." The United States has blunted Communist propaganda campaigns against our superior weapons by

the "feat of producing a 'clean' thermonuclear weapon." Now
we can discuss the "logic of nuclear strategy, in the defense of
West, . . . more reasonably and therefore more intelligently."
Now we can pretty well concentrate "on military targets without
endangering whole populations." Thus the Utopians had reverted to the original concept of massive retaliation: the use of
the H-bomb in tactical situations. Clean up H-bomb fallout and
the strategy can be made palatable. The question soon arose that
if our H-bomb was so clean, why not let the Russians in on our
secret and thus purify thermonuclear war? Nothing much came
of that suggestion.

According to Murphy, in the fall of 1957 "the American
strategic position, vis-à-vis Soviet Russia, is being steadily improved. . . . The master requirement of U.S. strategy clearly
should be to maintain and intensify the deterrent power." He
then directed a bit of advice to President Eisenhower: "If ever
it made sense for the U.S. to hold fast to the long-haul strategy
devised by the President and the Joint Chiefs of Staff during the
first years of his Administration, it certainly does now, when the
U.S. power margin is widening."

Admiral Radford spelled out his interpretation of the strategy
of limited atomic war in the only news conference he held in the
four years he had served as the nation's highest military strategist: "There has been no change in concept. The basic problem
has not changed. If you have a little war, you want to win it as
soon as possible. You don't want to drag it out."[6]

And he was correct. Two weeks before the Russian ICBM
the United States had ditched the Geneva understanding of
1955. We had, thanks to clean H-bombs and small tactical
atomic weapons, reverted to our 1953–1954 position. It was
now possible to carry out a strategy based on a wide range of
nuclear weapons. Radford's timing was off too. He became
chairman of the Joint Chiefs of Staff about the time the Russians
exploded their advanced H-bomb, and he left office little knowing that his entire strategy would be invalidated by an advanced
Russian ICBM, launched a few weeks after his retirement.

On August 26, 1957, came the Tass announcement that opened the Age of Deterrence: "A super long-distance inter-continental multi-stage ballistic rocket was launched a few days ago. The tests of the rocket were successful. They fully confirmed the correctness of the calculations and the selected design. The missile flew at a very high, unprecedented altitude. Covering a huge distance in a brief time, the missile landed in the target area. The results obtained show that it is possible to direct missile [sic] into any part of the world."

The Russian announcement went on to say that it would now be possible to reach remote areas "without resorting to a strategic air force, which at the present time is vulnerable to up-to-date means of anti-aircraft defense."

Dulles, when asked for a statement, commented: "We have no particular reason to doubt the veracity of the announcement . . . although . . . the words were very carefully chosen and could cover much or could cover little. . . . In general, the Soviet statements in this area have had some supporting fact."

The October Sputnik brought a host of "I told you so's" from the Utopians. Unfortunately, the Eisenhower Administration caught a bad case of foot-in-mouth disease by referring to the Russian space achievement as a "scientific trick" or an "outer-space basketball game."

Joseph Alsop carped: "The Administration has known, in short, that the Soviets have been rapidly outdistancing this country in the ballistic missile race, whose outcome will predictably determine the future balance of world power."

Air Force in November 1957 was exceedingly harsh toward President Eisenhower. "Knowing how easy it is to criticize from the sidelines, one is reluctant to place the blame squarely in the lap of the President. Yet, there is no other choice." Robert Hotz proclaimed that "this country cannot continue to survive as the free world's leader in face of the Communist challenge without leadership that has the integrity and courage to face up to the grim facts provided by our intelligence system."

Now the pitch for counterforce began in earnest. The extremely broad campaign included demands for more B–52's, for placing all space and ballistic missiles under the Air Force, and for a vast shelter and recuperation program. The leaked Gaither Report was essentially a plea for counterforce, with heavy Utopian service and political overtones.

Everything could be solved by a reorganization: American education, science, industry, and, as usual, the Department of Defense. The Pentagon remedies were the same old tired ones: single service, single Chief of Staff, single military plan.

The Utopians, who had banked on America's continuing technological lead, were even more frustrated than the rest of the American people, which is saying a great deal. America, the land of Benjamin Franklin, Robert Fulton, Eli Whitney, Thomas Edison, the Wright Brothers, and Henry Ford, had been surpassed by an atheistic, materialist, Communist Russia — the home of vodka, caviar, leather boots, and the concentration camp. In 1957 the last illusion of our technological superiority faded into the heavens, in which Sputnik was spinning. Yet reality was blurred. If the Russians could achieve a technological breakthrough, why couldn't we? Instead of demolishing our faith in gadgetry, Sputnik only increased the impression that our electronic miniaturization, free society, and industrial know-how would make up for those scientific secrets the Russians had looted when we "let them" take Germany.

As part of a calculated campaign to use the post-Sputnik fear in order to create the counterforce that the Eisenhower Administration had so far refused to build, *Air Force,* December 1957, featured an anonymous article, "How Much Time is Left?" The editors claimed its authors were "highly placed individuals" who were charged with the responsibility of attempting to insure the survival of this nation in the face of nuclear attack. "We can no longer catch up," and "a shift in the balance of nuclear striking power is inevitable . . . *no matter what action the United States may take in the meantime."* We have a little more than a year left. *"By mid-1959 we will definitely be in this period of blackmail, if indeed we are not already."* By

1959 to 1961, the article predicted, the Russians will have a substantial lead over the United States and will be able "to strike without warning at all the targets in this country which might be used in retaliation against them." If they cannot get what they want through blackmail at this time it "would also be the most advantageous time for the USSR to initiate war." And there is nothing the United States can do to close the gap.

The inference was plain: The United States must launch a preventive or pre-emptive war before the Russians get the ICBM's to hit us in a thermonuclear Pearl Harbor. More preventive war agitation would appear in 1958.

General Power, speaking to an Air Force Association seminar in December, told the faithful that the Russians will attack the United States "when they think they are stronger than we are." The general predicted that by the end of 1960 the Soviets will have a large stockpile of ICBM's, and

it is my considered opinion that as this stockpile [Russian missiles] grows, so does the threat of general war. . . . The United States has been and still is their major obstacle. It, therefore, stands to reason that the Soviets will make every effort to eliminate that obstacle as soon as they have attained — or believe they have attained — the capability of doing so with impunity.

General Power asserted that since moral considerations will never divert Russia from the horrors of nuclear war, such a war was only a matter of time. "They will initiate aggression as soon as they consider it expedient to do so." The bomber general then used an argument which would become a key one in the strategic struggle. "The Soviet rules [sic] will accept even sizeable losses in Russian lives and property as long as such losses will not jeopardize their own positions and welfare or impair the achievement of their goals."

If the B–47 and B–52 become obsolete and not capable of performing the job, "the resulting gap will weaken our military strength-in-being to such an extent as to actually invite aggression."[7]

And so 1957, which began so hopefully with Eisenhower wishing the Russian people well, ended on a note of desperation and the strong possibility of thermonuclear war within the next year or so.

7

1958 — The Birth of the Missile Gap

AMERICANS WERE UNNERVED BY THE SHOCK OF SPUTNIK, and their frustration was compounded by Vanguard's spectacular televised failure. Senate and House investigators probed the military services and the Department of Defense, hoping to diagnose the disease before the patient died. There was great uneasiness in the air and American institutions received a searching examination. TV and radio specials were devoted to "where we stand." CBS editorialized: "The challenge of Sputnik — of which Sputnik, of course, is only a symbol — is a challenge to our way of life and to our very survival. . . . We may have to change the climate of American society. In a sense, we must restore some of the attitudes and values of our Founding Fathers."

Special ad hoc groups, like the Rockefeller and Gaither Committees, reported their findings to the American people and the President. The President's State of the Union message was eagerly awaited by a nervous America, but what really calmed the nation was Explorer I's successful orbit on January 31. An almost audible sigh of relief spread across the land, similar to the Free World's reaction to Commander Alan Shepard's first space flight.

The Eisenhower Administration gained time to prevent a headlong rush into unthought-out policies. The Democratic party and Military Utopians attempted to take advantage of congressional and public support to exploit the defense issue to their partisan interests. In his State of the Union message Eisenhower had promised a reorganization of the Department of Defense. Traditionalists of all varieties fought the commander-in-chief on this issue and won. The JCS were preserved as a corporate body with the right to appeal directly to Congress, a provision labeled "legalized insubordination" by the President. The services remained intact, and Congress preserved its control over defense purse strings. Utopian centralizers were not appeased, and future challenges to the traditional defense structure were indicated.

Early in 1958 preventive and pre-emptive war once again were proposed as a solution to our dilemma. A basic reason for this was the confusion in the American mind concerning the ballistic missile's military significance. The deterrent and offensive functions of thermonuclear weapons, once completely interrelated when the bomber was queen, now began to diverge rapidly as the ballistic missile's true function was realized. The process was greatly accelerated in this country because the first reaction to the Russian ICBM was to speed American counterparts. Without the challenge of Russian missiles there seemed no doubt that the Utopians would have continued building bombers, and the two very different functions of thermonuclear weapons would never have been clear.

In regard to "the deterrent" the Eisenhower Administration turned Traditionalist. The concepts of "adequacy," mobility, and invulnerability were the guidelines that Eisenhower adopted. The real Eisenhower answer to Sputnik and the Russian ICBM was Polaris and the concept of deterrence it implied. Polaris was a calculated risk that paid great dividends. Its basic assumption was that there would be no gap between the end of the usefulness of manned bombers and the introduction of enough invulnerable missiles to inflict unacceptable damage upon the aggressor nation in a retaliatory strike. Navy Traditionalists were pleased, but Army Traditionalists were unhappy because they were still starved for funds needed to create the million-man Army they felt the nation's commitments absolutely demanded.

General Gavin resigned and wrote *War and Peace in the Space Age,* which helped forward the limited war concept. General Taylor was to quit in bitter disillusionment in 1959 and to write *The Uncertain Trumpet,* which popularized his views on the strategy of flexible response in the election year 1960.

Military Utopians and their liberal allies were also extremely unhappy with the Eisenhower Administration. They gave tacit support to the great missile gap controversy of 1958, triggered by Joseph Alsop and abetted by assorted Air Force officers, Democratic politicians, including Senator John F. Kennedy, and Utopian writers, such as Drew Pearson, Jack Anderson, and C. J. V. Murphy.

On one point only could the Utopians agree with the Eisenhower Administration, and in this Military Utopians found themselves strongly allied with Conservative Utopians — Democratic and Republican alike. This was on the question of limited nuclear war. To a man they agreed that there should be no more Koreas; any future challenges should be settled by our superior atomic weapons. But once again Eisenhower let the Utopians down as he reverted to a Traditionalist position in refusing to sanction the introduction of even the smallest nuclear weapons at Lebanon, and rejected, after slight hesitation, any extension to others of his control over atomic weapons. Only strong executive action and use of conventional weapons surmounted the Lebanon and Quemoy crises. The long, laborious attempt to make atomic weapons conventional came to naught in the summer of 1958, when the Eisenhower Administration in effect scuttled its own new new look strategy as it had the old new look in 1954–1955 over Dien Bien Phu and the Tachens. Unfortunately, scrapping the new new look left us relatively naked in Europe. For his own reasons Khrushchev did not press his six-month Berlin ultimatum announced on November 27, 1958. In-

stead of a crisis in Berlin and a conference in Geneva, Khrushchev came to the United States, was fêted at our most exclusive
clubs, and sparked the Camp David spirit of peaceful coexistence.

During the lull, Traditionalist doctrine advanced in the
spheres of both total war and limited war. Navy Traditionalists
went on the offensive with their new strategic doctrine molded
around the Polaris Fleet Ballistic Missile, a weapons system only
thirteen months old. The Lebanon and Quemoy crises made a
sea power believer out of Secretary of Defense McElroy but did
not quite convince the Eisenhower Administration of the need
for broader limited war forces.

Admiral Burke and other naval spokesmen of 1958 stressed
three major naval concepts: (1) Polaris and deterrence, (2)
limited war, and (3) dangers of Defense Department centralization. They also continued condemning preventive war.

The 1958 campaign for the concept of balanced deterrence
was foreshadowed in a speech before a Reserve Intelligence
Division in New York on December 11, 1957. Admiral Burke
declared:

"Limited" action can destroy us just as surely as nuclear war, unless
appropriate force can be administered precisely and rapidly to stop
or to confine local disturbances. And in supplying this "limited"
pressure we must be careful not to apply too much pressure,
for this may cause a limited action to expand into one of
major proportions.

In other words, the admiral cautioned against using atomic
weapons in limited war, a concept eventually known as the
"doctrine of escalation." Instead, we should rely on the conventional fire-power of fast carrier task forces to provide the "flexible mobile instrument of graduated military power by which we
can project our nation's military policy over much of the earth's
surface." In closing, the admiral made a veiled plea for legalized
dissent in the Joint Chiefs of Staff, anticipating the drive for
centralization of the Department of Defense in 1958. "We must

steadfastly defend the system which maintains freedom to express eccentric ideas, 'non-conformist' ideas, from which we are privileged to choose those 'best' ideas."

In January 1958 the Navy's long-range objectives group issued an unclassified summary of Naval Warfare Group Study Number 5 ("National Policy Implications of Atomic Parity"). This document, along with the "Résume of Major Strategic Considerations" (NWG 62–60) by T. E. Phipps of the Naval Warfare Analysis Group, represented two of the most important doctrinal statements of the broad strategic concepts that underlaid the alternative to counterforce. Among the anonymous thinkers who helped prepare and popularize this dissenting strategy were Dr. Douglas L. Brooks, Dr. Thomas Milburn, Dr. John Craven, Dr. Robert Osgood, and Dr. J. T. E. Thompson. They made a great, but largely unnoticed, contribution to the West's security while their doctrinal opponents, Herman Kahn, Albert Wohlstetter, Stefan Possony, and assorted Rand Corporation representatives, became famous, or infamous, as proponents of counterforce.

The 1958 Naval Warfare Group document began with the realignment of strategy to the Age of Deterrence, which the ICBM had ushered in: "The loss of the U.S. monopoly in high yield nuclear weapons, coupled with Russian advance in long-range delivery systems has created a new situation in which the classical goals and concepts of military power require modification. Military *superiority* in unlimited war no longer connotes ability to 'win' — nobody wins a suicide pact. Thus all-out war is obsolete as an instrument of national policy." Yet such a war can occur either through miscalculation or an irrational act. What the West needs to do is find a solution that takes into consideration Soviet hostility, "yet leads to a mutual deterrence of all-out war sufficiently stable to survive occasional periods of tension." Our current strategic retaliatory forces are very large and highly vulnerable. Russian missiles have made the old "blunting or disarming" function of our strategic forces meaningless. But Russia can "plan a surprise 'blunting or disarming mission' against *us*." One solution would be to increase the "size of our striking forces to offset their vulnerability," but this would lead to an "arms race and also an invitation to the enemy for preventive war adventurism."

How do we make sure that "his calculation of our residual strength after his attack will agree with ours well enough to deter him"? Once we have provided ourselves with striking power as nearly secure against surprise as possible, "the invitation to preventive war will be withdrawn." So too will the need disappear for huge United States strategic forces. America's elected leaders will gain "time to think" because when "our retaliatory forces are invulnerable, retaliation will lose this nightmarish, semi-automatic, 'hair-trigger' quality." The document then discussed two ways to guarantee the security of our strategic forces against surprise attack: the "fortress concept" and mobility and concealment. The Navy Traditionalist thinkers analyzed the deficiencies of the fixed, land-based system:

The "fortress concept" of *invulnerability to presupposed level of attack* involves "hardening" and active defense of fixed installations; that is to say, burying them in concrete deep under ground, and surrounding them with anti-missile batteries, both at tremendous expense. This concept merely promotes an arms race. It challenges the enemy in an area (endless mass-production of higher-yield, more-accurate missiles) where he is ready and able to respond impressively. Fortress-busting is always possible, since any fixed defenses, including all foreseeable anti-ICBM defenses, can be overwhelmed by numbers. Once embarked on this course, we will be committed to build installations and defenses faster than the enemy can build missiles to knock them out.

The long-range advantages of relying on sea-based mobility rather than land-based hardening were then discussed:

By contrast, security against surprise, when achieved through mobility and concealment, discourages an arms race. This concept challenges the enemy in an area (military intelligence) where he can clearly be frustrated, *e.g.*, by submarine or mobile land-based missile systems. Numbers of missiles will avail the enemy nothing, if he does not know the location of his target. We in effect take an initiative which he can overcome only by maintaining hour-to-hour fine-comb surveillance of all our land areas *and* the vast oceans.

Phipps carefully reviewed the relation between specific deterrence systems and the arms race:

To the extent that we rely on the fortress concept to achieve security against surprise, we commit ourselves to an eternal, strength-sapping race in which the Soviets have a head start. But we *can* get off the arms-race treadmill at the start. We can decisively lessen the chance of all-out war through enemy miscalculation. We can do so by adopting for our next-generation retaliatory systems not merely the broad requirement of "invulnerability," but more specifically the requirement of *invulnerability through mobility and concealment.*

To avoid needless and provocative over-inflation of our strategic forces, their size should be set by an objective of generous *adequacy for deterrence alone* (*i.e.,* for an ability to destroy major urban areas), not by the false goal of adequacy for "winning."

When this has been done, Soviet recognition of the resulting thermonuclear stalemate can be expected to induce them to vent their aggressions only at lower levels of conflict than all-out war. As a result U.S. military capabilities for wars of *limited* objectives and means (in the Indo-China, Suez, or Korean pattern) will become more rather than less, essential in the age of absolute weapons — if we are to avoid being "nibbled to death." The sizeable reductions in strategic forces permitted by their security against attack, *if we elect to procure secure forces of the type discussed above,* should in time free funds to build up those badly-needed capabilities for deterring limited wars, and also for competing with the Soviets in other areas, such as political and economic warfare, space travel, etc., where we now offer them a less-than maximum challenge.

The whole alternative strategy (slowly adopted from 1957 to 1963) is summed up in this document. It would be slightly modified during the next three years, but its significance as the first major strategic pronouncement by the Traditionalists in the Age of Deterrence is beyond question.

Meanwhile, George Kennan took a look at the nuclear arms race and concluded that the "technical realities of this competition are constantly changing from month to month and from year to year." He was very dubious about the "frantic" schemes being devised for defense against atomic attack. "Are we," Kennan wondered, "to flee like haunted creatures from one defensive device to another, each more costly and humiliating than the one before, cowering underground one day, breaking up our cities the next, attempting to surround ourselves with elaborate electronic shields on the third, concerned only to prolong the length of our lives while sacrificing all the values for which it might be worth while to live at all?"[1] Kennan thus rejected the fortress concept solution to our strategic deterrent problem.

Another example of the new strategy and its acceptance by the Navy Traditionalists was found in the Naval Institute's prize essay for 1958 by Commander Ralph E. Williams, long a proponent of the alternative strategy. Commander Williams wrote in the March *Proceedings:* "Some time prior to 1960 a crisis of the first magnitude in its national security policy" will take place in the United States. "The crisis compounds both a budgetary and a strategic dilemma." He pointed out that we need two almost mutually exclusive types of forces for general and limited war, in order to prevent the erosion of our world position and our isolation in a hostile world. Commander Williams anticipated the post U–2 international situation when he wrote, "The years ahead will inevitably see a progressive disassociation of our overseas allies from any responsibility for the American strategic striking capability." What will be our answer? Will our actions "commit us irrevocably either to a sound and balanced strategy, still at the service of the Free World alliance, or to the discredited, outmoded, and self-defeating concept of a Fortress America?" By basing our delivery forces in the continental United States, it "will inevitably draw down counter-battery fire upon it." This makes the United States the world's most perfect target, he argued, and helps simplify the enemy's problem by providing him with fixed targets of known locations. How much better it would be to stress sea mobility and ocean depth concealment. It is infinitely cheaper, easier, and quicker for our enemy to build missiles than it is for us to build bases. This is a race we cannot possibly hope to win. To base our retaliatory force on land would force the nation into an armed camp, "for on land there is not only no place to hide, there is no place to go. . . . If . . . our retaliatory forces are secure, there is no measurable increase in order of damage to be received, no matter how greatly the enemy increases his offensive force, and therefore no requirement to increase our own on this account. The problem, once solved, tends to stay fairly well put, and we shall be left with adequate resources available to apply to lesser contingencies." This means that we will have some place to stand between the extremes of retreat and total war.

To the Traditionalist the major problem of 1958 was not the missile gap, which obsessed the Utopians, but the proper and adequate creation of limited war forces and the production of invulnerable mobile-based deterrents. Rear Admiral William F. Raborn, Jr., director of the Polaris program, addressed himself to the problem in *Air Force,* April 1958. The Admiral reminded his readers that "mobility is synonymous with the naval operation . . . The submarine, married to a missile that approaches a range of almost 1,500 miles, provides a rather tremendous effort because the sea areas outflank all land masses. . . ."

In the early days of airpower the Utopians, accusing Mercator of subversion, redrew the map so that the polar projections would dominate. With the advent of the ballistic missiles the Traditionalists returned to the globe, and the Utopians embraced Mercator. The Mercator projection makes the continental United States look much larger than it really is, thus giving the illusion that there is plenty of space to hide the Minuteman, Atlas, and Titan from the one-hundred-million-megaton rockets of our Communist enemies. The globe accurately depicts our four per cent of global space and the seventy per cent that is sea, thus making it the favorite of Traditionalist strategists.

Admiral Burke's Press Club January 17 speech indicated the Chief of Naval Operations completely accepted the new strategy.

When Polaris goes to sea it will be able to reach most of the significant targets in the world. Its location will be unknown and unpredictable and hence it will not be predetermined for any enemy's missiles. It will operate entirely under U.S. control. The Polaris submarine travels alone. The system is economical as such systems go.

The Polaris system, because of its mobility, its fast reaction time, and unknown locations under the sea can become a very strong deterrent to a Soviet decision to launch ICBMs against us or an IRBM against our allies. This system does deserve a substantial portion of the nation's reliance in its defense.

As the year went on, Burke spoke of the economy and "sufficiency" aspects of Polaris:

It is a comparatively cheap retaliatory system. It won't be necessary to maintain large residual forces of Polaris submarines against the possible destruction of surprise attack.

It won't take very many to destroy the enemy if there should be another war. This is one good way the Navy can equate the rising cost of weapons of war. . . .[2]

On December 10 at the Naval War College, Admiral Burke made a surprisingly direct attack on massive retaliation, first by criticizing the sloganeering aspect of that strategy:

Massive retaliation, which became a slogan, reigned for a time under the guise of a practical concept and a simple solution. What happened? The Communists continued the expansion of their influence and prestige, regardless of our ability to destroy them, regardless of the strategic nuclear threat. . . .

It is clear that if the Soviets had an intention to build up as rapidly as possible to attack the United States, their long-range air force would have long since been a true intercontinental force. They have demonstrated their capability of building this equipment, but intercontinental types of aircraft still constitute only a small part of their long-range air force.

I am not emphasizing these factors to challenge the necessity for preparedness against a sneak attack. That is necessary. But that preparedness has been over accomplished. We are over-insured for that one contingency. I simply stress that we must widen our sights to include the necessity for adequate preparedness against the more probable enemy courses of action. These enemy courses of action, which can be decisive in the long run, fall far below the flash point of general war.

Secretary of the Army Wilbur Brucker sounded a similar theme in his opening statement before the Senate Preparedness Subcommittee:

Limited War on the ground remains the most probable immediate threat to the security of the nation and its allies. We must give at least as much attention to the forces we are likely to use as we give to those forces which we hope never to use.

We cannot withdraw to a fortress America, cock our long-range missiles skyward and abandon collective security. . . . We cannot abandon, to the Communists, our allies with their vital lands, their industries, their scientific resources and their desire to be free. It would be a national suicide for this nation to retract its forces to the confines of the North American Continent where they, together with our people and our industries, would constitute an extremely vulnerable target. . . .

This serves to illustrate the importance of the Army's role in a balanced, tri-dimensional force which is indispensable to victory.

Army magazine reminded its readers in February and March 1958 that the only setbacks the Communists had experienced since 1945 "have occurred when land armies bore the brunt of resistance to aggression." General Taylor was quoted as saying that SAC has kept the "big peace," but only the Army can keep the "little peace" and in the process prevent the big war. To create this little peace force, *Army* called for a one-million-man army.

In early June six weeks before the Lebanon landing, Secretary of Defense McElroy was reported "somewhat annoyed" at Army officials who were continually talking about limited war forces because he felt they were "adequate."

But by November McElroy was praising the limited war potential of the Navy. One of the lessons of Lebanon and Taiwan, he told a news conference, was that future "probing" attempts by the Communist world would be in peripheral areas "reachable by us only by air or by sea. We have a real job for the Navy" since even the Air Force was handicapped by poor airfields in the area. The *Washington Daily News* commented on November 14, 1958: "In this age of H-bombs and missiles it has been a long time since anyone at the Pentagon — except the Navy itself — has spoken almost urgently of the greater need for seacraft."

The Traditionalist doctrine was on the verge of a renaissance, thanks to the Polaris and the ever-probing nature of the Communist drive for world empire, which made it clear that weapons other than nuclear were needed to stop the expanding Red tide.

Still Utopians clung desperately to the concept of a nuclear counterforce so superior and diversified that it could handle either total or limited war. A mix of manned long-range bomber and ballistic missiles was visualized as the type of deterrent force for the coming decade. Thus the Utopians effectively confused the concept of deterrence with that of the air offensive. Utopians considered "stability" and mutual deterrence to be pernicious doctrines and preferred to talk in terms of instability and "winning" the thermonuclear exchange. As the counterforce doctrine broadened, it included vast shelter programs and recuperation schemes in order to add to the credibility of the all purpose air-nuclear force.

A main plank in the Utopian program was the unification of the armed services and creation of a single Chief of Staff. Only then, they reasoned, would the nation be able to free itself from the Traditional obscurantists who refused to adapt and re-organize all their forces for the coming nuclear war.

In 1958 the Utopians also coined the word "aerospace." Space was an extension of air, they contended, and hence the natural medium of the Air Force. Thus the domain of the Air Force stretched from earth to infinity. Eisenhower's crucial decision, continued by President Kennedy, to make space exploration a civilian enterprise for peaceful purposes was resented by the Military Utopians, who wanted to carry the arms race into space by creating bomber satellites and moving the deterrent concept into the outer reaches of space.

Central to Utopian strategy — indeed, without it there could be no counterforce — was the problem of convincing the American people, Congress, and the executive branch of the government of the necessity of constructing the tens of thousands of bombers and missiles that a second strike nation needs if it is to "win" a thermonuclear exchange.

Counterforce continued to gain many adherents in 1958. The supporters of the missile gap controversy were unwitting or unconscious confederates of the Military Utopians as they made one last great effort from 1958 to 1962 to sell their radical and revolutionary strategy.

C. J. V. Murphy (*Fortune,* January) launched the 1958 missile gap controversy. This supposed confidant of the Eisenhower Administration and Republican party continued his campaign to discredit the President's underlying strategic assumption and thereby to give aid and comfort to the Democratic enemy by creating the missile gap issue for 1958 and 1960.

In 1958 as at other times, intelligence estimates were used by Utopian partisans to further their counterforce case — a phenomenon which leads one to suspect that CIA estimates are as accessible to selected reporters as the weather report is to the man on the street. The motives of the CIA and military intelligence community in making these figures available are also suspect, considering the possibility of their use for partisan political and industrial gain.

Eisenhower's new strategic estimate, Murphy explained, was supported by gleanings of United States intelligence. The intelligence community stated "that possibly as early as late 1959 the U.S.S.R. could deploy enough intercontinental ballistic missiles to smash or paralyze the Strategic Air Command's U.S. bases. The attack could occur with a warning of no more than ten or fifteen minutes." This represented a change in the original peril date of from 1961 to 1962. Murphy asserted that SAC with its bases and stockpile was still effective; in fact, the size of the United States stockpile was so great that "if disclosed, would dumbfound the world." Unfortunately, he added, the Russians need only 100 to 175 ICBM's to wipe out SAC.

Murphy obliquely but cleverly attacked President Eisenhower for his words to the National Security Council at the height of the post-Sputnik crisis. "I can't understand," the President reportedly said, "why the American people have got so worked up over this thing. It's certainly not going to drop on their heads." Murphy was pleased that the Gaither Report and Sputnik II forced "a new sense of urgency" on the Eisenhower Administration. As a result, SAC was dispersed, reaction time quickened, strategic early warning pushed, and ICBM production speeded up.

Air Force in April 1958 began to develop the relationship of the manned bomber to the philosophy of "winning." "Ideally, missiles would seem most suitable against large industrial complexes," wrote Major General James Ferguson. He warned that

this alone, however, is not sufficient to defeat an enemy. A balance of missiles and aircraft of varying performances is needed to produce the greatest threat to an aggressor and the one most difficult to defend against.

In warfare, victory demands the ability to render enemy military strength ineffective. The enemy will protect his military resources. They will be hardened, camouflaged, and dispersed. It will be necessary to ferret them out and attack them with high orders of accuracy and large weapons. Needless to say, we must provide ourselves with this capability.

Fortunately, the Air Force had just the weapon, the B–70, "to ferret out small targets of uncertain location which are critical elements of military strength."[3]

The spring *Air University Quarterly Review,* while welcoming missiles into the Air Force family of weapons, cautioned airmen "to keep them in perspective. . . . The first strategic missiles will be directed against relatively soft, heavily defended targets where extreme accuracies and yields are not stringent requirements and where fast reaction times and invulnerability to enemy defenses are important. The smaller, harder targets will still be left to the manned bombers, which can destroy them more efficiently." Thus the Air Force saw the need for bombers and missiles to enable it to "win" the total war.

The implications of the developing counterforce doctrine were clear. Concepts like the "balance of terror" and mutual deterrence, once a part of the Utopian doctrine, were now shunned like the plague because they implied stability and a leveling off of the arms race, at least on the thermonuclear or total war level. General LeMay, like most Utopians, was disturbed by these new concepts and argued: "The Air Force believes in deterrence. We do not, however, believe in the false security that derives from believing in the myth of *mutual* deterrence. In our view there *is no* similarity between the U.S. and the Communist bloc when it comes to the use of aggression as a national instrument. . . . As to deterrence, there is no more transitory state in world affairs than that of stalemate."[4]

The Utopians' launching of the missile gap campaign, from which it was hoped that counterforce would flow, was timed for the beginning of the 1958 congressional campaign. Joseph Alsop was the willing vehicle in a series of nationally syndicated columns appearing in late July and early August. He began dramatically:

At the Pentagon, they shudder when they speak of the "gap," which means the years 1960, 1961, 1962, and 1963. They shudder because in these years, the American government will flaccidly permit the Kremlin to gain an almost unchallenged superiority in the nuclear striking power that was once our specialty. The persnickety facts that prove this terrible charge are as follows.

First and most horrifying there is the guided missile picture. . . .

According to Alsop during the "gap" years the United States would have thirty to one hundred and thirty missiles and a few Polarises. The Soviets would have five hundred to two thousand missiles. In bombers SAC would have five hundred B–52's, fourteen hundred B–47's, and seventy B–58's. The Soviets would have three hundred fifty Bison and one thousand Badgers plus a new six-engined supersonic bomber. Soviet air defense would also be better than ours, and they would be "employing anti-aircraft missiles in the satellites." Alsop claimed the "Administration has of course chosen the most optimistic estimates, which are almost surely wrong on past experience." With a striking power superiority of five and ten to one "no wonder they shudder at the Pentagon."

On August 1 Alsop became even rougher with the Eisenhower Administration.

The time has come, once again, to take a very grave step in this space. It is time to say quite bluntly that the Eisenhower Administration is guilty of gross untruth concerning the national defense of the United States. . . .

The time of deadly danger will begin soon, during the period the Pentagon calls "the gap" — the years between 1960 through 1963 or 1964. Massive orders for hardware must be placed immediately — indeed, they should have been placed last winter — if we are going to make the feeblest pretense of "keeping abreast" during the years of the gap.

He listed the alleged missile gap as 0 to 100 in 1959, 30 to 500 in 1960, 70 to 1000 in 1961, 130 and a few Polarises to 1500 in 1962, and 130 and more Polarises to 2000 in 1963. In face of these figures he sarcastically asked, "If this is 'keeping abreast,' one would like to know how the Administration defines 'falling behind.' " Alsop on August 1 concluded, "At this instant, the last chance to save ourselves is slipping through our hands."

Two days later he continued his criticism of the Eisenhower strategy. "It is now the Eisenhower Administration's policy to permit the Kremlin to gain an overwhelming superiority of nuclear striking power in the next five years. This is the true, though unadmitted, response to the warning of the sputniks." How could the President do such a thing? Was it the mystical hypnosis of ex-Secretary of the Treasury George Humphrey? Well, yes, partly. But the real culprits were the Army and Navy theorists who sold Eisenhower on "overkill." "This theory has been put forward by the Army and Navy in order to protect their own appropriations from the competition of the needed vast expenditures to strengthen our nuclear deterrent."

What, then, is this theory of "overkill"? In essence, it is the argument that you do not need the power to "overkill," if you already have H-bombs and the means to deliver them in quantities sufficient to destroy the Soviet Union.

Being childishly simple, it sounds convincing. This is nonsense, all the same, because it slurs over the operational realities and altogether ignores the political-psychological realities.

Alsop then used an argument which the Rand Corporation would refine to an article of faith: the supposed willingness of Communist leaders to "accept" twenty million casualties in order to obliterate capitalism: "As the Defense Department's . . . Raymond Garthoff has pointed out, the Kremlin's standard of damage that can be expected in order to win the war was set in the last war. The Soviet Union then survived a holocaust of tens of millions of its people, and the destruction or semi-destruction of most of the cities of European Russia."

Thus Alsop maintained that the Russians would be able to strike a first blow and accept the relatively small amount of damage equal in amount to her World War II losses that our surviving forces would be able to inflict. This was the main line of attack devised by Rand Corporation strategists for the Utopians to use against the Army-Navy concept of finite deterrence.

On August 14, 1958, Alsop's charges against the Eisenhower Administration were reflected in a speech on the missile gap by the junior senator from Massachusetts — John F. Kennedy. Senator Kennedy compared our loss of the nuclear striking power advantage to the British loss of Calais in 1558. The British recovered from their loss by building the world's greatest navy, which swept the Spanish from the seas. America should rise to her challenges and sweep the Communists from the skies. The senator told his colleagues: "We are rapidly approaching that dangerous period which General Gavin and others have called the 'gap' or the 'missile-lag period' — a period, in the words of General Gavin, 'in which our own offensive and defensive missile capabilities will lag so far behind those of the Soviets as to place us in a position of great peril. The most critical years of the gap would appear to be 1960–64.' " Kennedy was afraid that the deterrent ratio during the later period would be heavily weighted against us. "There is every indication that by 1960 the United States will have lost its Calais — its

superiority in nuclear striking power. If we act now to prepare
for that loss, and if, during the years of the gap, we act with
both courage and prudence, there is no reason why we, too, cannot successfully emerge from this period of peril more secure
than ever."

The years of the gap would demand a rejection of massive
retaliation and exercises in "brink of war diplomacy." Senator
Kennedy said Eisenhower's years from 1953 to 1957 were lost
ones. They were "the years the locusts have eaten, and it is quite
obvious we obtained economic security at the expense of military
security, and that this policy will bring us into great danger
within the next few years." To solve our defense problems, Senator Kennedy wanted additional bombers, missiles, air lift, sea
lift, and manpower — more of everything. He was still groping
for an alternative to massive retaliation, little realizing that the
counterforce he advocated was but the hated Dulles strategy
updated.

By October 1958 the new 1960 budget was cranking its tor-
tuous pathway through the Pentagon. C. J. V. Murphy wrote
another analysis of the military problem entitled, "Defense: The
Converging Decisions." It was a clever acceptance of the Democratic and Military Utopian–inspired concept of the missile gap,
and it played down limited war. "Among the chiefs, whenever
they negotiate with their JCS hat on, the case for a greatly expanded limited-war capability does not loom so large as the
'Young Turks' in the Army and Navy would have the public
believe."

According to Murphy, Eisenhower's big problem was not
limited war forces, but "whether the general-war capacity is going to stay great enough in the years immediately ahead."
Murphy approvingly quoted Senator Kennedy and Joseph Alsop
on the missile gap and significantly added: "As ICBM figures
go, it was clear that Alsop's stuck fairly close to the mark." Thus
we can infer that Murphy got next to the same "agreed" intelligence estimates that Alsop did.

Because of missile reliability factors, Murphy informed his readers, it would be difficult in the next few years to launch a surprise attack against all the United States' retaliatory strength. "Beginning in 1962, however, the gap could indeed become critical for us. . . . It's up to McElroy to prevent the years after 1962 from being those of the 'widening gap.' "

The December 1958 issue of *Fortune* featured an article, "Civil Defense is Possible," prepared with the assistance of Herman Kahn. For five hundred million dollars Kahn and his Rand associates maintained:

It is also possible to build shelters that will protect their inhabitants from the blast created by thermonuclear weapons. Not only the people of the U.S. but their physical assets and industrial capacity can be given substantial protection, and the U.S. economy could recover rapidly from a thermonuclear attack. . . .

It [the federal government] could initiate something like the $500-million program *without instigating a great national debate.* Decisive action by the federal government would serve to strengthen its own hand in dealing with the Russians. Almost any civil-defense program, if pursued vigorously, would be a reminder to the Russians that the U.S. will not submit to thermonuclear blackmail — that it is prepared, should the need arise, to accept the possibility of a big war with big bombs. If this point were brought home to the Russians, then civil defense could itself serve to make that war less likely. (Italics mine.)

In 1958 the Military Utopians continued their support of limited nuclear wars, even though the conventional engagements at Lebanon and Quemoy seemed to be swinging the emphasis toward a greater need for conventional war preparations.

In February C. J. V. Murphy was enthusiastic over the nuclear NATO alliance, claiming the Russians were trying to weaken NATO "by creating a nuclear vacuum in the heart of Europe." According to Murphy, George Kennan was helping the Russian cause by his BBC broadcast in favor of disengagement in Central Europe.

Dr. Edward Teller, "Father of the H-bomb," in *Foreign Affairs* in January 1958, claimed there were "good reasons to believe that a limited nuclear war can be fought in a humane way — if any aspect of war can be called humane."

General White devoted an entire speech to backing up Dulles's 1957 position that nuclear weapons can deter local aggression.

He concluded by claiming that the United States cannot afford to have "two tremendous capabilities" — one nuclear and the other conventional. And if we attempted to fight a conventional war it would take years to end and "the suffering involved would be indescribable. The American investment in lives, resources, and effort would be tremendous." The only solution to our dilemma was nuclear weapons.

The Utopian strategist De Seversky wholeheartedly agreed with General White:

I am convinced that:

1. We cannot win a limited war fought with traditional forces regardless of whether conventional or nuclear weapons are used because of numerical lack of our manpower.

2. We can make limited war impossible if we make clear to the world that we possess a retaliatory force with the strategic scope and tactical flexibility to crush local aggression anywhere on the globe.[5]

It was apparent that the Military Utopians had not modified their views on limited nuclear war in spite of the vivid case studies in the conventional use of force at Lebanon and Quemoy.

8

1959 — The Conflicting Strategies Ripen

T HE YEAR 1959 WAS ONE IN WHICH A REPUBLICAN VICE president addressed, from Siberia, his fellow party members and engaged the Russian premier in a famous kitchen debate. East-West relations began stormily with the second Berlin crisis and ultimatum hanging over our heads. The year ended with a fat and jolly Russian premier romping through Iowa cornfields. Outside of a minor Laotian crisis, which sent the Sixth Fleet scurrying into Southeast Asian waters and the Bamboo curtain creeping down over Tibet, the world's "normal" trouble spots were quiet in 1959. The Russians failed to display any new weapons in their flyovers of May and November 1959.

The Utopians continued to criticize the alleged missile gap, and Republicans and Traditionalists insisted that the deterrent gap did not exist. In the continuing strategic debate between Utopians and Traditionalists the conflict sharpened. The two-year span from early 1959 to January 20, 1961, represented the high point in post–World War II strategic ferment, beginning with Wohlstetter's "Delicate Balance of Terror" in 1959 and ending with Hanson Baldwin's summary articles in the *New York Times* in January 1961.

Army-Navy strategists drew closer together as they watched

their Air Force colleagues head for the "wild black yonder" of space. Finite deterrence became a full-blown strategy backed almost to a man by Military Traditionalists. Military Utopians solidified behind the doctrine of counterforce. On May 9 the first fleet ballistic submarine was launched at Groton, Connecticut, and the U.S.S. *George Washington* was commissioned on December 30. The great new counterforce weapon, the B–70, ran into political and scientific trouble, and its future seemed dubious. The F–108 long-range interceptor was canceled in September 1958, so that the only weapons of true counterforce remaining were the B–52, armed with the undeveloped Skybolt, and backed by the untested Minuteman. A strategy without a weapons system to carry it out was next to useless as the Navy could attest from its 1948–1949 experience with the Louis Johnson–scrapped supercarrier U.S.S. *United States,* which naval strategists hoped would complement the intercontinental B–36 in the strategic delivery of the nuclear deterrent. The prize plum, Space, was split between military and civilian agencies, and Von Braun's Redstone team was transferred with the Army's belated blessing to the National Aeronautics and Space Administration.

The limited war doctrine was stalemated and submerged by Pentagon preoccupation with the strategic deterrent. General Taylor resigned in disgust to write his prescription for flexible response, eventually proving that the pen is mightier than a JCS hat.

The year 1959 also saw a renewed outburst of preventive–pre-emptive war advocacy. The missile gap scare helped reinforce extremists in and out of uniform who wanted to believe in this solution to our defense problems. As usual, the Utopians harbored most of the pre-emptive warriors. As in the past the need for a pre-emptive war pretext was the controlling factor — provided we still had a military superiority (though ragged around the edges) to carry out the first strike to its satisfactory conclusion. The Berlin crisis offered the perfect pretext if only the Russians would try something. Western ground forces had been so reduced in NATO that a nuclear response was the only one possible to a major Russian move against Berlin or West Germany. Utopian reasoning, war gaming, and theory called not for a limited tactical nuclear strike at Russian ground armies but rather for using this threat to our vital interest as the *cause célèbre* to launch the long-desired pre-emptive war.

In other words, Berlin was the great issue that would allow the Utopians to exercise initiative and catch Russian strategic air forces on their bases. To delay a year would give the Soviets time to amass the vast numbers of ICBM's the missile gap proponents claimed the Russians were building. Hence, the one last time to launch a disarming, or blunting, attack against the U.S.S.R. was in 1959. We had the well-honed weapon, and Berlin looked like the perfect issue. Ships and planes were put on alert in late May, but Khrushchev's May 27 deadline passed and our forces went back to their normal training exercises.

Thus passed the one last clear chance to wage preventive war with a minimum of American casualties. Henceforth, Utopians would stress the tremendous damage such a war would cause, but with proper civilian defense measures recommended by the Rand Corporation, the thermonuclear exchange would not be half so bad. As the Donnelly Report, *United States Defense Policies in 1959,* stated, "The tenor of the RAND report is that it is possible to live through a major nuclear war and even to reestablish a national economy and society but that much careful planning is needed to find the proper program to make it effective."

The Military Utopians made two major statements on preemptive war in 1959. One, a book by General Power on national defense, never saw the light of day; the other was an article (*Air Force,* March 1959) by Colonel Robert C. Richardson, III, "Do We Need Unlimited Forces for Limited War?" At the end of his clever piece were the words, "The views expressed in this article are the author's own and do not necessarily reflect the views of the USAF or the Department of Defense." But Colonel Richardson was no obscure Air Force colonel; he was intimately connected with the Air Force Chief of Staff and the Long-Range

Objectives Group, which he eventually headed until his alleged implication in the Rusk memo leak of early 1961 forced his rather hasty exit to Paris. (Secretary of State Rusk's private memo to Secretary of Defense McNamara suggesting increased limited war forces caused Utopian extremists to leak the information to Richard Fryklund and Earl Voss of the *Evening Star* in February 1961.)

This action was not surprising in light of *Air Force Basic Doctrine* of December 1, 1959, which was emphatic: "It follows, therefore, that the best preparation for limited war is proper preparation for general war. The latter is the more important since there can be no guarantee that a limited war would not spread into general conflict." Both Colonel Richardson's article and the *Air Force Manual* stressed the necessity for taking the initiative — a euphemism for preventive or pre-emptive war.

Colonel Richardson stated his basic point early in his article: "I propose to argue that a policy of deterring war — all types of war — may well be served by a diversified general-war capability, supported by a well publicized willingness to use it effectively to deal with major acts of aggression anywhere in the free world. In the final analysis it is the general-war capability that contributes most to deterring major limited acts of aggression and not the real or alleged ability to deal locally with such acts."

Colonel Richardson welcomed a major military test in Europe. "The ability of the strategic force to attack and destroy the existing long-range bomber and missile threat to this country, *given the initiative,* is the major deterrent to aggression, particularly in Europe." (Italics mine.) Richardson equated massive retaliation with SAC's ability to retaliate against enemy cities after absorbing the first blow. The massive retaliation concept, therefore, only deterred a direct attack on the United States. But to solve the security problem of NATO and other vital areas, a counterforce was needed.

What has deterred aggression in Europe and in other vital allied areas for the past ten years has been primarily the counterforce aspect of the general-war capability, backed up by the expressed willingness to use any and all forces to defend the free world if it should become necessary. . . .

On the other hand, the counterforce capability of the strategic general-war forces constitutes the one threat to an aggressor which, if exercised effectively, would lead not to mutual destruction but to defeat of the aggressor.

Colonel Richardson then made a veiled appeal for pre-emptive war:

An enemy nation will be most effectively deterred from attempting major acts of limited aggression if and when he can be made to realize that the US has both the *will* and the *physical capability* to retaliate, with our general war forces, and that, should we do so, the resulting possession of the initiative, will lead to our destroying the enemy's general-war capability without invoking massive retaliation, but in such a way as to prevent him from achieving his limited objectives.

February and March 1959 witnessed an outbreak of pre-emptive war hysteria in Washington, which, though the President tried to silence it, only made matters worse. David Lawrence's March 3 column titled " 'Pre-emptive' War by U.S. now Called a Possibility," was based on an exchange between Secretary of Defense McElroy and Representative McCormack of Massachusetts before the House Space Committee. "Mr. McElroy emphasized that the present policy is not to strike the 'first blow' but 'whether that always will be true is another matter.' " Representative McCormack commented that he was encouraged to hear America might change its strictly defensive policy under certain conditions.

President Eisenhower, asked about McElroy's statement and whether he could "foresee any circumstances in which we might . . . strike the first blow against a possible aggressor," replied on March 5:

No . . . That is why, I will discuss that for a moment in this fashion: The right of self-preservation is just as instinctive and natural for a nation as it is for the individual. Therefore, if we know we are, at any moment, under a threat of attack, as would be evidenced by missiles or planes coming in our direction, then we have to act just as rapidly as is possible, humanly possible to defend ourselves.

But when you go beyond that point, I don't know exactly what this conversation meant, for the simple reason that I'm quite sure the Congress is not thinking of amending the Constitution and putting in the hands of the President the right to declare war. . . . But I do point out that when you have got certain circumstances that put your life or could put your life or the nation's life right at stake, then there is no time and whatever would be necessary, the President would then order.

The *Evening Star* (Washington) had pointed out editorially the day before that our policy decision not to strike first in event of war imposed a considerable handicap on this country, but it felt this was the right policy, for adopting the concept of preventive war would probably increase the likelihood of Russia striking first.

Doris Fleeson's interpretation of Eisenhower's remarks was that "for the first time in the history of the republic, the President of the United States has said that this Nation might strike the first blow of a future war." Yet on April 13 in Phoenix Admiral Burke told an audience, "The world well knows that it is a firm United States policy that we will not initiate the destruction of a large part of the world by launching a general nuclear war."

The preventive war talk was not lost on the Russians. *Red Star* charged that certain congressional hearings on the effect of atomic attacks were designed to prove that the United States "must not wait to be attacked." The Russian military newspaper claimed "the American military command is now endeavoring to frighten the broad masses, placing before them the question: Either we attack the Soviet Union or they will destroy us first."

The Utopian apologist Jack Anderson, reporting the ban on General Thomas S. Power's book on defense policy by the Eisenhower Administration, summed up General Power's thinking on pre-emptive war:

Our military strategy is essentially defensive. This does not preclude the possibility that we may have to strike the first blow. But while preemptive action on our part might initiate open warfare, it still would not represent offensive strategy because it would be undertaken only in self-defense.

There is relatively little likelihood of a preemptive war against the Soviet Union because so long as there is the slightest hope that we can prevent a Soviet attack through diplomatic means or a strong posture of deterrence, our government, backed by the majority of the American people, would be opposed to more drastic means.

Representatives Holifield and McCormack in a civil defense debate in July looked approvingly on the first strike doctrine. Representative Holifield said that "unless we are clearly willing to use, in extreme necessity, our deterrent striking force, that force is not really a deterrent. . . ."

Dr. Eugene Rabinowitch, examining the causes for the rash of preventive–pre-emptive war statements, concluded (*Bulletin of the Atomic Scientists,* November 1959) they were due to the vulnerability of our nuclear striking forces. He saw great danger of war by miscalculation occurring during times of crisis when our and the enemy's retaliatory forces are on "alert."

The Strategic Air Command . . . has long entertained the idea that it is not going to wait for enemy missiles or bombers to rain destruction on its bases. Rather, it would like to strike first, when it becomes clear the other side's preparations indicate that an attack is imminent. This is the strategy of pre-emptive war.

There is no reason to assume that the President and the National Security Council have accepted this doctrine, but there is no doubt that the Strategic Air Command is dedicated to it, and that their reasoning is convincing enough to make its adoption in some future contingency feasible.

Only when the United States acquires an arsenal of solid fuel rockets, which could be fired rapidly from launching pads deep underground or from movable platforms at sea or on land, will the arguments for pre-emptive attack lose their persuasiveness, but this will require several years.

In anticipation of such a breakthrough, Utopian strategists began to attack finite deterrence and the Polaris system upon which the strategy was based. A counterforce strategy is an impossibility if the concept of stability, adequacy, or invulnerability become accepted parts of a national defense policy. In other words, if the executive branch of the American government, for whatever its reasons, comes to the conclusion that an arms race is senseless in the age of invulnerable ballistic missiles, it follows that there will be a demand for a finite level of weapons systems for total war. Stabilization of the arms race becomes the object. Arms control becomes feasible; even unilateral arms control is a possibility.

Albert Wohlstetter of Rand Corporation in January's *Foreign Affairs* examined the stability of the thermonuclear balance and concluded: "The balance . . . is in fact precarious. . . . Deterrence in the 1960's is neither assured nor impossible but will be the product of sustained intelligent effort and hard choices responsibly made. . . . While feasible, it will be much harder to achieve in the 1960's than is generally believed."

In conclusion, Wohlstetter told of the difficulties in the path of the "automatic deterrence" theory based on the balance of terror. He warned: "It is a contribution to the rhetoric rather than the logic of war in the thermonuclear age. The notion that a carefully planned attack can be checkmated almost effortlessly, that in short, we may resume our deep pre-Sputnik sleep, is wrong and its nearly universal acceptance is terribly dangerous."

Yet in 1959 the Eisenhower Administration was trying to relax international tensions. Nixon and Khrushchev exchanged visits, and the President was scheduled to make a triumphant tour of Russia in 1960. An unenthusiastic Wohlstetter commented: "Almost everyone seems concerned with the need to relax tension. . . . Relaxation, like Miltown, is not an end in itself. Not all danger comes from tension. To be tense where there is danger is only rational."

The Utopians were encouraged when Defense Secretary McElroy testified that the Soviets would probably have a three to one superiority in ICBM's by 1961.

Robert Hotz, asking, "Will we close the missile gap?" (*Avia-*

tion Week, February 23, 1959) maintained that the most con-servative (official) figures placed the unfavorable ratio at three to one, whereas Senator Symington claimed they would be four to one. Hotz urged Congress, Defense, and the White House to "immediately tackle a concrete plan to narrow the ICBM gap with the Soviet Union in . . . the critical time period we face. The alternative is to allow the Soviets to build an ICBM force capable of smashing both our own small ICBM capability and the grounded bombers of SAC in one swift 30-minute blow."

Eisenhower reacted to this and similar criticisms as the oppo-sition fueled up the soaring missile gap issue. In a late February press conference the President once again accepted the Tradi-tionalist concept of balanced forces: "And remember our system is a balanced one. We should not concern ourselves so much with one single item. Somebody makes a demagogic talk about a missile, or somebody else about a different submarine or a piece of radar. You have got a whole level of balanced types of equipment, training, organization and strategy that we believe fits our system."

Contrary to Eisenhower's strategic views, C. J. V. Murphy (*Fortune,* November 1959) outlined the Air Force's justifica-tions for the counterforce strategy and weapons system: "It wants the B–70 for reconnaissance, for assessment of damage in the midst of war, and for precision attacks on enemy missile sites and command centers. Underlying the argument is a doctrine which holds that the ICBM's are essentially city destroyers and that the desirable role for the Air Force is that of a counterforce to concentrate on an enemy's means of war."

As predictable as the coming of spring, another C. J. V. Murphy defense article appeared in April, summing up the Utopian arguments of the preceding season. Beside a picture of "the embattled Mr. McElroy" were the following highly signifi-cant words: "[The Eisenhower Administration's interest in a balanced budget] is holding down the U.S. output of ICBM's, thereby forfeiting a dangerous offensive advantage to the Rus-sians."

Murphy asserted that because of the missile gap the United States' deterrent had been undermined and the United States had been exposed to ballistic blackmail over the Berlin crisis. The Utopian popularizer rode Eisenhower hard. "For the trouble that now surrounds the military budget (and McElroy), Eisenhower is in no small part to blame." The United States could have three times as many ICBM's in three years. But, said Murphy, the Administration had neither the "intention or policy" to match "missile for missile" the Russian production. Murphy, like *Aviation Week,* hinted about the existence of the U–2 reconnaissance aircraft. "The military-budget decision was made in light of what U.S. intelligence has gleaned of Soviet progress by means of long-range radar and *other techniques."* (Italics mine.) Murphy revealed that United States intelligence had found only a dozen or so ICBM's and that on the ICBM range "an absolute blank descended." This meant, in effect, that the Russian ICBM estimates would have to be changed downward, i.e., 10 ICBM's early 1959, 100 early 1960, and 500 mid-1961. United States planners came to the conclusion "that the Russians were not striving for a large capability as early as first estimated."

Utopian strategic literature received a tremendous boost with the publication of the Stanford Research Institute *Journal* for the Fourth Quarter of 1959. Included in that issue was Herman Kahn's "The Nature and Feasibility of War and Deterrence," which was eventually reprinted by two different congressional committees and appeared in expanded form in his book *On Thermonuclear War.* Kahn set forth his theme that a thermonuclear exchange would not necessarily end in "mutual annihilation." *"We concluded,"* Kahn optimistically wrote, *"that for at least the next decade or so, any assumption of total world annihilation appears to be wrong, irrespective of the military course of events."*

After proving thermonuclear war feasible, Kahn set forth his three famous types of deterrence. Type I protected the nation against a direct attack; Type II deterred extreme provocation; and Type III deterred moderate provocation. Kahn and the counterforce school of Utopian strategists maintained that by and large the United States should have thermonuclear forces so superior that all three types of deterrent contingencies could be taken care of.

The same issue of the Stanford *Journal* contained an article by Rogers Cannell entitled "The Strategic Role of Civil Defense." The brunt of his argument was that civil defense preparations "can be a positive war-deterrent force, and they are a prerequisite to survival in any total-war situation." He went on to aver that the United States "has the technical know-how to save 90 per cent of the population in nuclear war" and that civilization can recover from total war.

What the Utopians hoped to accomplish by civil defense and enormous quantities of thermonuclear weapons, the Traditionalists sought to effect by invulnerability and quality.

Admiral Burke observed: "In making our retaliatory force secure from enemy attack, we do not need great numbers of missiles and bombers. Whether the USSR has one-half as many or several times as many missiles as the United States, is really academic as long as we have the assured capability of destroying Russia and as long as the Soviets know it and are really convinced of it."[1]

Some Congressmen attempted to explain these highly complex and emotional strategic issues. Representative Gubser told his fellow representatives that "we are worrying about the wrong missile gap." Instead of trying frantically to match the Russian missile for missile, we should worry about the Polaris gap. He likened the Air Force concrete ICBM fortresses foisted upon America by the "polished words of Air Force public relations experts" to twentieth-century equivalents of the Great Wall of China, Rhenish and Scottish castles, or the walled city of Quebec. He warned: "The famous Maginot Line of France presents a more recent monument to the same mistake. Even in the 20th century man has still to learn that the impregnable fortress of today will certainly be bypassed or splintered by the weapon of tomorrow."

The Traditionalists in their drive for Polaris and a new total war deterrent strategy did not overlook limited war. Nearly all Admiral Burke's speeches in 1959 contained either a positive statement on limited war or a reference to it. In a May 6 Kansas speech the admiral remarked: "Twice in 1958 American sea-power demonstrated its powerful influence in the maintenance of tranquillity in troubled waters. Twice United States naval forces, the SIXTH FLEET in the Mediterranean, and the SEVENTH FLEET in the Far East, created an environment of strength in a local area in which free nations were able to act in their own be-half to prevent critical situations from deteriorating into chaos or spreading warfare."

Captain Brown Taylor called conventional forces "the lesser deterrent." His essay on this subject in the August 1959 *Proceedings* was essentially a plea for a "truly credible combat-ready mobile force of Army and Marine Corps troops" big enough to handle another Korea.

General Maxwell Taylor retired from the Army and prepared his case for flexible response, which included a deterrent to thermonuclear war and a credible though equally important de-terrent to limited war. *Look* published excerpts from *The Un-certain Trumpet* in the late fall. By the end of 1959 both the Army and Navy Traditionalists had placed their cases for bal-anced deterrence on the record.

Also helping the Traditionalist cause was Hanson W. Bald-win, who opened his significant article on limited war in the May 1959 *Atlantic Monthly* with a famous quotation from Admiral "Cat" Brown:

In early 1959, a three star admiral publicly admitted the most significant politico-military heresy yet confessed by a man in uni-form. Vice-Admiral "Cat" Brown answered a question at the National Press Club in Washington with a simple negation which struck at the heart of many of the nation's military policies. "I have no faith," he said, "in the so-called controlled use of atomic weapons. . . . I would not recommend the use of any atomic weapons, no matter how small, when both sides have the power to destroy the world." Admiral Brown added that he did not believe there was any dependable distinction between tactical, or localized and restricted, target or situations and strategic, or unlimited, situations.

In some strategic circles this has become known as the "Cat" Brown thesis, which is drastically opposed to Utopian thinking on the use of atomic weapons in limited war.

The stage was set for the great strategic debate of 1960. Counterforce versus balanced deterrence would grapple for public, congressional, and service acceptance. The real target of the debate was the new Administration, which would take office in January 1961. For in the final analysis a strategy can be successful under our form of government only if the executive branch is wholeheartedly behind it. A new strategy, or an old one given new life, is in its early stages a hothouse plant. Domestic politics, technological breakthroughs, international events and personalities all conspire to modify, stunt, or kill a fledgling strategy.

9

1960 — The Continuing Strategic Debate

1960 WAS, ABOVE ALL, AN ELECTION YEAR. IT SEEMED APPAR-
ent that the Republicans were going to campaign on a platform
of Three P's — Peace, Prosperity, and Progress — with Vice
President Nixon leading the ticket. Eisenhower's summit conference in May was to be followed by a triumphant tour of
Russia near enough to election day to be remembered. But by
mid-summer both Peace and Prosperity had turned to ashes,
leaving only a questionable Progress on which to campaign.

The Democrats developed issues out of the missile gap, the
declining state of the national economy, and American prestige
in order to wrest the White House from the Republicans.

The calm and serene first quarter of 1960 exploded in the
next months into a series of international crises that have yet to
run their course. The shooting down of Francis Gary Powers in
a U–2 over Sverdlovsk, Russia, triggered a series of foreign
policy reverses and crises: the abortive summit conference, the
overthrow of Syngman Rhee, the Tokyo riots, the civil war in
the Congo, the deteriorating situations in Cuba and Laos, and
Mr. Khrushchev's shoe pounding at the United Nations.

It was inevitable that the continuing strategic debate between
Utopians and Traditionalists over the proper type of deterrent
strategy would become entangled with partisan politics. Ever
since 1954 the Democratic party had been using a series of

"gaps" to cast doubt on the wisdom of the Republican party's handling of America's defenses, and in the process they hoped to cut President Eisenhower down to size. The most glamorous and fearful of these "gaps" concerned the number of ICBM's the Russians had, or would have, in the next three years. Utopians and most Democrats unquestioningly accepted the missile gap as a matter of faith.

Scholarly works and articles by the score were based on the assumption that such a gap indeed existed. These works suggested four solutions to the problem: (1) pre-emptive war, (2) airborne alert, (3) a crash program for fixed-based ICBM's, and (4) mobile sea-based deterrents. Utopians and most liberals accepted the first three solutions, though some liberal Democrats were opposed to pre-emptive war. Traditionalists, most Republicans, except extreme Conservative Utopians, and some Democrats favored the fourth solution.

Putting one's faith in Polaris and the strategy it represented was made easier when on July 20, 1960, the U.S.S. *George Washington* successfully fired two Polaris ballistic missiles from an underwater launching site off Cape Canaveral. The first two Fleet Ballistic Missile submarines U.S.S. *George Washington* and U.S.S. *Patrick Henry,* were on station by January 1, 1961. During 1960 the Utopians campaigned furiously for their counterforce strategy, which was now broad enough to include *all* aspects of defense and offense. The Traditionalists saw the international technological events of 1960 as added proof of the validity of their balanced deterrence strategy. The need for mobile sea-based deterrents and modernized, mobile, limited war forces was apparent to all but a few Traditionalist strategists.

Secretary of State Christian Herter, in an address to the American Bar Association, September 1960, listed four means by which the United States hoped to carry out its foreign policy aims: "(1) We maintain an invulnerable strategic deterrent. (2) We maintain a secure and diversified capability for responding to, and suppressing, a wide variety of lesser threats to the

peace. (3) We maintain collective security arrangements . . .
(4) We seek safeguarded arms reduction which will diminish the
risk of war resulting from a continuing and spiralling arms race."
The Secretary of State had tellingly summed up the Military
Traditionalist position on the purpose of flexible armed forces.

But again in 1960, as in other years of the post–World War
II era, came the call for preventive war. The doctrine of pre-
emptive war received official sanction on April 29, 1960, when
George H. Mahon, chairman of the Committee on Appropriations, submitted Report 1561 on defense appropriations. Included in the otherwise technical report was a clear rationale for
pre-emptive war:

In the final analysis, to effectively deter a would-be aggressor, we
should maintain our armed forces in such a way and with such an
understanding that should it ever become obvious that an attack
upon us or our allies is imminent, we can launch an attack before
the aggressor has hit either us or our allies. This is an element of
deterrence which the United States should not deny itself. No other
form of deterrence can be fully relied upon.

The major news weeklies understood this as a call for pre-
emptive war despite Mr. Mahon's protests to the contrary.

Thus *Newsweek,* May 9, 1960, commented, "In the long and
bitter debate over defense, the strategists, all seemingly qualified
men, have differed widely." The Air Force argued vehemently
for what was generally known as a "preemptive war strategy."
"Its case as offered by the Strategic Air Command: the only
deterrent that Soviet Russia will respect is the ability to strike
first, if necessary, and with such power that it would bring
Russia to her knees almost instantly."

Time, May 9, 1960, pushed the doctrine of pre-emptive war
in its most naked form. It insisted that "the slow, careful phrases
of Chairman George H. Mahon, a tough-minded Texan" were
"miles away from the concept of 'preventive war'. . . . The
committee's statement was a defense of what has been called
'preemptive war.' "

In its slickest fashion *Time* then editorialized and played God, State Department, and American history revisionist: "The Mahon committee's position was in conflict with prevailing doctrine that the U.S. must suffer the first blow in order to justify counter-warfare. . . . Defenders of pre-emptive war hold that U.S. intelligence can and will know when an enemy is preparing to strike — just as it had advance evidence of Japanese intention to attack, though not specific knowledge of where and when, on the eve of Pearl Harbor."

In a similar vein Robert Sprague, a member of the Gaither Committee, said in a May 24, 1960, television discussion he believed that "if we have strategic intelligence that the Russians are planning a strike against us that we certainly should make the first strike." Mr. Sprague maintained that the United States had a greater relative superiority "over Russia than it has ever had, or will have again." Then he presented his case for pre-emptive war:

Now with the enormous power of nuclear weapons and ability to deliver them over long distances, if we suffer the first strike this would wipe out a very large percentage of our military capability, and in this position we do not have the superior power position. . . .

If war appears to be imminent and Russia, for example, for her own reasons isn't making the progress of peaceful means that she wants to make, and decides on military means, in that event it is absolutely essential we strike first if we possibly can.

The Donnelly Report, *United States Defense Policies in 1960*, bluntly and correctly connected pre-emptive war, although it is called pre-emptive strike or attack, with counterforce. The 1960 report stated:

Another concept which is closely related to the counterforce strategy is the preemptive strike or attack. The theory here is that when a nation is positive that it is about to be attacked, its chances for survival are likely to be much greater if it can get in the first blow. This is "getting the drop" on an opponent when a fight becomes inevitable. Advocates of this doctrine point out that knowledge of an imminent attack is sufficient justification for protective measures, including knocking an adversary out before he can strike and perhaps cause such weakness that an effective counterblow would be impossible.

General Power was again given the task in 1960 of opposing all at the same time President Eisenhower, "minimum deterrence," and Military Traditionalists. A series of remarks were prepared for General Power to give at the Air Force Association gathering in San Francisco.

Today, more than ever before, the advantage lies with the nation that has the initiative, that is, starts the war. . . . This means that, merely by passing the initiative to the Soviets, we degrade our capability by two-thirds. . . . On the other hand, we must never permit the Soviets to conclude that they have a monopoly on the initiative. If they could be sure that we would not take the initiative under any circumstances, nothing would stop them from taking over Iran, Turkey and the rest of the Free World.

The Utopians studiously avoided scrutiny of the costs of preemptive war or its effect on democratic institutions.

Presumably, the United States attack would be delivered without benefit of congressional declaration of war, and a heavy responsibility would be on the decision-makers — the President and the top military — to be sure that they were not wrong about the enemy's intentions and actions. But it is doubtful United States intelligence, or anybody's intelligence, can ever be that effective. In the past ten years there have been a number of notable intelligence gaps that reportedly have caught our intelligence completely off guard: the Chinese intervention in Korea and placing of two hundred thousand "volunteers" behind the Eighth Army; the speed with which Russia developed nuclear weapons and jet bombers; Nasser's seizure of Suez; the coup d'etat in Iraq; the Russian Sputnik and IRBM; Syngman Rhee's ouster; and the ill-fated Cuban invasion.

Pre-emptive war would require decision-making power to be consolidated into fewer and fewer hands, namely, the President and the chairman of the JCS or a single Chief of Staff, for the compelling reason that the decision to launch the preventive attack would have to be made in "one helluva hurry" — between the time that the intelligence reports irrevocably indicated that the Russians were about to launch an attack and the one-half hour or less flying time of the ICBM.

As to the cost of pre-emptive war, *Newsweek,* May 9, 1960, noted that "high officers, including President Eisenhower, have grave doubt about the strike-first strategy. They insist that it would cost such fantastic sums to carry out that it would bankrupt the nation. The Strategic Air Command alone would cost $30 billion a year."

The adoption of a philosophy of pre-emptive war would trigger an untold and fantastically expensive arms race of a completely new order and of an infinite nature. The idea of a peaceful, civilian control of space would be cast aside, and NASA would inevitably be absorbed by the USAF. There would not be enough funds left over to equip conventional or limited war forces. Instead, the 1953–1954 era of the new look, with its fanatical obsession over suicidal hydrogen weapons and its massive retaliation strategy, would be perpetuated into the seventh decade of the twentieth century but on a grander and vaster scale.

The main themes of the Utopians during 1960 were the missile gap, counterforce, and the weapons needed to resolve both. The Military Utopians went on the offensive and exercised the greatest of initiative by developing "the gap," the strategy, and the weapons system.

General Power opened the year's debate in a speech before the Economic Club of New York on January 19 with a hair-raising announcement that the Russians would need only three hundred ballistic missiles to wipe out our entire nuclear strike capability within one-half hour. Joseph Alsop and some Democratic senators pounced on and popularized the SAC general's largely unnoticed address. Secretary Gates and President Eisenhower responded that there was "no deterrent gap." Once again Military Utopians had teamed up with the Democrats to make defense a highly political issue. The bomber gap was dead, but not many noticed it because a much more glamorous and dangerous gap was opening up before the American voters. United States intelligence estimates had revised the Russian long-range bomber strength downward once again. In 1959 the Russians were officially estimated to have: 500–1000 Badgers (twin jet medium bombers); 250–500 Bison (heavy 4-jet bombers); and 100–200 Bears (4-engine turboprop long-range bombers). In 1960 the Russians were officially estimated to have: 1000 Badgers, 100–120 Bison, and 60–70 Bears. These figures explain why the Russian bomber gap of 1954 to 1957 had disappeared. But all this was forgotten now because 1960 was an election year, and the Democrats controlled Congress and the investigating committees.

General Power's speech, which so antagonized General Eisenhower that he called the head of SAC a "parochial" general, included the following assertions, as outlined by Joseph Alsop on January 25, 1960:

If (the Soviets) [sic] could effectively threaten us from a position of such military superiority that we would feel unable to defend ourselves, our capability to resist . . . would be greatly reduced, if not nullified. (Such) military strategy superiority would be achieved through accumulation of (enough) ballistic missiles to destroy our retaliatory forces before they could be launched. Surprisingly, this would not take very many missiles under present conditions . . . the total number of installations and facilities from which we can launch nuclear-armed aircraft or missiles at this moment is only about 100. All of these facilities present "soft targets" — that is, they could suffer crippling damage even (from) a near miss.

Alsop then repeated the key parts of General Power's attack on the Eisenhower Administration:

It would take an average of three missiles, in their current stage of development, to give an aggressor a mathematical probability of 95 per cent that he can destroy one given soft target, from 5,000 miles away. This means that, *with only some 300 ballistic missiles, the Soviets could virtually wipe out our entire nuclear strike capability within a span of 30 minutes.* (Italics are General Power's.)

To further heighten this threat, only about half these missiles would have to be ICBMs. The rest could be smaller intermediate range ballistic missiles.

The Utopian Mr. Alsop concluded his article with a suggestion that the Eisenhower Administration was risking the very future of the nation, indeed, of Western civilization. "Twining and Gates have derived [their] comforting conviction from the national intelligence estimates. But are the national estimates correct? And is it permissible to gamble the whole national future on mere estimates?" This represented a strange switch for Mr. Alsop, who only a few years before had used the same intelligence estimates to support his campaign for building thousands of bombers to fill the "bomber gap."

President Eisenhower at a press conference in January gave his harsh opinion of his defense critics: "I've spent my life in this and I know more about it than almost anybody . . . because I have given my life to it . . . I believe that the matter of defense has been handled well . . . and I think those people that are trying to make defense a partisan matter are doing a disservice to the United States."

When the President made those remarks, even his friends derided him. *Newsweek* remarked that "a growing sense of national uneasiness could be detected last week — and the politicians seized on it eagerly. In a Presidential election year, national defense was far too good an issue for the Democrats to pass up." The *New Republic* sarcastically commented, "The President, who recently reminded us again that he knows more than most about such matters, indignantly rejects the accusation that the nation's security is being neglected for budgetary or other reasons."

In late January Joseph Alsop continued "unmasking" Eisenhower's approach to defense, accusing the Administration of "literally playing a gigantic game of Russian roulette with the national future." Alsop quoted General Power to prove this very strong statement. To save the nation, Alsop recommended General Power's solution: more early warning and immediate full airborne alert. Once again for good measure, Alsop damned the national intelligence estimates.

General Power returned to criticizing his commander-in-chief's defense views at the American Legion's National Security Commission on January 28. The commander of SAC directly attacked the President on four issues: airborne alert, B–70, military uses of space, and Polaris. Power said that SAC needed all of these regardless of what the President thought. Senator Jackson and General White agreed on one of the points and demanded one billion dollars to place SAC on a twenty-four hour airborne alert now. Immediately after his American Legion speech General Power flew back to his concrete dugout at Omaha.

Robert Hotz, editor of *Aviation Week,* made a visit to General Power's SAC headquarters and used the occasion to call Eisenhower a "misinformed, tired old man who will not be contradicted." Hotz said that the B–70 cutback was "one of the most stupid decisions ever made [and predicted] we will be driven by the sheer lunacy of their decision to reinstate the full program."

On February 8 Air Force Secretary Dudley C. Sharp reiterated the Administration position that there was "no deterrence gap." But Congressman Mahon announced that funds for airborne alert would be multiplied to about 350 million dollars.

Sides were being drawn; loyal Republicans and Military Traditionalists in all services backed the Administration position that there was no deterrent gap. They also gave the impression that the intelligence estimates on which the missile gap was based might even be revised downward again. Military Utopians in their drive for counterforce were utilizing the Democratic party and vice versa. The Navy was moving at flank speed to make the U.S.S. *George Washington* operational so that the alternative strategy would have an operational weapons system to carry the strategy forward into the sixties.

The Military Utopians realized that the "pernicious" doctrine, which they called minimum deterrence, had to be discredited, and failing this, the Polaris weapons system would have to be absorbed. They tried to do both. The first tactic was to label the finite deterrent supporters "city-busters." The gambit for accomplishing the second proposal was to have the Polaris included in a single strategic command headed by SAC. The Utopians were unsuccessful in both campaigns. The real stumbling block was the President and the JCS. As long as strategic dissent was allowed by law, there was always the possibility that unpopular ideas would get to Congress and to the President. The long-range answer, as the Military Utopians indicated in the Air Force's "Black Book of Reorganization Papers," was to unify or merge the three services. The surface reason was to achieve efficiency and economy through elimination of waste, duplication, and overlapping. The real purpose was to enforce a "ruthless purge" (in the words of the Air Force Association) of the old-fashioned Traditionalist ideas no longer suited for the Aerospace Age.

Brigadier General Robert C. Richardson, III, in an article in the spring issue of *Air University Quarterly Review* attempted to refute "minimum deterrence," "nuclear stalemate," and charges of "overkill." According to the General the basic difference between the strategies was that with counterforce, the nation could win a thermonuclear war by penetrating Soviet defenses and finding mobile missiles with our B–70's. But if the United States insisted on building a minimum deterrent, we "may not take the initiative in general war under any circumstances, including receipt of unequivocal warning of attack." What General Richardson meant was that the United States could not engage in pre-emptive war if we developed a "minimum deterrent." Another major criticism of minimum deterrence was that it would make limited war more likely. To the Military Utopians this was a horrible fate, for they believed, as did General Richardson, that "general war is clearly more likely in the future than it has been to date. . . . A national policy dedicated to deterrence of war, or to victory if deterrence should fail, must therefore be concerned first with the problem of general war and secondly with lesser wars. An ideal solution would be a security system that could deter effectively all types of war." This was the old Utopian position of using the H-bomb to cover all contingencies.

General Richardson condemned a countercity targeting strategy for general war as violating two basic principles: (1) "The only rational military objective in war is the enemy forces or targets that affect the forces"; and (2) "destruction which does not affect the outcome of the war in one's favor is irrational and politically and morally unjustifiable." The only way to have victory in the Thermonuclear Age is through the ability "to destroy *his existing* capability for delivering destruction."

General Richardson turned his argument to NATO and claimed that minimum deterrent advocates tended to "discredit the validity of our approved national security strategy with respect to the NATO area. . . . These statements are, at the very least, irresponsible in that they *invite* limited aggression by increasing Soviet confidence that we will not retaliate against their homeland . . ." If this happens, General Richardson warned, our limited war forces would have to be greatly increased, and we would return to the "classical land warfare of attack and counterattack."

In the same spring issue General Frederick H. Smith listed various uses of nuclear weapons in limited war. He suggested a new type of target called "situation control" targets, which included rain forests, mangrove forests, bamboo groves, karst areas, valley routes, mountain defiles, close-contact siege or redoubt, and beach or amphibious landings. General Smith argued that

. . . we must not deprive ourselves of the unique advantages offered by imaginative employment of nuclear weapons. We have been quite clear and firm in expressing our determination to use nuclear weapons in total war. Now we need to speak out with equal clarity in affirming that we can and will use nuclear weapons in limited war when such weapons best serve our broad interest and meet the demands of the tactical military situation. . . .

I believe we can prevent future limited aggression by the Soviets or their satellites if they become equally convinced that we can and will employ nuclear firepower from the outset.

General Smith's prescription for using nuclear weapons from the outset represented a 1960 attempt to reinvigorate a policy that the Eisenhower Administration was allowing to die by inaction.

Utopian strategy had been reduced by the end of 1960 to the following concepts: A thermonuclear war, the most likely form of war because of the Russian buildup, could be won if we had a true counterforce that would deter all forms of war. But if deterrence failed, counterforce would win any nuclear war, which would and should be nuclear. The only way to have a counterforce is to have a mix consisting of thousands of cheap, hardened, solid-fueled Minuteman missiles and manned B-70 bombers to "ferret" out mobile and hidden Russian missiles. Pre-emptive war, or exercise of the initiative, is highly desirable. Civilian defense, recuperation, and recovery programs are a vital part of winning a total war and should be encouraged. The best way to achieve this new strategy is by having a single military service; the three service systems can no longer be tolerated. The most important question remaining for the Utopians was whether President Kennedy would accept this Military Utopian doctrine, and his past remarks left this an open question.

For Traditionalists 1960 was the year of the Polaris. Traditionalist doctrine was concerned with defining and defending the finite deterrent, total war aspect of balanced deterrence, which became crucial when President Kennedy was elected. From its earliest conception in 1955 the Polaris had been developed under the protective shield of President Eisenhower and the Republican Administration. Since military aviation had been the product of Democratic Administrations until 1952, there had been qualms in some aviation quarters as to the effect of a Republican Administration upon it. Their fears were unfounded, for the Eisenhower Administration initially attached greater importance to the manned bomber than even its most enthusiastic supporter could have dreamed possible. Similarly, the fears of seapower advocates that President Kennedy's new Democratic Administration would not be sympathetic with the Polaris and the oceanic deterrent concept were unfounded.

The Navy had stolen a march on the Air Force and the Soviets by first realizing the advantages of mobility and solid-propelled ballistic rockets. Five years of fantastic technological achievements, coupled with a slowly developing alternative strategy, resulted in an operational weapons system that could be offered to the new Democratic Administration for acceptance or rejection. It was by no means a foregone conclusion that President Kennedy would accept General Taylor's concept of flexible response, which the Navy called balanced deterrence. For President Kennedy, like most Democrats, had spoken on both sides of the strategy issue. The safe course was to come out for more of everything, which most liberal Democrats did, and the result was a mixture of both strategies.

Generally speaking, Army Traditionalists (on active duty) lay low in 1960, preferring to let Navy Traditionalists slug it out with Air Force Utopians. General Taylor in *The Uncertain Trumpet* and General Medaris in *Countdown for Decision* made their positions as supporters of finite deterrence unmistakably clear. General Taylor also advocated a great increase in the conventional non-nuclear limited war force, which he saw as vital a part of the flexible response as the thermonuclear deterrent. Both Medaris's and Taylor's books helped the Polaris concept by focusing public attention on the "adequacy" of thermonuclear deterrents and pointing out the senselessness of "overkill." Both retired generals' books were condensed in *Look,* which helped disseminate their ideas.

A vital task of Navy Traditionalists was to protect the Fleet Ballistic Missile from being absorbed by the Air Force and pressed into the service of the counterforce strategy. The Traditionalists also were forced to refine finite deterrence, for the Utopians were determined to label it a "city buster" strategy and its advocates unpatriotic or disloyal for not planning to win a thermonuclear war. A third task was to prevent the Utopians from carrying out their plans to reorganize the Department of Defense into a single service with a single chief of staff. The focal point of the bitter wrangle was the Symington "Defense Task Force Report" of early December 1960.

The Utopians realized that the 1961–1962 period would be the crucial one for achieving their organizational goals, but once these were achieved they would then have control over the selection of weapons and, ultimately, strategy. Defense tasks of the three services, instead of becoming more similar with the advent of missiles, were becoming more diversified. The rise of the doctrine of limited war, which increased the importance of the land fighting soldier using conventional or unconventional weapons, made it more and more unlikely that the foot soldier could be dispensed with as was once believed during the heyday of the new look and massive retaliation. The increasing importance of the oceans for total war deterrents and limited war forces mobility meant that the peculiar nature and skills of the sailor would be needed. Kissinger's ideas concerning the feasibility of unification in *Nuclear Weapons and Foreign Policy* were now outdated. It was the Military Utopians who were finding it difficult to carve out a comfortable niche in the new strategic environment; therefore, it was not surprising that the Military Utopians and their supporters deemed it necessary to achieve a single service while they were still at their peak of public popularity and commanded the lion's share of the defense budget.

President Eisenhower's State of the Union message of 1960 was a hopeful statement about the increasing chances for world peace. The President accepted the Traditionalist view concerning the nature of a total nuclear war. "With both sides of this divided world in possession of unbelievably destructive weapons, mankind approaches a state where mutual annihilation becomes a possibility. No other fact of today's world equals this in importance — it colors everything we say, plan, and do."

On January 25, 1960, Senator Leverett Saltonstall remarked, "I do not agree that there is this great missile gap." But it was essential for the Utopians to create the missile gap, for without it increased funds for airborne alert, more B–52's, and ballistic missiles would hardly be forthcoming. If the American Congress and the American people could be convinced that in one red "bolt from the blue" the United States could be disarmed and left defenseless, sufficient funds would be provided to build the counterforce that previous circumstances had conspired to prevent.

The "missile gap" was based on the mysterious and sacrosanct world of intelligence estimates in which nobody agrees and compromise abounds. It was a perfect issue on which men of good will could and would disagree.

Secretary Gates confused the entire situation by explaining that the new intelligence estimates had been revised downward because they were based on "what the Soviet Union probably would do, as opposed to former estimates which were made on what they are capable of doing."

Senator Mundt, in a weekly report to his constituents, announced that he believed some of the defense criticism was based on "political opportunism." On January 31 Secretary of Defense Gates admitted that the Russians would have "moderately more" missiles in production and operation until the United States presumably began catching up in 1962. But Gates told his press conference that the ICBM missile gap, which the Utopians had been protesting about, was being offset in other ways: "We are expanding our missile program, putting missiles on our bomber force and bringing into operation Polaris submarines which we believe will offset any so-called missile gap, at least from the point of view of the validity of our deterrent. . . . We are in a first rate first position."

Lyndon Johnson disagreed, and after hearing a briefing by Allen Dulles, claimed the Russians would have "an enormous advantage in missile striking power in the near future."

Merriman Smith asked President Eisenhower at a February 3 press conference what he thought about recent statements by generals concerning our lag behind the Russians. The President used this occasion to elaborate further his theory of adequacy.

"I am always a little bit amazed about this business of catching up. What you want is enough, a thing that is adequate. A deterrent has no added power, once it has become completely adequate, for compelling the respect of any potential opponent for your deterrent and, therefore, to make him act prudently."

When Rowland Evans, Jr., asked the President what he thought about General Power's testimony before Congress that his heavy bombers could not be properly safeguarded without a full air alert, the President replied:

No, I'm — there are too many of these generals have all sorts of ideas; but I do point this out: I have got the Secretary of Defense, whom I trust, and who I know is honest in his study, analysis and conclusion.

That is Secretary Gates. And beneath him, assisting him, is the Chairman of the Chiefs of Staff, whom I similarly trust; and the Joint Chiefs of Staff, with those two, are my military advisers. And I have been long enough in the military service that I assure you that I cannot be particularly disturbed because everybody with a parochial viewpoint all over the place comes along and takes and says that the bosses know nothing about it.

Now, I don't think anyone's trying to impugn the patriotism and the earnestness and the integrity of the group I have just mentioned. And I think, myself, that they are the ablest people we could get. That's the reason they were selected.

Senator Symington was not satisfied with the official explanation of the change in intelligence estimates and protested that the Soviet lead in 1962 would be more than three to one.

General White helped calm the furor caused by General Power's three hundred ballistic missiles speech by saying that the commanding general of SAC was speaking of a purely "hypothetical" situation. Other military men testified that the Russians would have to "salvo" all three hundred missiles simultaneously. Otherwise tactical warning would be given to our forces. Furthermore, the Traditionalists were happy to point out, Power had finally admitted that SAC and fixed bases are highly vulnerable to ICBM's. The solution seemed to be to move the deterrent off the American continent and place it in mobile, concealed platforms. General Power had unwittingly given the finite deterrent concept a great boost in an attempt to win the short-range benefit of air alert.

Admiral Burke and Navy leaders quickly seized upon Power's speech to prove that mobility was the answer. In a February 21 interview with the *San Diego Union,* the Chief of Naval Operations spelled out the significance of SAC's vulnerability.

A deterrent is no longer a deterrent if the enemy believes he can destroy it or it cannot be used. . . . The Navy is virtually a most elusive target and provides inevitable retaliation. . . . You must have some installations and bases that have no fixed addresses. The Navy can provide a substantial portion of these with great effectiveness — because of its mobility. And no matter what destruction the enemy may have inflicted through surprise attack, the Navy ships at sea can deliver powerful retaliation. They will be somewhere where they can retaliate.

On a television broadcast with Senator Jackson, Admiral Burke called for forty-five Polaris submarines. This was no figure pulled from his seabag but a carefully calculated number representing the end-product of the thinking and planning of the Naval Ordnance Test Station, Operations Evaluation Group, Special Projects, the Chief of Naval Operations, and other scholars.

On February 11 it was revealed, or leaked, that the Air Force had taken exception to the estimate prepared by the National Intelligence Board.[1] The Military Utopians had credited the Russians with a greater advantage than that conceded in estimates presented to Congress. Major General J. H. Walsh, head of Air Force Intelligence, testified that he had filed a dissent from intelligence estimates on Soviet missile strength.

Senator Prescott Bush criticized Senator Symington and "the disclosure of much too much information to the enemy about our plans and our estimates of their plans." The Republican National Committee charged that if Symington made public secret intelligence estimates of Russian missile power, it would be "an act of total reckless irresponsibility."

Admiral Burke discussed the difficulty of launching one missile, let alone 150 or 200 simultaneously. Representative Clarence Cannon made an amazing speech on the House floor evidently based on General Power's and Joseph Alsop's hypothetical and inflated figures. The head of the House Appropriations Committee claimed that the Russians had enough ICBM's to destroy all our cities and probably SAC bases as well, and he blamed our perilous state on his own committee and "the admirals" who still regarded the Navy as the first line of defense.

Symington notified Admiral Burke that if the Navy did not change its stand and support the B–70 bomber, he might not go along with the increase of Polaris. Eisenhower again denounced the "leaks" and parochial officers who were publicizing their personal opinions. The President wrote a letter to Representative Jessica Weis:

These reactions are difficult for me to understand because not just every once in a while, but every single year, during the appropriations season, we go through defense disputes of this kind, and they get especially spirited the closer we get to elections.

They seem to me to be an intermixture of political opportunism and the perpetual military yearning for more than can be reasonably expected.

A few days later at his February 17, 1960, press conference, the President had a difficult time controlling himself as he answered Symington's charges. On January 27, 1960, the Missouri senator had accused the Administration of the "manipulation of data" and in a Senate speech declared that "the American people are being enticed down the trail of insecurity by the issuance of misinformation about our deterrent power and especially about the missile gap."

President Eisenhower responded emotionally: "If anybody — anybody — believes that I have deliberately misled the American people, I'd like to tell him to his face what I think about him. This is a charge that I think is despicable, and I have never made it against anyone in the world, and I wouldn't as long — unless he were in a bar of justice somewhere to be tried for something that was intolerable."

Symington, when asked to comment at a news conference, replied, "I don't like to get into personalities. I do like to get into facts." He also claimed he did not "know anybody who said the President misled the nation." This verbal exchange between the senator and the President ended the major aspect of the missile gap controversy in the first half of 1960.

Then Hanson Baldwin revealed on May 6, 1960, that "Washington experts declare that there is still no evidence of existence of any Soviet launching sites for long-range missiles except the two known sites at Kapustin Yar, near Stalingrad, and Tyuratam, near the Aral Sea. These two sites have been used for the launching of Soviet developmental missiles. No other operational sites are known to exist, *despite intensive and at least partly successful efforts to penetrate the Iron Curtain.*" (Italics mine.) The *New York Times* defense expert wrote this column on May 6 just before the truth about Francis Gary Powers and the U–2 burst on the world. There seems to be no doubt that the Eisenhower Administration based its low estimates of both Russian bombers and missiles on photographic intelligence gathered with U–2 reconnaissance aircraft that had been soaring and snapping pictures over Russia since 1956.

On July 20, 1960, almost fifteen years to the day after the United States exploded the world's first nuclear bomb at Alamogordo, New Mexico, the Navy successfully test-fired two solid-fueled Polaris ballistic missiles from a submerged atomic submarine lying off Cape Canaveral. The possibility of stabilizing the thermonuclear arms race became a reality. A new star of peace had jumped from the sea. The afternoon of July 20 had all the tension and drama of a final World Series game. The league in which the Polaris was playing was truly a global one, for billions of dollars and hundreds of millions of lives were in balance. "Hot lines" to Cape Canaveral buzzed with the news of "holds"; the countdown was started, stopped, and then

started again. Finally, after hours of sweating and minor technical delays, the button was pressed, and Polaris rushed upward,
propelled by a slug of compressed air. The bottle-shaped missile
entered the air sideways; momentarily the alternative strategy
hung precariously. Then its first stage ignited, the gyros took
over, straightened the missile, and the Polaris raced downrange
into the "pickle barrel." The alternative strategy would have a
modern operational weapons system to usher in the Age of
Deterrence.

Serious questions remained: Who would have operational
control? Would the full fleet of forty-five boats be built so that
Polaris could become the primary Free World deterrent? Would
funding of Polaris be at the expense of counterforce or limited
war forces? Would the Polaris cause a major strategy shift in
the new Administration?

The Utopians had been campaigning to place Polaris in a
strategic command and make it a part of the Air Force counterforce strategy. After long and bitter wrangling Secretary Gates
created a Joint Targeting Committee at Omaha, still under the
command and control of the Joint Chiefs of Staff.

In the realm of strategy the Traditionalists realized that the
strategic battle had been joined at last. Support for the Traditionalist viewpoint now came from many quarters. The House
Committee on Government Operations issued a report on July 1
on civil defense and post-attack recovery, in which the two
competing views on strategy were analyzed:

If the Air Force cannot claim a capability to knock out enemy
strategic forces *before* they are launched against us, the extremely
expensive missile-bomber force of the Strategic Air Command
inevitably loses some of its appeal to the American public. If all
that is required to maintain a general deterrent is the capability of
inflicting punishment on the enemy after the fact, then a much
smaller force — aimed only at the enemy's cities — could do the job.

The subcommittee refused to draw the obvious inference that
"the 'counterforce' strategy as formulated by the Air Force [has]

an implication of the doctrine of the preemptive strike; that is, a first attack rather than a retaliatory action."

But the report took the argument up to the brink:

In short, the "counterforce" doctrine implies an ability to blunt an enemy attack by hitting his military bases before the attack is launched against us. To do this requires enough missiles and bombers to strike all his strategic bases in a first effort. If this mission is accomplished the enemy's counterblow will be drastically reduced and its impact on the American population would not be as great as it would be otherwise.

Simply put, if the United States could get in the first strike, we would save one hundred million lives and be victorious. Seldom has the relation of counterforce to pre-emptive war been as clearly stated. The Utopians attempted to sanitize and sweeten their doctrine by introducing the prospect of "winning" a thermonuclear war.

On August 26, 1960, General LeMay in a Fort Worth address opened what promised to be a full scale attack on the United States Navy, Polaris, and the finite deterrent strategy. LeMay recalled, for the Air Power Council, the past glories of the B–36: "Back in the late 1940s you people here in Fort Worth were keenly interested in the now famous 'B–36 case.' As Commander in Chief of the Strategic Air Command, I, too, had more than a casual interest. History has proven us right in our faith in the Convair B–36. . . . There were many indictments of strategic bombing made at that time, yet public opinion and national purpose were strong and united."

There is no doubt that this was a direct attack on the Navy of the past. General LeMay then flayed the Navy of 1960: "Unfortunately, there are people in this country who advocate reducing U.S. strategic forces to a small, somewhat mobile, retaliatory capability suitable only for destroying cities." LeMay continued: "Our forces, therefore, must be sufficient, prepared and able to destroy any aggressor's military power to the extent that he no longer has the will or ability to wage war. This is the type of military force we must maintain — a counterforce — a force that can win — the kind of military force that is essential to true deterrence."

A United Press International dispatch from Fort Worth reported: "Air Force General Curtis E. LeMay lashed out at Navy strategic theories in a major policy speech tonight, saying in effect they were wrong a decade ago and still are today."

Traditionalists were given moral support by B. H. Liddell Hart's book, *Deterrent or Defense: A Fresh Look at the West's Military Position,* and its review by Senator John F. Kennedy in the *Saturday Review,* September 3, 1960. The senator's excellent analysis of Liddell Hart's book gave an accurate preview of the Kennedy shift of 1961:

The central problem we face is clear enough. The Soviet acquisition of nuclear weapons and the means for their delivery anywhere on the face of the planet now makes certain that a nuclear war would be a war of mutual devastation. . . .

The grand theme of Hart's book comes to this: The West must be prepared to face down Communist aggression, short of nuclear war, by conventional forces. . . . Behind this theme is a judgment: that responsible leaders in the West will not and should not deal with limited aggression by unlimited weapons whose use could only be mutually suicidal. . . . I share Captain Hart's judgment . . .

Senator Kennedy, having agreed to the need of conventional forces, then discussed the

. . . security and effectiveness of the American nuclear deterrent. We face a real problem over the next several years in guaranteeing that our deterrent is safe from sudden attack and capable of effective penetration of Soviet defenses. We have no right to tempt Soviet planners and political leaders with the possibility of catching our aircraft and unprotected missiles on the ground, in a gigantic Pearl Harbor. This is our first defense problem.

Senator Kennedy saw great virtue in weapons like the Polaris and Minuteman. "The relative security from attack which the new mobile missiles allow should diminish the need for hair-trigger decisions and should give the United States, and the world as a whole, a greater degree of stability."

In this remarkable review Senator Kennedy accepted the

entire Traditionalist strategy: (1) impossibility of "winning" thermonuclear wars, (2) need for greater amounts of nonnuclear conventional forces for limited war, (3) necessity of invulnerable second strike forces, (4) desirability of building military forces for stability rather than instability, and (5) realization of the danger of hair-trigger responses and decisions, which could lead to accidental or pre-emptive war.

As fall advanced toward winter and the World Series and the presidential campaign ended, the conflict over strategic doctrine heated up. President-elect Kennedy's exact outlines on strategy and organization were unclear. Wild rumors, new appointments, task force studies, and great unresolved questions made the Pentagon most uneasy. The military services were holding their collective breath while waiting for the first concrete signal marking the way the new Administration would lean. For grand strategy is all; weapons systems and organization can be molded, at some cost and difficulty, to be sure, but the controlling decision of any Administration can be reduced to one or two words: containment, liberation, balanced forces, or massive retaliation. Semantics were all important. Both Traditionalists and Utopians scanned press reports from Palm Beach in hopes of garnering clues as to the nature of Kennedy's defense policy. Nitze, Gilpatric, and McNamara were appointed to key defense posts. The Symington "Defense Task Force Report" was forwarded to the President, while the Pentagon waited, wondered, and kept on talking and writing about the relatively safe topic of deterrence.

The Traditionalist view was outlined at the end of the year in the "Résumé of Major Strategic Considerations," written by T. E. Phipps when he was a member of the Naval Warfare Analysis Group, a team of civilian scientists managed by the Massachusetts Institute of Technology, which conducts operations research studies related to problems of long-range naval planning. The key to Phipp's paper and to the entire alternative strategy was the capability to "strike second" after receiving the first surprise blow. "The advent of nuclear parity could thus imply a strengthening of mutual deterrence of all-out war, particularly if both opponents had the assured 'strike second' capability." Phipps maintained that the Western powers "can unilaterally put an end to the nuclear arms race, when certain conditions are met:

(1) The concept must win broad public and governmental acceptance that in "all-out" nuclear warfare there is such a thing as enough; *i.e.*, that a finite number of nuclear weapons *predeterminable independently of enemy* offensive capabilities, will (if successfully delivered) fully satisfy the requirement of retaliation.

(2) The futility and/or undesirability of attempting direct attack on enemy missile sites must be generally acknowledged.

(3) We must have a known "strike second" capability for all-out war, *i.e.*, we must be sure that the desired number of nuclear weapons can obviously survive any surprise attack on us, as well as any at-target defenses the enemy may establish.

(4) We must provide ourselves with adequate military capabilities to fight limited wars, without gross over-reaction to the provocations that give rise to them.

In the first two weeks of the new year a number of articles appeared and events took place which helped forward the balanced deterrence strategy that Phipps had outlined so brilliantly.

Hanson Baldwin wrote a series of three articles that succinctly analyzed the various strategic positions of the Army, Navy, Air Force, and the then current strategy. Thomas B. Ross of the *Chicago Sun-Times*, with an eye like Baldwin's on the new Kennedy Administration about to take office, headlined a summary article, "Great Debate of 1961 Centers on Strategy." *Life* unexpectedly added its support to the limited war doctrine and the vital half of balanced deterrence with an editorial called, "Who Fights Brush-Fire Wars?"

About the same time Henry Kissinger in his new book, *The Necessity for Choice*, moved away from limited nuclear war that he had popularized in 1957 to a dual capability concept (nuclear and conventionally equipped army) with a new stress on non-nuclear forces. The "missile gap," on which Kissinger predicated a great deal of his thermonuclear deterrent argument, melted before the deep Washington snows did. Eisenhower gave it the coup de grâce when he noted in his State of the Union message that "the 'bomber gap' of several years ago was always a fiction, and the 'missile gap' shows every sign of being the same."

Then in early February 1961, Secretary McNamara, in a famous background briefing for the Pentagon press, gave the Kennedy Administration's blessing to burial of the missile gap with his preliminary analysis, never repudiated, that the missile gap no longer existed. Although few realized it at the time, the old era had ended. The age of the air offensive, during which the manned bomber could both deter a total war and win a total war for the United States of America, was over.

10

1961 — The Kennedy Shift

THE THIRTY-FIFTH PRESIDENT OF THE UNITED STATES assumed office on a bright and bitterly cold Friday in January, following a fierce blizzard and a monumental traffic jam. Kennedy's inaugural address was eloquent, and Washington experienced the strange and bewildering tinge of welcomed inspiration and wonder as New Frontiersmen swooped down on Washington and Georgetown like better-born and better-mannered Jacksonian Democrats. Nikita Khrushchev, who felt kindly toward the young and vigorous President, released the three captive RB–47 pilots as a symbol of another thaw and a new beginning in East-West relations.

Unfortunately, during the spring and summer of 1961 American morale and confidence plummeted as nearly everything went wrong on the international scene: Two Russians, Majors Titov and Gagarin, were the first earthlings to orbit the mother planet; the situation in Laos deteriorated; American troops came within a Siamese cat's whisker of being committed in Southeast Asia; and the Cuban invasion was a spectacular failure. It was 1953 with the Berlin riots and 1954 with the Indochina crisis all over again. The Big Two Conference in Vienna merely confirmed the worst fears concerning the third Berlin crisis: the Russians were in no mood to compromise. The monstrous Russian nuclear tests of late summer added to the near hysteria.

A frightening shelter scare, encouraged by the President, Luce magazines, Rand Corporation publications and publicists, and Utopian strategists, swept the nation. A few Americans fled to Australia and New Zealand before it was too late; others bought bomb shelters from the score of contractors and hucksters who mushroomed during the fallout-laden late summer days; others lined their recreation rooms with lead, or purchased guns to keep their neighbors out, should the time come. Many joined the John Birch Society, tried to impeach Earl Warren and, for good measure, slandered Eisenhower and Dulles. Others signed up with the Minutemen and started their watch on the Mississippi for Russian gunboats. Still others emigrated to California to set up Utopian colonies leeward of the missile sites.

Fortunately, the vast majority of Americans refused to be panicked during this conscious attempt to scare Khrushchev by using shelters to increase the credibility of the deterrent. Commander Alan Shepard's suborbital flight gave the Administration and the nation something to be proud of and revived hope that we were not hopelessly behind the Russians in space after all. The President handled the third Berlin crisis — wall and all — deftly and carefully. The Eisenhower response to the Berlin riots of 1953 and the Hungarian revolt of 1956 had been to do nothing militarily but cut conventional forces. Kennedy's response to increased Russian belligerency was to increase our non-nuclear conventional forces and to make the second strike total war deterrent more secure, controllable, and invulnerable. In doing this he has carried out the Forrestal prescription of 1948 and the Acheson strategy of 1950–1951, summed up in the Acheson Plan submitted by the ex-Secretary of State during the summer of 1961 and thoroughly approved of by such Traditionalists as Admiral Burke and General Taylor. One of the key features of the mobilization was calling up 150,000 reservists — a successful "quick fix," but political dynamite.

Finally, in early fall 1961 the Russian premier lifted his Berlin ultimatum and widened the doctrinal gap with Mao Tse-tung over the control and direction of world Communism. American sanity and balance were further restored when the Congo operation seemed to be going our way, and the United States Fleet appeared off Santo Domingo, thus preventing the reinstatement of a military dictatorship in the Dominican Republic. Democratic victories in congressional and gubernatorial elections added to the general return of Administration confidence. Returning prosperity and the phenomenal popularity of the President and his clan helped make the last quarter of 1961 a pleasant one for the Kennedy Administration.

The strategic struggle between the Traditionalists and the Utopians continued unabated in 1961 but generally was muffled within the Pentagon as Defense Secretary McNamara took the services' measure and they took his. It was not until 1962 that the smoldering conflict flared up over the "muzzling" issue, the B–70 (redesignated the RS–70), and the national military strategy that went with it. Beneath the surface another titanic conflict raged between the Air Force Utopians and the National Aeronautics and Space Administration over "military space."

In the battle to change basic national military strategy, President Kennedy and his Defense Secretary revealed themselves as basically Liberal Traditionalists. As Eric Larrabee pointed out in his perceptive essay, "The Politics of Strategy," in the March 1962 *Bulletin of the Atomic Scientists,* Kennedy

has done all the right things. In McNamara he has at last a Secretary of Defense who means to be master in his own house, which is the first and foremost victory. "Conventional" forces are being strengthened and perhaps may even . . . someday acquire the airlift to transport them rapidly abroad. The Polaris submarines and the Minuteman are within sight of providing us with second-strike retaliation, and the most extravagant of the Air Force's demands for still more piloted bombers are being resisted . . .

Mr. Larrabee might have added that President Kennedy increased our paramilitary forces to cope with the ever possible "wars of liberation." The Eisenhower emphasis on the peaceful uses of space with specific prohibitions against bomber satellites and other offensive weapons was also continued by the Kennedy Administration.

Fortunately, the Administration from its very first days realized the implications of the nuclear stalemate, and its response was twofold: to build up the invulnerable thermonuclear deterrent and to increase non-nuclear conventional forces. The testing of John F. Kennedy came quickly over Berlin. Thirteen years previously Secretary of Defense James Forrestal had faced the same dilemma: to use the A-bomb or to do nothing because of the deficiency of conventional forces. At the height of the Berlin crisis (July 6, 1961) President Kennedy pledged that this nation intended "to have a wider choice than humiliation or all-out nuclear action." Kennedy had thus resolved Forrestal's dilemma the only way possible this side of a thermonuclear exchange or the most dangerous and precarious form of brinksmanship. In a sense, Kennedy's Berlin message marked the end of a one weapon, one response strategy.

The Kennedy Administration, in one of its first official defense acts, put the missile gap out to pasture, where it joined the bomber gap in retirement, having served its purpose of dramatizing a legitimate but improperly defined and accentuated issue. The missile gap was stressed and exploited by Liberal Utopians and their military allies, and it proved exceedingly useful. This, coupled with Russian space advances through superior rocket power, created a slight uneasiness in the American voter, which Kennedy tapped with his talks of our declining prestige and the need to "get America moving again."

By soft-pedaling the missile gap, purchasing less of the very missiles that were supposed to close the gap by 1963, Kennedy, in effect, ratified the Eisenhower decision on "adequacy" of the thermonuclear deterrent force.

The Utopians were stunned, for they had expected just the opposite action by the Democrats. During the first months after Kennedy's election the future had looked bright for Utopians. The President-elect was himself one of the formulators of the missile gap. He had asked Senator Symington (former Air Force

Secretary under President Truman) to make a task force study of defense reorganization needs, sending shivers up and down Traditionalist backs, for the dreaded single Chief of Staff–single service seemed just a decision away. Vice President Johnson was a known supporter of the RS–70 and hailed from a state with extensive aircraft and missile contracts. All the top Department of Defense appointees were either ex-Air Force Secretaries (Gilpatric), ex-Air Force officers (McNamara), sympathetic strategists or Rand Corporation alumni (Paul Nitze, Albert Wohlstetter, Henry Rowen, Charles Hitch), or Air Force Laboratory Directors (Harold Brown). And the greatest Utopian bomber general of them all, Curtis LeMay, was appointed Chief of Staff of the Air Force.

Thus the Pentagon seemed to be stacked in Utopian favor, and Congress was filled with supporters of the Air Force weapons system and strategy. But once again as under Eisenhower the Utopians had failed to capture the White House staff or the presidency. As in 1953–1955 when international events conspired to doom any sole reliance on massive retaliation, so the events of 1961 (the Cuba, Berlin, Congo, Laos and Vietnam crises) precluded reliance on counterforce to meet the real contingencies of the global struggle. Eisenhower, instead of adding conventional forces to our armory, cut them back and reduced the defense budget. President Kennedy, to the contrary, added seven billion dollars to the defense budget, resulting in a "45 per cent increase in strength of conventional forces."

The Utopians reacted as could be expected: thrashing around trying to get their counterforce or controlled thermonuclear war strategy accepted; attempting to force a refunding of their counterforce vehicle, the RS–70; making overt grabs for the National Aeronautics and Space Administration program; boldly attempting to undercut the peaceful uses of space; and cleverly moving to sabotage a non-nuclear strategy. Their coalition had been reformed with reduced support from Liberal Utopians, basically because most of the older Liberal Utopians were not as emotionally committed to Utopian military strategy as they were to the Democratic party. Utopians failed to realize that the Kennedy strategy was being made the test of party orthodoxy. Thus Military Utopians were left with their natural allies, the Conservative Utopians, and with whatever support they could get on local "pork barrel" issues from time to time from Conservative and Liberal Traditionalists.

Unfortunately for the Military Utopians, they could not offer economy for their strategy or weapons system. Indeed, for the first time in a decade and a half, they were on the side of the "big spenders" and vast new outlays. By unimaginative tactics, occasioned by blind faith in strategic air warfare, they had finally been caught in the unwieldy position of being in direct opposition to a popular President and Secretary of Defense. They offered as an alternative strategy a single, expensive, simplistic solution to defense and foreign policy issues that even the most uninitiated were likely to view as very complex.

Utopians earnestly believe that with their strategy a thermonuclear war can be won. "Winning" is the key argument used against the Utopian-coined term, "minimum deterrence" (which the Traditionalists call balanced deterrence). Utopian strategy contains potential overtones of a future McCarthy-like attack on Traditionalists, similar to the 1954 assault on the Army for attempting to block the new look. The tack is simple: The finite warriors do not offer total victory over world Communism; instead, they have adopted a "no-win" strategy. We, the infinite counterforce and pre-emptive warriors, can guarantee that victory. It is true that there will be some damage to our homeland, but the resulting eradication of world Communism will far outweigh the destruction of New York, Washington, and Chicago. Furthermore, we can absorb an atomic or thermonuclear exchange better than the Russians if we spend the necessary money on recovery and rehabilitation programs. While we are constructing counterforce weapons, the process of exactly locating Russian fixed and mobile targets should begin.

This may very well be the outline of the continuing assault on the Kennedy shift with the first attack directed at the Liberal

Traditionalists surrounding the President. C. J. V. Murphy's exposé on the Cuban invasion in *Fortune* September 1961 was directed at Chester Bowles, Adlai Stevenson, Dean Rusk, and the President. (His February 16, 1962, *Life* article on nuclear testing added General Taylor, McGeorge Bundy, Hans Bethe, and Jerome Wiesner to his hatchet list.)

Utopian thinking at its most bellicose was revealed in September 1961 at the Air Force Association's annual meeting in Philadelphia. Besides coming out for the RS–70, bomber satellites, and increased numbers of thermonuclear delivery systems, the Air Force Lobby resolved:

Freedom must bury Communism or be buried by Communism. Complete eradication of the Soviet system must be our national goal, our obligation to all free people, our promise of hope to all who are not free . . . We are determined to back our words with action even at the risk of war. We seek not merely to preserve our freedoms but to extend them. . . . Soviet aims are both evil and implacable. The people are willing to work toward, and fight for if necessary, the elimination of Communism from the world scene. Let the issue be joined.

Military and Conservative Utopians, with tacit support from certain Liberal Utopians, continued to advocate their strategy, their most favored defense organization, and the needed weapons systems. Summed up, Utopians of all varieties demand total victory over world Communism. If this means preparing for a total thermonuclear war, then, by all means, let us start preparing.

Generally speaking, events of 1961 tended to isolate the Conservative Utopians, leaving them huddled around the far right. The Military Utopians were finally smoked out, and their leader, unsurprisingly, turned out to be the brusque, cigar-smoking bomber general — Curtis LeMay. Unfortunately for General LeMay, he picked the wrong time, the wrong strategy, and the wrong President against whom to revolt. The *New Republic* of March 19, 1962, titled LeMay's fight for the B–70, "LeMay's Last Stand." Even staunch friends and past supporters like Joseph Alsop kicked the dying king. In the unkindest cut of all Alsop compared General LeMay, the fire bomb B–29 hero of Tokyo and the B–36 hearings, to a "battleship admiral."

The President answered the Utopians by deriding their "no-win" accusations. In his press conference of February 14, 1962, the President eloquently remarked:

Now, if someone thinks we should have a nuclear war in order to win, I can inform them that there will not be winners of the next nuclear war, if there is one, and this country and other countries would suffer very heavy blows. So we have to proceed with responsibility and with care in an age where the human race can obliterate itself. The objective of this administration, and I think the objective of the country, is to protect our security, keep the peace, protect our vital interests, make it possible for what we believe to be a system of government which is in accordance with the basic aspirations of people everywhere to ultimately prevail and that is our objective and that is the one that we shall follow.

Three days later the Secretary of Defense elaborated on the National Security Council meeting of January 18, 1962, at which the President had described his strategic philosophy.

McNamara's February 17, 1962, Chicago address to the American Bar Foundation referred to Khrushchev's January 6, 1961, speech entitled, "For New Victories of the World Communist Movement." The Soviet premier had analyzed three categories of wars: "world wars, local wars, and liberation wars or popular uprisings." He had admonished his fellow comrades "to work out the correct tactics with regard to these wars" and concluded that "world wars" (total wars) and "local wars" (limited wars) were too dangerous to play the role of "midwife to revolution." "But," he predicted, "liberation wars and popular uprisings will continue to exist as long as imperialism exists", and good Communists should have "a most positive" attitude toward such wars of liberation.

McNamara then explained the Kennedy strategy, designed to create the tri-level military stabilization that General Taylor had alluded to on January 15, 1962, in a speech in New York.

Joseph and Stewart Alsop subtly misinterpreted this strategy in newspaper columns and a magazine article.

According to McNamara, for total wars the United States had adequate power, "which is able to survive a nuclear surprise attack and strike back with sufficient power to destroy the enemy target system." McNamara stated that our policy's first requirement is to "maintain our nuclear strike power as a realistic, effective deterrent against Soviet initiation of major wars." But the deterrent of the future, unlike that of the past, can no longer be achieved "merely by maintaining a larger stockpile of nuclear weapons." Instead, our deterrent "must be hardened, dispersed, and mobile." In other words, it must be made as invulnerable as possible, a difficult and expensive thing to do.

The Secretary of Defense then discussed the new "command and control" machinery that must be able "to survive an attack and to apply the surviving forces in consonance with national security objectives." The narrow line between the Traditionalist controlled response (or flexible response) and the Utopian controlled thermonuclear war was never narrower than when McNamara attempted to describe the advantages of this "protected command and control system." He hypothesized:

We may have to retaliate with a single massive attack. Or, we may be able to use our retaliatory forces to limit damage done to ourselves, and our allies, by knocking out the enemy's bases before he has had time to launch his second salvos. We may seek to terminate a war on favorable terms by using our forces as a bargaining weapon — by threatening further attack. In any case, our large reserve of protected firepower would give an enemy an incentive to avoid our cities and to stop a war.

On the second level of military stabilization (limited war), the Secretary was less ambiguous. It was clear, he stated, "that we require a wider range of practical alternatives to meet the kind of military challenges that Khrushchev has announced he has in store for us." We require non-nuclear conventional military strength to "provide us with the means to meet a limited challenge with limited forces." McNamara continued in the manner of a balanced forces advocate:

Our policy is aimed at achieving the best balance of military capabilities — over the entire range of potential conflict, in the various areas of the globe where the Free World has vital interests, and over the years as far ahead as we can reasonably plan. I firmly believe that the non-nuclear buildup will — by improving and expanding the alternatives open to the Free World — reduce the pressures to make concessions in the face of Soviet threats.

And the Secretary significantly added:

As we develop a balanced, modern non-nuclear force, ready to move rapidly against aggression in any part of the world, we continue to inhibit the opportunities for successful conduct of Khrushchev's "local wars." It is tempting to conclude that our conventional forces will leave us free to compete with communism in the peaceful sphere of economic and social development, where we can compete most effectively.

The Kennedy Administration, realizing the danger of accidental war had greatly increased through the years, took major steps to reduce this possibility. Stewart Alsop called this new strategic concept the "doctrine of the controlled response."[1] This was not the same as controlled thermonuclear war, for there is a fine but vital line between these two semantically similar phrases. The "doctrine of controlled response" was directed against accidental war, whereas "controlled thermonuclear war" attempted to preserve thermonuclear war and the threat thereof as an instrument of national policy. Unfortunately, similar control mechanisms are used for both strategies. The real difference between the strategies is in the *number* of thermonuclear delivery systems required, targeting selection, passive defense measures, and the fact that the "controlled response" assumes a rapid, non-nuclear, conventional, limited war buildup. Controlled thermonuclear war, like its predecessors, massive retaliation and counterforce, attempts to use atomic and thermonuclear weapons as substitutes for conventional arms, preferring instead to "limit" thermonuclear war. "In other words," wrote Stewart Alsop, "if nuclear war comes, our reaction must not be an automatic thermonuclear spasm designed to reduce the other side to a 'waste howling wilderness.' Retaliation for its own sake is irrational. It should be selective and controlled — 'an eye for an eye, a tooth for a tooth, a Minsk for a Hartford.' "

Utopians understand, if nobody else does, that the only way to wage a winning thermonuclear war is to have some way either to "ferret out" and destroy the mobile Russian missiles by "hunter-killer" aircraft; prevent them from getting through to us by some sort of anti-ICBM; or make preparations through shelters to *minimize* the damage done if their missiles do get through. The Kennedy Administration, by killing the RS–70 and refusing to sanction offensive uses of space for bomber satellites (another method of locating mobile Russian ICBM's and triggering a military space race in the process of which the Utopians would try for a counterforce) and by its renewed stress on non-nuclear conventional forces (which reduced the likelihood of a tactical nuclear exchange from escalating into a total thermonuclear war and thereby eliminated an excuse for launching the first nuclear strike) cut the heart out of counterforce, leaving only an outside possibility that still gives hope to Liberal, Conservative, or Military Utopians within and without the Administration that their doctrine still might prevail.

Controlled thermonuclear war is an actionist offensive strategy fought *instead* of a limited conventional ground war. That is, instead of responding in kind to a conventional Russian attack on Berlin or Iran, the United States would take the initiative and immediately escalate the war by taking out a single Russian strategic target or series of targets with nuclear weapons to prove we mean business. If the Russians respond by striking one of our cities, we would return the fire, always being careful to keep the retaliation proportional. Another strategic option would be an immediate escalation to total thermonuclear war and guaranteed total victory over world Communism by "an exercise of the initiative" (pre-emptive war). These are the Utopian alternatives to increasing non-nuclear conventional forces.

The unexpressed Utopian assumption in 1961 was that the only way to guarantee America's future was to protect Berlin and the rest of the Free World by building a vastly superior thermonuclear force and bankrupting the Russians, who with their lower gross national product, could never keep up with us. In other words, we can afford that type of arms race and should engage in it. This is also the reasoning behind increased civilian defense expenditures. The strong possibility that this new and expanded arms race would make total war thinkable and thus all the more likely is consciously not taken into consideration. Instead, we are told that we will be given victory and more security since our weapons are purely defensive. These recommendations are considered by some Traditionalists to be a proto-Fascist solution to our defense dilemma as they lead inevitably to a variety of national socialism through complete government intervention into all levels of the social fabric and economy of the nation.

The problem President Kennedy faced — and this is one of the reasons for his assault on right-wing military extremists — was how to neutralize the various competing military and political groups who wanted to use the crises of the 1960's to engage in a great preventive war crusade for total victory or who wished to divert the national treasure into nonproductive technical by-ways in hopes of creating a true counterforce. Trevor Gardner, former Assistant Secretary of Defense for Research and Development, on August 16, 1961, said that it was wishful thinking to believe that science and technology would produce a decisive weapons advantage for the United States during the coming decade.[2] James Douglas, Secretary of the Air Force from 1957 to 1960, agreed that overoptimism exists as to the effectiveness of various weapons systems in all three services.

But Alexander De Seversky dissented and in his book, *America: Too Young to Die!,* one of the Utopians' greatest popularizers campaigned for the United States to develop an "electronic curtain" so that we could get the drop on the Communists:

If we develop a positive defense against the Russian military threat, we can in effect knock the revolver out of the enemy's hand and thus force her to build more guns and more defenses against our own threat. Thus we could compel Russia to continue to commit her entire industrial base to military effort. . . . We can defeat Russia's purpose only by facing her with a supreme challenge in aerospace warfare, on a magnitude with which her limited military economy cannot cope and do it within the framework of a totally new philosophy, weapons, strategy, and tactics opened up by science and new technology.

This excerpt gives another insight into the difference between Utopians and Traditionalists vis-à-vis the arms race. Utopians believe in a never-ending race with our shadow in an attempt to regain our lost primacy. If it ends in great instability, they are sure that our superior industrial and technological base will enable us to "win." Traditionalists are not so sure that the arms race works in our favor and would rather have the West use its technological genius to find ways to stabilize the arms race before the human race puts an end to man's history.

The Utopians are caught in a dilemma. Their last hope, to find an "advantage of some kind" in nuclear weapons, is behind the Utopian drive for a neutron bomb, a fusionless everyman's hydrogen bomb, a death ray, or some other "absolute weapon." A non-nuclear alternative would be to engage in an extensive, non-lethal chemical research and production program, for chemicals would save both *people* and *property*. Military Utopians and their allies are somehow revolted at even the thought of gas, preferring to kill the enemy by nuclear blast, heat, or radiation. This is a perfect example of vested military and industrial interests attempting to prevent a logical evolution of military weapons.

During the early years of our atomic dominance, Finletter, Symington, Gilpatric, McCone, Strauss, Teller, Dulles, and Radford had been blinded by the brilliance and awed by the magnitude of the nuclear power our scientists had created. Unfortunately for the Free World, what technology could create in one industrially advanced nation could be duplicated in another. The nuclear power that the Utopians had so counted on to give us a decisive edge in 1945–1950 and 1953–1955 had become almost our own downfall. Thus the years 1957 to 1961 represent the nadir of American usable strength. The paradox of weakness amidst plenty is an old one for the United States as our post-World War I history testifies. Thus a surfeit of unusable power, had Kennedy not made heroic changes in the spring, summer, and fall of 1961, most assuredly would have allowed Berlin and Vietnam to go the way of Laos and Cuba: neutralized or lost to the West. Whether the Kennedy shift would be able to permanently reverse this historical trend was an open question basically because the complex strategic debate had not yet been resolved *within* the Kennedy Administration. Until the clear choice was made between balanced forces or counterforce, the Russian response would likewise be highly ambiguous, for Kremlin leaders follow American strategic pronouncements very closely and understand clearly the crucial semantic nuances even if the American public does not.

11

1962 – The Rise and Fall of Counterforce

In MANY RESPECTS THE DEFENSE POLICIES OF THE KENNEDY Administration paralleled the first two years of the Eisenhower Administration. The "bad old chiefs" were removed and replaced by a new and more "trustworthy" set; a new chairman of the Joint Chiefs of Staff was appointed, and, like Admiral Radford, he had the President's fullest confidence; a revised strategy of deterrence was promulgated and promptly modified; an industrialist Secretary of Defense tore into that "nest of eels," the Pentagon; Imperialist Communism continued probing the West's frontiers (and backyard) with renewed vigor; and increasing tension caused policy makers to re-examine the usable military forces available to the United States.

The strategic struggle continued to be a contest between balanced forces and "massive retaliation up-dated," or *counterforce.* In its first year the Kennedy Administration succeeded in accomplishing two top-priority tasks: It made the deterrent more invulnerable and increased our "conventional options." However, late in 1961 in response to the third Berlin crisis, civilian strategists and theoreticians were faced with an almost unresolved problem. Berlin had been saved, temporarily at least, but the calling up of 150,000 reserves had created a delicate political situation at home. Furthermore, the cost of "conventional options" (especially our 400,000 troops in Europe) was having a highly adverse effect on the balance of payments. Was it possible to arrive at a new, less costly, and even more effective strategic solution?

In addition, since the infamous bomber and missile gaps were, surprisingly, now a Russian worry, we had an enormous nuclear superiority of about four to one. Indeed, any controlled thermonuclear warriors would have at their disposal in the near future roughly 2260 intercontinental bombers, 300 carrier-based bombers, 162 ICBM's, 100 IRBM's, and 144 Polarises. Soviet Russia, on the other hand, was believed to have operational only about 150 intercontinental bombers (in addition to 450 to 600 medium-range bombers, which, in a pinch, could make one-way trips to the United States), 100 ICBM's, 700 IRBM's, and a handful of submarines with short-range, surface-fired nuclear missiles.

In view of this tremendous superiority, the argument ran, why not squeeze political-military advantage out of the strategic forces before they went to seed? This argument, well documented with thick and scholarly technical studies and buttressed with wargaming statistics, was remarkably similar to the Radford-Dulles reasoning of 1953–1954. It had great influence in high places and evidently, for a while at least, carried the day. During the eight-month period from October 1961 to June 1962, high Defense officials, engaging in a massive psychological campaign, issued a series of declaratory statements aimed at educating the Communists (and our Allies) to the strategic implications of our nuclear superiority. In February and again in late March 1962, journalistic enthusiasts for counterforce strategy asserted that the President and the United States had adopted a new strategy by which, at times and places of our own choosing, we could "exercise the initiative," a euphemism for waging preventive, or, pre-emptive war.

This global "education" program culminated in the famous McNamara doctrine of counterforce, which the Defense Secretary enunciated at the University of Michigan at Ann Arbor on June 16, 1962. Like Dulles's doctrine of massive retaliation, its blood brother, the McNamara doctrine of counterforce hoped to harvest a political "spillover bonus" from our fantastic nuclear superiority. The deterrent effect of nuclear weapons could, he hoped, protect Berlin and other critical areas of the Free World.

The Russians responded to the new deterrent theory in 1962 as they had in 1954: by immediately challenging our doctrine and forcing us literally "to put up or shut up." They manufactured the fourth Berlin crisis, resumed thermonuclear multi-megatonnage weapons testing, turned Cuba into an armed Communist camp, and accused the United States of preparing for preventive war. McNamara, like Dulles, quickly modified his doctrine. But here the similarity between the Kennedy and Eisenhower defense policies ended. During the Eisenhower Administration, conventional and unconventional forces were cut in half by implementing the new look (1954–1957), and the official atmosphere was definitely hostile to "any more Koreas" or limited wars anywhere.

Throughout 1961–1962 the Kennedy Administration accorded the alternative doctrine of balanced forces equal status, and these balanced forces flourished in an uneasy coexistence with the more technocratic and glamorous counterforce. In its quest for alternatives to "humiliation or holocaust," the Kennedy Administration tolerated the two strategic concepts within the defense establishment. Actually, the United States, or any nation for that matter, can never make a clear choice between strategies; it is, rather, a question of emphasis. However, since three of the "pure counterforce" implications — massive civil defense including blast shelters, unlimited and accelerated *thermonuclear* arms race, and greatly increased danger of pre-emptive war — are so filled with danger to our democratic society, it is apparent that if our security and worldwide national interests can be protected or forwarded by another grand strategy, then that strategy should be adopted.

A high point in the evolution of balanced forces was General Taylor's January 15, 1962, speech to the New York Printers Association, in which he sketched a deterrent concept consisting of: (1) Total war (a first strike Russian thermonuclear attack or a massive conventional Russian thrust in Europe) is deterred by invulnerable second strike deterrent forces configured for *retaliatory* counterforce; (2) limited war (Korea) is deterred by adequate, mobile, and available dually-equipped forces; (3) "wars of liberation" (Vietnam and Cuba) are deterred by proper prognosis before the situation becomes critical and, if unsuccessful, fought by "special and unconventional forces"; and (4) Taylor implied that political-economic challenge is countered by imaginative and "good policies," such as the Peace Corps, civic action, Interdependence, the Trade Expansion Act, and Project Apollo. Three days after General Taylor's speech President Kennedy apparently ratified this strategy by eloquently setting forth his famous "strategic guidelines" to an expanded National Security Council gathered at the White House.

But whatever the President may propose, the vast bureaucracy still disposes, and where such a vital concept as strategic guidelines is concerned, the entire federal bureaucracy is involved. Civilian members of the Defense Department throughout the first half of 1962 hinted that what the President *really* meant by his January "guidelines" was counterforce. Sympathetic journalists also tried to convince the public that counterforce was indeed what the President had had in mind. Phrases like "exercise of the initiative," attributed to the President, received quick, heated denials. But the proponents of "no-win" were unappeased, and as the year wore on the demands for total victory over world Communism, even if it meant nuclear war, were heard in the land. Old-fashioned diplomacy, backed by traditional military tools, was not sufficient for these modern warhawks, who seemed to demand an atomic showdown — the sooner the better.

Denials or no, the famous Ann Arbor speech in June 1962 by Secretary McNamara appeared to confirm the view that henceforth balanced forces, although useful, were of secondary importance, and thermonuclear counterforce would be used to solve our outstanding political-military problems. To sophisticated and unsophisticated alike it seemed that the United States, for the first time in her history, had officially adopted an aggressive first strike strategy. For there was no doubt about it, a counterforce strategy had triumphed. This strategy, which had been fighting for acceptance since the first primitive atomic bomb was dropped on Hiroshima in 1945, was now official doctrine of the United States of America. In Secretary McNamara's words: "The US has come to the conclusion that to the extent feasible, basic military strategy in a possible nuclear war should be approached in much the same way that conventional military operations have been regarded in the past. That is to say, principal military objectives, in the event of a nuclear war stemming from a major attack on the Alliance, should be the destruction of the enemy's military forces, not of his civilian population." And a few sentences later the Secretary of Defense offered the so-called Marquis of Queensbury rules to the Russians. "In other words," McNamara stated, "we are giving a possible opponent the strongest imaginable incentive to refrain from striking our own cities."

Thus the United States announced to the world that we were going to preserve the *option* of fighting a controlled thermonuclear war, and from this capability it was calculated by some of the Pentagon "Whiz Kids" that the United States would reap the same political benefits that the Soviets allegedly receive from Khrushchev's "rocket rattling." Americans, like Communists, under this theory would use the threat of a thermonuclear war as an instrument of foreign policy. The inherent difference, which some technocrats and so-called hard liners find difficult to understand, is that the United States is a Western democracy operating under representative principles and backed by 2000 years of Christian-Humanist traditions. She cannot brandish the threat of thermonuclear Armageddon with as much facility or credibility as a Communist nation. In a sense, the leaders of the

Western democracies are captives of the many-millennia-long process that Walter Lippmann calls our "heritage of civility." Paradoxically, this heritage is, as far as waging controlled thermonuclear war is concerned, the West's greatest weakness; but when it comes to creating a consensus within the Western world and influencing the behavior of the "third world," this civility is perhaps the West's greatest strength.

McNamara's advisors, high priests of the new deterrence theology, had not taken into consideration these deep traditions or international political realities. The price America would have to pay to preserve her heritage would be almost instantaneous modification of the McNamara doctrine of counterforce and its replacement by a new grand strategy backed by balanced forces.

Sharp and totally unexpected European reaction to his speech caused Mr. McNamara to make the first of many modifications to it. Quickest to protest were the British, who pointed out that Mr. McNamara's "scathing" denunciation that "relatively weak national nuclear forces . . . operating independently are dangerous, expensive, prone to obsolescence, and lacking in credibility as a deterrent" did not apply to the Bomber Command. The London *Sunday Times* on June 24, 1962 remarked: "It was surprising that Mr. MacNamara [sic] should have been quite so outspoken about independent nuclear deterrent, just when his colleague, Mr. Rusk, was landing at Paris on his European mission. . . . Everyone assumed that this was an open criticism of French policy and only less of British."

That same day McNamara clarified the intent of his counterforce speech by explaining: "What I said at Ann Arbor was . . . separate nuclear capabilities operating independently were dangerous. But Britain's bomber command aircraft with their nuclear weapons have long been organized as part of a thoroughly coordinated Anglo-American striking force and are targeted as such. . . . I was, therefore, not referring to Britain."

Harold Watkinson, Britain's Defense Minister, confronted by the opposition swirling in on all sides, reaffirmed that Britain had the unchallenged right to use its nuclear force independently if it wished.

French reaction was slow in coming and took the irreversible form of a De Gaullean parliamentary victory for the French independent deterrent, the *force de frappe,* during the July debates over the funding of a new gaseous diffusion plant — Pierrelatte. Like John Foster Dulles's "agonizing reappraisal," occasioned by too obvious American pressure that effectively killed the European Defense Community, Secretary McNamara's attempt to go over the head of the French government was a resounding failure. As Raymond Aron observed, Frenchmen find it hard to understand why it is safe for the independent deterrent to cross the Atlantic but "dangerous" and "inimical" for it to cross the English Channel. Aron also maintained that the French independent deterrent was conceived before De Gaulle came to power and would be continued after his departure. The French said, in effect, that the *force de frappe* exists, and they intend to make the most of it.

President Kennedy quickly sized up the political realities better than Mr. McNamara's "young technocrats," who, in the words of the French writer A. Delcroix, "have a tendency to underestimate the purely political because of the contempt in which they hold things political." Therefore, on July 4 at Independence Hall in Philadelphia, the President made his revolutionary offer of "partnership" and "interdependence" within the Atlantic Alliance. However, if this concept means anything at all, it presupposes a realization of the truth of which *The Times* (London) wrote:

Western Europe as a whole has the resources for a nuclear armament no less economical, up-to-date or convincing than America's.

As European unity grows, these technical resources will surely be matched by power ambitions. The time has already come to consider the pattern of nuclear arms within an Atlantic Alliance in which, so Mr. Heath has foretold, there will be two great partners, North America and Europe.

Nothing less than equal status for these two could meet the need in this supreme defensive sphere.

This observation was similar to President Kennedy's splendid vision: "We see in such a Europe a partner with whom we can deal on a basis of full equality in all the great and burdensome tasks of building and defending a community of free nations." He also noted that "building the Atlantic partnership now will not be easily or cheaply finished." James Reston hinted, and the President later confirmed the fact, that the United States would be willing to consider a uniquely European nuclear solution, providing it were integrated with our deterrent and were something more than a collection of independent national deterrents.

Two days later on July 6, 1962, Secretary McNamara took another backward step away from "pure" counterforce when he told a press conference that the Ann Arbor speech, far from being a primer on Marquis of Queensbury rules of nuclear warfare, was instead an outline of a "flexible strategy" because "we can't be certain how a nuclear war would develop." Therefore, the United States might spare Soviet cities or it might not. The *New York Herald Tribune* on July 9, 1962, editorialized on "Mr. McNamara's Modified War," and knowledgeable counterforce strategists were greatly dismayed that the pure counterforce doctrine had been scrapped so soon. Indeed, C. L. Sulzberger on July 9, 1962, categorically reported from London that counterforce "is now dead." The reasons were simple. Partnership, which implies equality with our allies, would be impossible if America retained control of strategic nuclear weapons and, more importantly, the Russians announced they would not play our game. Finally, such a strategy, in Henry Kissinger's analysis (*Foreign Affairs,* July 1962), is technologically infeasible, since the adversary can make his deterrent invulnerable, thereby depriving your counterforce of any targets to counter.

Radio Moscow in early June spelled out Russian reaction: "Mr. McNamara . . . dropped the hint that nuclear war might be conducted along gentlemen's lines and might, as a result, be almost a civilized one . . . Mr. McNamara attempts to draw a line between local wars fought with tactical nuclear weapons and the world wars, when no such line can be drawn."

Further proof that the Russians were buying neither counterforce nor its concommitant, controlled thermonuclear war, was supplied by Premier Khrushchev in an address on July 10, 1962, to the World Conference on General Disarmament and Peace. Khrushchev declared that "the league of war-industrial monopolies, the 'death merchants,' and the zealot militarists — this military-industrial complex as ex-President Eisenhower described it — is heating up the arms race to a frenzy." Khrushchev directly answered the Ann Arbor doctrine: "Lately, the militarists talk more and more about thermonuclear war. Take Defense Secretary McNamara's speech of June 16. He says in it that an understanding may be reached to use nuclear weapons solely for striking at the armed forces, and not at the big cities. The U.S. press says that McNamara's statement had the approval of the White House, and interprets it as a sort of proposal to the Soviet Union on 'rules' of conducting a nuclear war."

Premier Khrushchev then remarked: "It is a monstrous proposal filled from beginning to end with a misanthropic disdain for men, for mankind, because it seeks to legalize nuclear war and thereby the murder of millions upon millions of people."

During the course of his speech, the Soviet prime minister also spoke of a "global rocket" with a multi-megaton warhead "practically impervious to defense" and, for good measure, he accused the United States of planning to wage preventive war when the American press talks of taking the "initiative."

Further clarification of the Ann Arbor doctrine was not long in coming. Marquis Childs, after an exclusive interview with the Secretary of Defense, reported that McNamara was "surprised" that anyone would conclude from his Ann Arbor speech that the United States was preparing a pre-emptive strike, and to support his position he quoted President Kennedy's mid-February press conference: "Now if someone thinks we should have a nuclear war in order to win, I can inform them that there will not be winners of the next nuclear war, if there is one, and this country and other countries would suffer very heavy blows . . ."

McNamara reiterated to Mr. Childs that he does not believe

that a "nuclear war can be won" and that although we keep our deterrent guard strong and invulnerable, we will never initiate a nuclear attack. The Defense Secretary now had changed significantly his original June 16 position with its overtones of a *counterforce first strike* strategy to a much more sensible and traditional doctrine of *retaliatory counterforce.*

However, *Air Force,* July 1962, chose to regard McNamara's speech as a vindication of first strike and "an endorsement of the Air Force's doctrine of counterforce capability." Dr. Robert E. Osgood pointed out in the *New Republic,* September 10, 1962, that "some proponents of a counterforce strategy now advocate 'winning' a nuclear war by disarming the enemy in an all-out attack on his strategic nuclear weapons." Fortunately, most professional military men would seem to favor the interpretation that Secretary McNamara apparently accepted as a result of the Childs interview, when he rejected any preventive first strike or "war winning" overtones to his Ann Arbor speech. He now appeared to favor the concept that the United States would maintain a substantial superiority over the Russians in invulnerable "strike-second" delivery systems. We would use this superiority in only two instances: a direct thermonuclear attack on the United States or a massive conventional drive threatening to overrun Europe. And in both cases the *initial* American response would be a controlled retaliatory strike directed against enemy nuclear forces. In case of accidental war or "miscalculation," the United States would have sufficient insurance to engage in limited nuclear reprisal or retaliatory counterforce before exercising her "ultimate option" of an all-out attack on enemy cities.

After a particularly searching column, "Miscalculation and War," by Warren Rogers, Jr., in the *New York Herald Tribune* (July 19, 1962), Secretary McNamara in another interview modified counterforce even further. Curiously, the interview coincided with Hanson Baldwin's famous "leak" in the *New York Times* of July 26, 1962, which stated that the "Soviets were building shields at missile sites." This "hardening" was by above-ground "concrete coffins." The significance of the announcement was clear to the *New York Times* military analyst, who reported that the Soviets are building two types of missile forces — one consisting of "a few of their huge, ponderous and expensive first-generation missiles, but are deliberately fitting the largest possible warheads to them in order to achieve maximum political and psychological effect and, in case of war, widespread damage and destruction by means of pattern bombardment."

Secondly, Baldwin interpreted the invulnerable missiles this way:

The advent of Russian missile-firing submarines and hardened land-based missile sites indicates to many in Washington that Soviet strategic thinking is roughly along the same lines as our own. Moscow, like Washington, is trying to make its nuclear deterrent and retaliatory power less and less vulnerable to surprise attack.

As the invulnerability of missile launching sites increases and each side finds it impossible to knock out the other's nuclear capability by a surprise first strike, the stability of the deterrent is expected to increase . . .

According to *Newsweek,* Mr. Baldwin's story resulted in an FBI investigation and an order that Joint Chiefs of Staff officers "turn in detailed reports on all interviews — and even chance meetings — with newsmen."

Shortly after its appearance Mr. McNamara "confirmed" the Baldwin story and, ironically, took credit for the Russian missile "hardening." Rogers of the *New York Herald Tribune,* after a chat with Mr. McNamara, reported that "paradoxical as it may seem, the United States is hopeful that Russia will go underground or otherwise 'harden' its missile launchers. . . ." For with an invulnerable deterrent, the Russians, in the event of a serious international crisis, would feel more secure and less tempted to launch a pre-emptive strike.

Ross of the *Chicago Sun-Times,* apparently after another interview, continued speculating in the same vein: "Now, the Russians apparently realize they must follow the U.S. lead and shield their weapons — a development which, in the ironic logic of the cold war, does not at all displease McNamara." The Defense Secretary had thus confirmed that United States policy, which since 1945 had rejected an aggressive war against the Soviet Union, remained the official doctrine of the United States.

Even Jules Feiffer caught the "counterforce madness" heavily hanging over the Potomac during the summer of 1962. He depicted, not Pentagon generals, but two civilian intellectuals glibly discussing the advantages of counterforce. One scholar remarked: "The proper move would be to convince the U.S.S.R. that we will ignore THEIR population centers if they ignore OURS. If we can restrict nuclear war to each other's missile bases it may prove to be quite a civilized affair." To which the other scholar, barely restraining his enthusiasm, added: "Much NEATER than rival forms of war, really." And the two lay militarists smilingly drank a toast to "happy wars."

But one need not be a Jules Feiffer or even an Albert Wohlstetter or Herman Kahn to understand that once the Russian deterrent is invulnerable, a counterforce strategy is a technological impossibility (and this state, Henry Kissinger, maintains is rapidly approaching).

Thus by August 1962 the Ann Arbor doctrine had been so modified and utterly confused, first by the President (in offering nuclear partnership to Europe) and second by McNamara (by reassuring the English and Russians) that a clarifying statement was needed.

General Taylor, Chairman Designate of the Joint Chiefs, made such a statement in Minneapolis, in which he returned to the same theme as his New York speech of January 15 and the views set forth in *The Uncertain Trumpet*. In mid-August General Taylor told the National Convention of Veterans of Foreign Wars: "We must be prepared to cope with general atomic war, with conventional war with or without the support of nuclear weapons, and unconventional war of the Vietnam type." The new chairman of the Joint Chiefs of Staff noted that if the Communists acted boldly in the days when America had an atomic monopoly, "we can expect even less restraint now that their atomic strength grows. It seems reasonable to expect that the provocations with which we will be faced will be more varied and at higher levels than in the past. To meet this possibility we must be able to offer a wide choice of response to our leaders, not merely the alternatives of giving way or resorting to general atomic war."

Now this was the voice of a truly professional military officer, and it implied that under his regime the Joint Chiefs of Staff would play a much greater role in the formulation of strategy, heretofore abdicated to the bright young "Whiz Kids," who, for the most part, have never known war or diplomacy and tend to be suspicious of anything that cannot be reduced to mathematical formulas or models. The abortive counterforce strategy was just such an end product. Fortunately, there are simply too many unknowns, too many imponderables in a nation's foreign and defense policy or war itself to make them susceptible to such a rational deterrent strategy as counterforce and controlled thermonuclear war. United States policy-makers had to formulate a more *politically* realistic strategy, better able to reconcile the new world to the new Europe.

This was done at Copenhagen on September 27, 1962, when McGeorge Bundy, President Kennedy's Special Assistant for National Security Affairs, told the delegates to the General Assembly of the Atlantic Treaty Association that the United States was no longer opposed to an independent European nuclear deterrent. Bundy promised that "if it should turn out that a genuinely multilateral European deterrent, integrated with ours in NATO, is what is needed and wanted, it will not be a veto from the Administration in the United States which stands in the way." In other words, carrying out President Kennedy's July 4, 1962, offer of partnership and interdependence, the United States would not veto and would undoubtedly aid an independent European deterrent on two conditions: that it be the deterrent force of a united Europe and it be integrated or coordinated with our deterrent.

Pure counterforce's final coup de grâce was delivered by Secretary McNamara in a series of ironic remarks delivered, fittingly, at a memorial dinner to America's greatest professional soldier, George Catlett Marshall. Before the Army Association on October 10 in Washington, the Secretary of Defense apparently completely disengaged himself from the Ann Arbor concept of counterforce. McNamara expressed his now traditional philosophy of deterrence with these definitive words of deterrent art: *"We deter the Soviets from using their growing nuclear force by maintaining a nuclear force strong enough and survivable enough to ride out any conceivable nuclear attack, and to survive with sufficient power to cause unacceptable damage to the attacker."* (Italics mine.)[1] By referring to Khrushchev's "much-quoted speech of 6 January 1961," in which he had remarked that "the problem of preventing a global thermonuclear war is the most burning and vital problem for mankind," McNamara acknowledged that both Russia and the United States desired to "prevent" thermonuclear wars, not "win" them. Like General Taylor, McNamara was sure that Khrushchev was still an "enthusiastic advocate" of wars of liberation and that America must have the proper forms of usable force in order to cope with the changing but relentless challenge.

Furthermore, Secretary McNamara revealed himself to be an enthusiastic advocate of balanced forces. ". . . the role of the Army," he remarked to the long suffering Army Association, "and even the role of the individual combat soldier, becomes not less but more important." "We require," continued McNamara in a sentence that might have been borrowed from General Taylor's *The Uncertain Trumpet,*

increasing capability to deter forms of political and military aggression against which the application of nuclear weapons may not be a credible response.

It is essential, in order to protect our own national security, as well as to meet our responsibilities as the leader of the free world, that we develop and maintain the forces to deter Communist aggression across the entire spectrum of military and para-military aggression — and, if deterrence should be unsuccessful, to stop that aggression dead in its tracks.

American strategic doctrine had travelled a long and difficult road in the first two years of the Kennedy Administration. The competing strategies, counterforce and balanced forces, were alternately in and out of favor. One can safely assert that the 14,000 American troops committed to saving Vietnam, the Second Fleet and Strike Force standing watch over Cuba, the Sixth Fleet protecting Europe's soft underbelly, the Seventh Fleet insuring stability in the Formosan Straits and Southeast Asia, the 400,000 American troops guarding Europe, the 6000 combat-ready soldiers in Berlin, the 150,000 reservists, and the Peace Corps volunteers everywhere are as vital to American deterrent power as are the Strategic Air Command's B–47, B–52, Atlas, Titan, the Navy's Polaris and A3D and A3J bombers.

This is what Secretary McNamara, General Taylor, and other strategists meant by balanced forces and the stabilized deterrence such forces help bring about. It is why, as Secretary McNamara reminded his Army Association audience, "countering Communist aggression requires the organized efforts not only of all the four military services but of all the agencies of government." Then and only then will America be able to achieve her key foreign policy goal of bringing about, in Secretary of State Dean Rusk's words, a "peaceful world community" in which "nations are free to choose their own future and political system — so long as they threaten no one else's freedom." Balanced forces rather than counterforce will help make this goal a reality in this century. The acid test for the Kennedy-McNamara strategy came with surprising swiftness, not in Berlin where everyone feared, but in that "American lake" — the Caribbean.

12

The Cuban Crisis: Theory in Practice

OF ALL THE "LESSONS OF CUBA" THE ONE OF GREATEST strategic significance was the realization by Washington policymakers of the unique utility of conventional forces. During the Cuban crisis President Kennedy, as commander-in-chief of the American armed forces, outgeneraled Premier Khrushchev, thanks to the skilled use of our conventional forces. The facts of the naval quarantine spoke for themselves. Utopians had to settle for supplying a part of the deterrent shield behind which the President manipulated the men and ships of the general-purpose forces. Herman Kahn's vision, the strategic use of thermonuclear forces, so assiduously bootlegged for five years within the Eisenhower and Kennedy Administrations, was relegated to the "think factories" where it had been developed. Instead, the artificial restraints introduced into modern war by the invention of the H-bomb and perfection of its ballistic missile delivery vehicle allowed President Kennedy to employ old-fashioned naval power off Castro's Communist fortress.

It should be noted that as late as August and September 1962 official Washington still thought of the "sword and shield" in their post-1953 sense; the sword was the blazing fury of an alerted, avenging, and victorious Strategic Air Command, and the shield was NATO ground forces, a "trip wire" or plate-glass shield, that would trigger with hardly a moment's hesitation the thermonuclear vengeance of the B–47 and B–52. Implicitly, this entailed a first strategic nuclear strike made in response to *any* type of Russian attack in Europe.

But the winds of doctrinal and technological change had long been stirring up an increasingly violent controversy in Washington and Europe. The famous Rusk memo of February 1961, which had suggested a greater emphasis on conventional ground forces in Europe, foreshadowed important strategic changes to come, as its Pentagon "leakers" well knew. The Berlin crisis of 1961 had been surmounted with an equivocal buildup of both nuclear and conventional forces. Happily, the nuclear forces purchased were basically "strike-second" (Polaris and Minuteman), but what the deciding factor had been that forced Khrushchev to loosen the screws on Berlin in the fall of 1961 was never absolutely clear. Fortunately, no such ambiguous interpretation was entertained after Cuba. Conventional forces carried the day, and in speech after speech Administration spokesmen proclaimed this truth.

But it was not until Secretary of Defense McNamara's address to the NATO ministerial meeting in mid-December that the switch in strategic theory became official policy; henceforth, thermonuclear weapons would be the shield and conventional weapons, the sword. American strategy had returned to its traditional postwar conception of the deterrent. Under the protection of the B–29 and B–36 with their atomic bombs, the Western world had recovered from the shock of losing eastern Europe and China and had rearmed itself slowly — militarily, economically, politically, and morally. World Communism was contained by the imaginative use of conventional force (Korea) and unconventional force (Berlin airlift, aid to Greece, and the Sixth Fleet in the Mediterranean). Under the protection of McNamara's new nuclear shield, created by invulnerable strike-second deterrents, the free world's increasing strength conceivably might be translated politically into another Renaissance.

One week after McNamara's speech at Paris in December 1962, President Kennedy met Prime Minister Macmillan in the Bahamas, where they drew up the historic Nassau Pact, by which they attempted to institutionalize the multilateral-multi-national solution for the nuclear problem as well as to recognize formally the changed status of the sword and shield.

Thus the Nassau agreements were the direct result of the Cuban experience; indeed, the Cuban crisis of 1962 was a tremendous global catalyst. The direct Russo-American confrontation, occurring simultaneously with the Chinese invasion of India, permanently and massively altered world history. Alliances and great power blocs — East, West, and Neutral — were shaken to their very foundations. Paradoxically, both the Western Alliance and the Communist bloc were weakened because of the smashing success of the Americans and Chinese. The Communist and non-Communist worlds ultimately will reform again, but the pattern will be changed, for the power equation within the world has been altered permanently by those fateful events in the blue Caribbean and the white Himalayas. Symbolically, on November 21 President Kennedy lifted the naval quarantine, and Communist China declared a unilateral cease-fire along the Indian border. Conventional sea power and manpower had been victorious, and both nations limited their victories for fear that by their very excesses everything won might be lost (as it was when President Truman permitted General MacArthur to pursue the retreating North Koreans across the thirty-eighth parallel up the narrow waist of Korea toward the frozen Yalu).

The Cuban catalyst affected military strategy, diplomatic policy, and domestic politics. With the change in sword and shield President Kennedy moved toward a "true deterrent strategy." Simply stated, this meant all first strike weapons systems would be phased out, and no new ones built. Instead, only those strategic systems that because of their invulnerability properly can be called strike-second or retaliatory weapons would be stockpiled and deployed. Secondly, and just as important, conventional and unconventional forces would be modernized and strengthened. This will be a very costly process, for recall that in 1953 it was the Army's conventional forces that had been pared from 1,600,000 to 860,000 as the quickest and surest way to honor the 1952 campaign promise to cut the budget by twenty billion dollars. President Kennedy and Secretary McNamara increased the Army to nearly a million men, bringing up its division strength from eleven to sixteen. The strategic doctrine that this two-pronged buildup operated within is called "mutual deterrence," which supposes, as Secretary McNamara first remarked in October and later in December at Paris, a level of adequacy in strategic forces beyond which it is pointless to build, for even if we double or triple our strategic forces, an enemy's invulnerable deterrent will remain to vaporize our exposed cities in retaliation.

Cuba changed also the style of American diplomacy and foreign policy. As President Kennedy expressed it on December 31 in a statement that created a minor transatlantic furor: "I don't expect that the U.S. will be more beloved, but I would hope that we could get more done." Globally, this meant unilateral United States initiative in the Congo, where the President sent General Truman from Joint Task Force Four to determine what "logistical" support the United Nations would need to send Tshombe packing and to unify the Congo. American initiative in trying to settle the Yemen revolution was another example of the new diplomatic style and bore a striking resemblance to that of Teddy Roosevelt except that President Kennedy operated less dramatically through his agents.

However, it was on our NATO allies that the carry-over from our unilateral Cuban crisis management had the greatest impact. The decision to cancel the bomber-launched Skybolt missile stemmed from political, strategic, and economic motives. Britain's Conservative government, which had known since September 1962 the decision was probable, stage-managed an elaborate reaction to the "perfidious" State Department decision while cleverly planning its own alternative to the original American

multilateral force concept of October 1962. The result of this
maneuvering was the Nassau Pact, which must rank with the
Monroe Doctrine and Hayes's Open Door Policy as a first-rate
British conception sold to overly anxious Americans. The British regarded Nassau as a halfway house on the road to an
English-preferred NATO nuclear trusteeship: an English-domi-
nated European deterrent within NATO but lacking the American veto.

France, sensing an "Anglo-Saxon" trap, rejected "integration"
of her national *force de frappe* as a condition for acceptance of
the Nassau policies, killed British hopes for immediate entry
into the Common Market, and wrecked President Kennedy's
grand design for an Atlantic Community, forcing the President
and his advisers to their fallback position of Atlantic partnership.

Meanwhile, the Germans, always ready to opt for strength
and supranationalism, were also distracted by the Cuban crisis.
The Adenauer-Strauss wing of the ruling Christian Democratic
party had been very pleased with Dulles's massive retaliation.
The Utopian Franz Josef Strauss wanted nuclear weapons for
the Bundeswehr, but others in Germany wished to see conventional forces strengthened. Previously, Defense Minister Strauss
and General Norstad at NATO had seen eye to eye on the general utility of nuclear weapons and the land-based MRBM in
Germany. With Norstad about to retire, the one last chance to
scuttle the Kennedy shift seemed to Strauss (and some American Utopians) to be over the issue of land-based MRBM's and
front-line Davy Crocketts (atomic bazookas or mortars).

Armed with these nuclear weapons and shored up by American Utopian theory, it seemed to Strauss NATO would have
"total deterrence" once again. The clock would be turned back
to before the Russian ICBM, when there were no "self-gen-
erated" doubts about the credibility of a SAC thermonuclear
response at the slightest Soviet aggressive move. To Strauss,
European and American Utopians, those were the good old days
of total deterrence or total war, when, thanks to American nuclear superiority in a "credible first strike capability," total vic-

tory over world Communism was a certainty. The total deterrence of Strauss and American Military Utopians was really Dulles's massive retaliation updated. Berlin and the German cities along the Iron Curtain offered a wonderful pretext for a pre-emptive strike to eradicate world Communism because it could be accomplished in the name of sacred NATO commitments. Strauss, Gaullist, and American Utopians bitterly resisted the reversal of the sword and shield concept because it implied that America was determined to have an alternative between "humiliation and holocaust" even if it meant fighting a limited war in Europe.

American Utopians received strong support from German, English, and French Utopians but for different reasons. English theoreticians fought the revision because it would cost a great deal more money, would mean the buildup of the Royal Navy at the expense of the Royal Air Force and Bomber Command, probably would necessitate the revival of conscription, and it was highly embarrassing politically, since the Conservative government would be forced to admit that it was wrong in adopting the Skybolt concept in the first place. The British, thanks to institutions like the Institute of Strategic Studies, were not deluded by the universality of thermonuclear weapons. Great Britain's relatively small size — four or five H-bombs would eliminate her — preordained that the *deterrent* effect rather than the war-winning aspect of thermonuclear weapons was the accepted rationale of these "megadeath" city busters. Super powers, like the United States and the Soviet Union, could separate the idea of deterring total war from fighting and winning total war, but smaller nations could not afford that macabre luxury. Herman Kahn's "forty or sixty" million "acceptable" casualties would completely wipe out France, England, or Germany even if, theoretically, it would only cripple the United States for a decade. Consequently, with the exception of Strauss and those German militarists sympathetic to him, hardly any European strategist reacted favorably to the McNamara doctrine of counterforce proposed at Ann Arbor in June 1962. British and French strategists immediately rejected it because it seemed to doom national deterrents, while American strategists condemned the doctrine for being so ambiguous that it suggested an aggressive first strike strategy aimed at fighting and winning controlled thermonuclear war.[1]

France's leading strategist, General Pierre Gallois, violently attacked the counterforce doctrine as full of contradictions and passionately defended the French *force de frappe,* which was endangered by the McNamara "no cities" doctrine, since its only conceivable targets were Soviet cities. McNamara had suggested at Ann Arbor that the United States would avoid hitting Soviet cities if the Russians would do likewise. In numerous articles Gallois pointed out that McNamara's assertions about the Polaris and invulnerable deterrents implied that neither the United States nor Russia would be able to destroy the opposing strategic forces; hence the only possible target would be enemy cities. Furthermore, Gallois maintained, the French *force de frappe* was designed from its bomb up to be a "city buster," to "rip off an arm," or to kill "millions and millions of men" in response to overt aggression.

French theorists, like their British counterparts, believe in the deterrent effect of nuclear weapons and maintain that if they are ever used, they will have failed their purpose; the complete destruction of the nation will be inevitable. They oppose American strategic doctrine because they believe the United States wants to deprive France of its "nuclear sovereignty" by "integrating" the French and American deterrents. They do not want to increase a conventional buildup because it would siphon too much money from their foremost priority — the *force de frappe.* To De Gaulle, Nassau looked like a resurrection of the "special relationship" between the Anglo-Saxon powers and a sellout of national independence for multilateral interdependence. In De Gaulle's eyes Macmillan was a traitor to Europe for allowing American predominance and direction in Europe to continue in the vital nuclear domain. Thus the startling success of President Kennedy in staring down Khrushchev and forcing the Soviet premier to beat a hasty retreat from his Caribbean adventure contributed to a lessening of world tension and afforded our allies the luxury of speculating openly and loudly about their future relationship with the most powerful nation in history.

The Cuban crisis had demonstrated to President Kennedy the absolute indivisibility of the nuclear defense of the Free World and the necessity for as few fingers on the nuclear trigger as possible. By rejecting pre-emptive war against Cuba or the Soviet Union as a possible course of action and by stressing conventional forces and an adequate strike-second deterrent weapons program, the United States set the stage for a much more rapid revision of American strategy than was planned or believed possible.

To Traditionalists after so many years in the strategic wilderness, the first two years of the Kennedy Administration were like reaching the Promised Land. First Berlin and then Cuba demonstrated beyond any possible contradiction the absolute utility of conventional, usable military force in the Age of Deterrence. From the international events of the fall of 1962, a new grand strategy for the Western world was formed. Beginning with General Lemnitzer's appointment as Supreme Allied Commander Europe and the almost simultaneous French funding of Pierrelatte for its H-bomb in July 1962, a great debate seized the Western Alliance, was propelled by the Cuban crisis, Skybolt cancellation, and Nassau Pact, and reached its thunderous conclusion in January 1963, when De Gaulle proclaimed his "double no" to the Polaris offer and British entry into the Common Market, forcing the United States to reappraise its entire European policy.

Throughout this ferment Utopians and Traditionalists began to lock horns in a titanic struggle that would make the B–36 versus U.S.S. *United States* conflict of 1949 seem like tiddly-winks, for the stakes were immense: appropriations for specific weapons systems worth billions of dollars; perpetuation of the United States Air Force as the dominant service; survival of many communities and local industries; salvation of so-called political advantages of a strategic nuclear war; maintenance of the psychological advantage of fighting and "winning" thermo-nuclear war; preservation of the option of pre-emptive war, the likelihood of truly significant tax cuts in the defense budget, the chance to abolish the JCS and to create a merged single military service, the possibility of manned orbiting bombers, and for some few Utopians, the hope of a garrison state created by a military coup d'etat.

After Cuba Secretary Rusk pictured the United States and the planet Earth as on the brink of a strange, new, and promising age. Although the Secretary of State did not amplify his rather veiled vision, it is possible that Rusk had glimpsed some of the golden opportunities of the Age of Deterrence: peace, freedom, prosperity, health, and happiness. How ironic indeed that through traditional uses of military force Utopia could be approached within the lifetime of the majority of the world's population without massacring twenty-five million to one billion human beings.

The key concept in this new Age of Deterrence, the mutual existence of invulnerable deterrents, was foreshadowed by the unfolding of the 1962 Cuban crisis. Both Traditionalists and Utopians could and did interpret October's awful events as justification for their long-held doctrinal views. In the broadest sense, the Traditionalist was convinced that Cuba demonstrated the limits of nuclear power and that as the two great global antagonists perfect their strike-second forces, these thermonuclear forces tend to cancel out each other, leaving the more conventional means of settling conflicts between nations the only alternative to mutual suicide.

Cuba then was merely the latest and potentially most explosive of a series of post–World War II political-military conflicts between East and West in what has been called popularly the Cold War. But the Cold War is actually a transitional state between total wars of the World War I and II variety (an institution of the Age of National Defense) and the new Age of True Deterrence. It is conceivable that Cuba was the climactic incident of the Cold War, since it represented a direct confrontation between American and Soviet military power. During the Cuban crisis the President, thanks to the existence of balanced military forces, chose to exercise the option of *strategic use of conventional force* under the protective shield of the deterrent.

To the Military Utopian this interpretation of the Cuban crisis is sheer heresy, for he has been weaned on *the strategic use of nuclear force*. This means simply using our "most modern weapons" (a euphemism for "nukes") in practically any situation, tactical or strategic, since our absolute superiority in both forms of nuclear weapons should allow us to use either with relative immunity and without fear of "escalation" or receiving a preemptive strike. American Utopians have been aware since late 1961 that the Soviets were in the process of hardening their ICBM's and moving part of their deterrent to sea. Soviet construction of an invulnerable deterrent, hinted at in Secretary McNamara's defense presentation in January 1962 and further alluded to in Hanson Baldwin's famous "leak" in July 1962, was officially confirmed in McNamara's January 1963 presentation to the House Armed Services Committee, in which he summarily rejected Utopian hopes of building a counterforce by stating:

Fully hard Soviet ICBM's and nuclear-powered ballistic missile launching-submarines would considerably detract from our ability to destroy completely the Soviet strategic nuclear forces . . . Even if we were to double and triple our forces we would not be able to destroy quickly all or almost all of the hardened ICBM sites. And even if we could do that, we know of no way to destroy the enemy's missile launching submarines at the same time.

What made this Soviet invulnerability especially galling to Utopians was that this strategic mutation finally forced them to draw the long obscured theoretical distinction between a purely retaliatory force and an aggressive first strike counterforce, both in terms of the enemy's deterrent forces and our own deterrent forces. In other words, the rationale for strategic force could no longer be confused. The distinction between defensive and offensive strategic forces became much clearer as the concept of mutual invulnerability and its far-flung implications were better understood.

Furthermore, if the Russians actually were hardening and dispersing their strategic forces and filling *their* deterrent or missile gap, the time for achieving the Utopian decade-long hopes of a *Pax Americana* was fast running out. The promise implicit in the Douhet-Mitchell-Trenchard doctrine of victory through airpower delivered by the heavy bomber soon would become a technical impossibility. There is no doubt that the American "aerospace" industry could produce thousands of "quick reaction" Minuteman ICBM's, hundreds of RS–70's and satellite bombers, and thereby attain any desired numerical superiority over any possible combination of opponents. The Utopians' problem was to find a rational military justification for this "overkill" capability now expressed in terms of "thousands of Minutemen." Such a justification, once the Soviet deterrent became invulnerable, would be an absolute necessity. The only conceivable solution was to change the targeting philosophy so that Utopian strategists could target four to eight Minuteman missiles to "dig out" each hardened Soviet missile, guarantee a 90 to 95 per cent kill ratio on a second strike, and follow up this massive strategic strike with postattack reconnaissance bombers designed to ferret out any surviving Soviet retaliatory weapons system.

Unfortunately for the Utopians, the only pretext for such a huge force could not be a retaliatory response to a Soviet first strike because our ICBM's would be hitting empty Soviet missile pits. The obvious answer was to find some political issue (such as Berlin or Cuba) and use any Communist aggression as the pretext to get in the first strike. Theoretically, this could be justified as a non-aggressive strike, since we would be responding to Communist aggression and carrying out our moral commitments. What Utopians overlook — in a typical American reaction to a war situation — is that we would be consciously committing aggression because we purposely utilized more force than was absolutely necessary. Once we had utilized a Russian conventional probe as a nuclear *casus belli,* it would be all too apparent to the world what we had perpetrated: a massacre of the innocents under the guise of hitting only Communist "military targets." But our politically exposed position, Berlin, would be protected by strategic use of our superior thermonuclear force.

As late as the second week of October 1962 it seemed that Berlin would be the logical place to carry out this "exercise of the initiative," for had not McNamara, Robert Kennedy, Rostow, and other Administration officials promised to use all weapons necessary in order to defend Berlin? Paradoxically, it was the victory of conventional forces at Cuba two weeks later that took pressure off Berlin and prevented a recurrence of another Berlin crisis with its high potential for triggering World War III. For President Kennedy at least, the issue that had been plaguing his Administration since its inauguration, the question of which to rely on in a real "crunch" — the strategic use of thermonuclear force or the strategic use of conventional force — finally had been resolved. Our Liberal Traditionalist President, after carefully studying the alternative strategies, had opted for balanced deterrence and balanced forces, which required four major policy decisions: carry out the logic of invulnerable deterrents, simultaneously build up conventional forces, resist pressure from the extreme right for pre-emptive war and from the extreme left for "total and complete disarmament," and, above all, be patient.

Within the National Security Council's Executive Committee during the Cuban crisis, the same strategic struggle that had raged during the days of the Democratic Advisory Council flared up again as men now in high position fought for strategic concepts rooted many years before. Liberal Traditionalists battled Liberal and Conservative Utopians over the best means for removing the Soviet threat to the Americas. Stewart Alsop and Charles Bartlett, in their infamous *Saturday Evening Post* article, called the Traditionalists "doves" and the Utopians "hawks." Adlai Stevenson, as well as Chester Bowles, was one of the first and severest critics of Dulles's massive retaliation speech, and

Stevenson has consistently backed modernized conventional forces as an alternative to nuclear weapons.

Like the Oppenheimer "exercise" of 1953–1954, the drive to "get" Stevenson over the issue of missile bases in Turkey and Italy was launched for two purposes: to remove an eloquent and formidable Traditionalist opponent of Utopian strategic concepts and to forestall the Mediterranean Polaris replacement for the forty-five first strike Jupiters in Italy and Turkey and thus preserve European-based B–47's. Stevenson's real "sin," like that of all Traditionalists since 1945, was to oppose a preventive, or preemptive, first strike against Communist forces in Cuba, which possibly might lead to a "winning" nuclear blow against the Russian heartland as well. When Rusk, McNamara, Robert Kennedy, and Sorensen backed Stevenson's "dove" position, they too became marked men in the bitter campaign launched by the Conservative and Military wings of the American Utopian establishment. Their aim was to discredit President Kennedy's Traditionalist supporters preparatory to taking on the President himself in 1964.

Just as the Stassen-led Utopians were frustrated in their attempt to capitalize on the Korean War in the 1950 congressional elections due to the brilliant Marine landings at Inchon, so too the Goldwater-led Utopians were stymied in their attempt to use the Cuban issue in the congressional elections of 1962 by the President's imaginative use of the naval quarantine. But Utopians tried to lay the groundwork for a winning issue by exploiting the American desire for a clearcut and final victory over world Communism in the shadow of the Cuban "political" compromise and the undeclared, bitter "illegal" war in Vietnam. Partisan exploitation had been eminently successful in 1952; why not in 1964 especially since there were highly available Utopians waiting in the wings: General Norstad, General Goldwater, or the Liberal Utopian, Nelson "Fallout Shelter" Rockefeller. Taking a leaf from the Democratic campaign of 1960, these Utopians could exploit the frustrations of the 'sixties, when for the first time in the nation's history, her armed services could not prevent destruction of her urban and industrial heartland, and there was even a new gap waiting for discovery: the "aero-space" gap.

Furthermore, public confidence in the nation's armed services could be undermined by staging, or forcing, a revolt of the bomber generals, a relatively easy "pony show" to produce. The struggle between Utopians and Traditionalists could be triggered simply by rigging questions when they testified before the House and Senate committees during the "military posture" presentations. The RS–70 and Skybolt issues were ready-made; top them with a spectacular Billy Mitchell–like resignation based on "special" intelligence reports and on "national survival," question the Joint Chiefs of Staff system, uncover "traitors" wanting still more Munichs or grander Yalta's, and the campaign of 1964 would be jet-propelled. This political-military fight promises to be the most bitter since the B–36 versus U.S.S. *United States* struggle of the late 1940's and the politically irresponsible attacks on the "limited war" in Korea throughout that conflict. Unfortunately for the Traditionalist politician who is confronted by a Utopian demagogue, the Age of Deterrence may produce more Koreas, Vietnams, and Cubas with their limited engagements, tacit agreements, and untidy compromises.

The only thing Traditionalists can hope for is a triumph of the sober second thought of the American people, their maturity, and their capacity to be educated to the somber truths of the Age of Deterrence. Unhappily, a cold and impartial glance at American history, especially at her wars, reveals a definite Utopian predilection for an "outraged innocence" approach to war and peace. But the Age of Deterrence permits no great crusade to make the world safe for democracy or a war aim of unconditional surrender, objectives that Liberal Traditionalist presidents, due to the totality of twentieth century war, were forced to pursue in order to gain their people's support, blood, and treasure. How ironic that our two Liberal Traditionalist Presidents, Wilson and FDR, were turned into Liberal Utopians by the vicissitudes of total war and that Harry Truman, a

Liberal Utopian before the Korean War, ended his term a Liberal Traditionalist, consistently resisting either a "peace deal" freeing the Red Chinese armies for other Asiatic adventures or a strategy expanding the war to China in the hopes of finding the chimeral total victory on the Asiatic mainland so long demanded by Conservative Utopians.

During the Cuban crisis President Kennedy faced a similar decision: whether to risk expanding a Cold War political conflict into a Russo-American military engagement by the direct confrontation of American and Soviet military power or to attempt to solve the crisis less spectacularly by using an old-fashioned, non-violent quarantine. The difference was between a relatively short military campaign costing thousands of lives and a long drawn out series of negotiations that might be highly damaging in the domestic political arena for years to come.

The Cuban time-bomb was deftly de-fused by the political use of conventional military forces operating under the deterrent umbrella of our thermonuclear forces. The rapid and successful resolution of the 1962 Cuban crisis is directly attributable to having the proper amount of usable force in the form of a battle-ready fleet backed up by balanced military forces. With this traditional diplomatic instrument President Kennedy was able to apply "the precise amount of pressure at the precise place and the precise time to serve our national purposes." What the President did with this gray steel diplomatic tool "was to adopt limited objectives which could be achieved by limited means."

When the Second Fleet and Task Force 136 tightened their vise around Castroland, the stage was set for a historical re-run of a long forgotten film. Scholars, historians, and international law experts hurriedly dusted off their textbooks to find precedents for a naval quarantine. Naval officers in dress whites, approaching the Lebanon-chartered freighter "Marucla" at "first light" in whale boats, called to mind a scene from another century. The clock of history seemed to have been turned back a hundred years to a simpler and more understandable time. Warning shots across the bow and boarding parties conjured up the image of

Thomas Jefferson or Teddy Roosevelt. Just how incongruous *was* the old-fashioned, conventional gray steel task force in the era of 100-megaton bombs and continent-spanning ICBM's?

Ironically, the Age of Deterrence spawns just such anachronisms; there has not been a crisis since 1945 that has not been resolved by old-fashioned, conventional, usable force consisting of naval warships, infantry, and relatively obsolete aircraft.

On the other hand, the prime function of wonder weapons during the past seventeen years has been a crucial if limited one: preventing local use of force from escalating into total war. There is every evidence to suggest that the United States naval quarantine of Cuba, far from being an atavistic throwback, represents the most likely form of military power utilization in the next two decades. Apparently this is precisely the major lesson President Kennedy drew from the events of October 1962. There had been a decided proclivity to make this major strategic shift early in the days of his Administration, but counterforce was kept alive as a possible alternative by the simple expedient of allowing both doctrines — balanced forces and counterforce — to co-exist within the White House staff, State Department, and Pentagon. Cuba apparently resolved this strategic indecision, at least in the President's mind. The weapons system choice, foreign policy moves, speeches of Administration spokesmen, as well as the anguished cries of the Utopians, created the unmistakable impression that American grand strategy has gone Traditional.

On November 12, 1962, Walt W. Rostow, counselor and chairman of the State Department's Policy Planning Council, hinted at the strategic switch under way. Rostow explained the "radical strengthening of the whole American military posture" by a military budget increase of fourteen billion dollars. "Taken altogether," he explained, "these moves gradually made clear that we are prepared to deal with any form of aggression that the Communists might mount — from nuclear to guerrilla war — and that we are prepared, in particular, to maintain a capacity to inflict decisive retaliatory damage upon the Soviet Union with nuclear arms."

Under Secretary of State George Ball, in his November 16 address to the NATO parliamentarians, was more specific in his defense of conventional forces as he, too, drew some lessons from Cuba. Significantly, Ball rejected the old Utopian concept of "controlled response" (which had become identified with counterforce and controlled thermonuclear war) and spoke instead of "the wisdom — indeed the necessity of the measured response." Secretary Ball related that President Kennedy could have eliminated the Cuban missile menace

by force — through a sudden air strike or an invasion. . . .

But President Kennedy chose not to take such action. . . . He chose instead a more limited response — a quarantine, interdicting the build up of offensive weapons in Cuba. Through that choice, we could avoid resort to an immediate use of force that might have led the United States and the Soviet Union, and with them their allies — up an ascending scale of violence. That choice also enabled the President to gain time — time to consult with our allies about the future steps we should take, time also to seek a political solution. Lastly, it enabled him to keep — and he still keeps — an option for further pressure if the situation should require it.

In short, the President applied a doctrine of measured choice and thereby minimized the risk of nuclear incineration. By establishing the quarantine he developed an effective weapon — a weapon with economic as well as military implications — that may usefully be included in the growing arsenal that provides for the free world the widest spectrum of response to military and political threats. . . .

Ball understood, without giving the new doctrine a name, that the United States had moved beyond massive retaliation. "The fact that my own country, within a very short period, has moved from reliance on massive retaliation to a search for the widest range of possible retaliatory measures is no accident of political fortune. It is an expression of the pace and the sweep of change that technology forces upon us."

Toward the end of his address Secretary Ball outlined the rationale behind the American suggestion that NATO increase her conventional forces. Ball, like Dean Acheson in a speech at West Point in December 1962 and in *Foreign Affairs,* January 1963, observed that NATO

in population and gross national product, . . . [is] more than a match for the Soviet Union and its east European satellites. NATO forces already dominate the sea. Our air strength is at least equal to that of the Soviet bloc. We do need more strength on the ground, not only in terms of man-power but in qualitative terms. . . .

There is no reason why the NATO countries cannot maintain in the NATO area conventional forces that are at least equal to those in eastern Europe. . . . If we do — always preserving intact the ultimate nuclear deterrent — we increase our ability to achieve the purposes of the alliance at the smallest risk of nuclear annihilation.

It was obvious from Secretary Ball's defense of the part conventional forces played in the Cuban crisis and of his pleas for an increase in NATO's conventional forces that the non-nuclear element of the Western defense posture was once again in favor in high places. The new look of 1953–1954 had been completely reversed. Conventional weapons had become the principal instrument of American diplomacy, but operating under the always ready nuclear deterrent shield.

McNamara had enunciated the semantical and theoretical switch in the NATO concept of the "sword and the shield" at the NATO Ministerial Meeting in Paris in December. Before that time the sword had been the vast nuclear power of the United States and the shield, conventional divisions in Europe. Thereafter, strategic nuclear power became the "shield" against all-out war. "At the same time, as proved to be the case in Cuba, it was the conventional forces — the local superiority in men, ships and planes — that did the 'sword' work of carrying out operations short of major hostilities."

Other spokesmen at the NATO meeting implied that the United States was willing to consider the ways and means for setting up a seaborne NATO multilateral force providing the Europeans wanted it and were willing to pay for it. Such a force, these spokesmen said, would fulfill an acknowledged political rather than military need. This promise to look with favor upon a NATO multilateral force would have great significance within a week because of the Skybolt cancellation. This air-to-surface strategic missile was under development by Douglas Aircraft Corporation for the Air Force's SAC and the RAF's Bomber Command. Theoretically, this air-launched ballistic missile (ALBM) would extend the life of the B–52 and Vulcan bombers into the early 1970's, when their strategic mission could be turned over to the RS–70 or bomber satellites. The cancellation of the program, according to Mr. McNamara and President Kennedy, would save two and a half billion dollars. The Administration claimed that all five tests were failures, which prompted Douglas Aircraft Corporation to publish full-page advertisements claiming "only successes for the missile." When asked about this claim on the highly successful televised two-year review of his Administration, President Kennedy revealed a bit of strategic philosophy that undoubtedly has had a tremendous effect on both his and Secretary McNamara's thinking about United States grand strategy. He asked the rhetorical question that Traditional strategists have been posing since 1949: "How much strategic nuclear power is enough?" or, in President Kennedy's own words:

There is just a limit to how much we need, as well as how much we can afford to have a successful deterrent. . . .

I would say when we start to talk about the megatonnage we could bring into a nuclear war, we are talking about annihilation. *How many times do you have to hit a target with nuclear weapons?* That is why when we are talking about spending this $2.5 billion, we don't think that we are going to get $2.5 billion worth of national security, now I know there are others who disagree, but that is our feeling [*sic*]. (Italics mine.)

Prime Minister Macmillan, fresh from a two-day meeting with General De Gaulle at Rambouillet, flew to the Bahamas to meet with President Kennedy to resolve the Skybolt crisis that was poisoning Anglo-American relations. Out of this three-day meeting at Nassau emerged a "whole new concept for Western defense." Three major facts that the United States had long sought to have recognized were accepted by Her Majesty's Government: the indivisibility of the strategic nuclear deterrent forces; the need for more emphasis on multilateral nuclear deterrents; and the need for conventional backup to strategic nuclear weapons themselves, for they are not universal military deterrents against all forms of aggression.

The actual mechanics of the Nassau Pact were deceptively simple: The United States agreed to sell Britain the Polaris missile in place of Skybolt; the British would equip the Polaris with their own nuclear warheads and build their own nuclear submarines to carry the missile. In return for the Polaris, Britain agreed that this weapons system would become a part of a NATO nuclear force and would have its targets designated by NATO. The so-called "escape clause" stipulated, however, that except where Her Majesty's Government "may decide that supreme national interests are at stake, these British forces will be used for the purposes of international defense of the Western Alliance in all circumstances." This important clause was actually the implementation clause setting up the first phase of the NATO nuclear force — the multinational contribution. The forces in the multinational unit "could include allocations from United States strategic forces, from United Kingdom Bomber Command, and from tactical nuclear forces now held in Europe." In the final paragraph of the Nassau communiqué, President Kennedy and Prime Minister Macmillan institutionalized the changed sword and shield concept first officially announced by Secretary McNamara at Paris a week before. The two Western leaders agreed "that in addition to having a nuclear shield it is important to have a non-nuclear sword. For this purpose they agreed on the importance of increasing the effectiveness of their conventional forces on a world-wide basis."

President Kennedy returned to Palm Beach for the Christmas holidays and Macmillan to a hornet's nest of controversy, immeasurably complicated by the "successful" Skybolt test announced by the Air Force the day after the Nassau Pact was

revealed to the world. The original Air Force release claimed
that the missile "impacted in the target area" after a perfect
launch from a B–52 bomber. On December 27 the Pentagon
corrected this false impression of success by noting that the Skybolt did not carry a nose cone and that the actual trajectory
would have dropped its missile eighty-seven miles off target.
Pentagon officials also corrected the Air Force assertion that "it
was the first time a ballistic missile was launched successfully
from an aircraft and flew its full mission under its own power
to a point 800 miles down the Atlantic Range." Pentagon
sources contended to the contrary that the Bold Orion missile
was fired 950 miles from a plane in 1958 but was still cancelled.

The Utopians took such a gamble, angering both the President,
who was reportedly "furious," and laying themselves open to
charges of meddling in foreign affairs, because their entire
strategy and future rode on the Skybolt and manned bombers.
Utopian theorists had known for years that "true deterrent"
weapons systems like the Fleet Ballistic Missile Submarine, if
ever purchased in sufficient numbers, would doom the massive
retaliation-counterforce strategy — weapons systems, base and
support facilities, and immense budgetary share, the entire kit
and caboodle — all remnants of the age of the air offensive,
when total war could be won without "unacceptable damage" to
a nation. Once mutual invulnerability of deterrent systems became the controlling philosophy of an American Administration,
it would be next to impossible to justify any strategic weapons
systems that were not strike-second.

In carrying out the logic of this philosophy, over a two-
month period the Administration announced many modifications
in the domain of strategic weapons. The Skybolt was cancelled,
which inevitably doomed the B–52 H because, according to
Joseph Alsop, the Soviets were building and emplacing "hundreds upon hundreds of SAM II's and SAM III's" (Soviet sur-
face-to-air missiles for defense against both high and low level
penetration). But more immediately, Turkey and Italy revealed
that they were willing and eager to have their forty-five "first

generation" liquid-fueled Jupiters replaced by three Mediterranean-based Polaris-firing submarines. In August the British had already announced that the sixty Thor IRBM phase-out would be accelerated. Early in 1963 the Pentagon reprogrammed MIDAS (early warning satellite) for financial, technical, and strategic reasons. When MIDAS was first proposed, most Americans believed that a missile gap existed and that we needed better warning than the one-half hour BMEWS (ballistic missile early warning system) would give; MIDAS promised to cut the warning time to fifteen minutes. But with the advent of a deterrent force that could ride out a first strike and retaliate, inflicting "unacceptable losses" to an aggressor, MIDAS became superfluous. The Navy's A3J's (Mach 2 medium bombers) were converted to reconnaissance aircraft and phased out of the strategic forces. Nearly one thousand obsolete B–47's were scheduled for retirement at a greatly stepped-up rate. By mid-February 1963 some B–47's had already left their British bases, and SAC was rapidly dissolving its B–47 squadrons.

Thus it could be predicted that by the end of 1963 most land-based American strategic delivery systems will be removed from their foreign bases. Bomber and missile bases in Spain, Morocco, Britain, Italy, and Turkey have become victims of technical and strategic obsolescence. The deterrent is now carried by the sea-based Polaris, hardened continental-based ICBM's, and B–52's, based for the most part in the United States.

Symbolically, On December 31, 1962, the Defense Department "handed down a formal death sentence . . . on the Air Force's bomber-launched Skybolt missile." The year 1962 would see the last of the heavy bomber's strategic predominance, which had lasted almost exactly two decades. Hence the Polaris-for-Jupiters exchange is an example of "weapons modernization" for the Age of Deterrence, and this switch related only indirectly to the Kennedy-Khrushchev exchange of letters during and after Cuba. Even without Cuba such a phase-out of first generation obsolete weapons systems would have taken place. In fact, it was the Berlin crisis of 1961 and the Cuban crisis of 1962 that extended the operational life of the B-47. American and European Utopians refused to be satisfied with this explanation of "weapons modernization." They, especially the Conservative Utopians, preferred to see "another Yalta," "atomic disengagement," or a "secret Cuban deal" in the retirement of Thors, Jupiters, and B-47's. What Utopians were really disturbed about was the Kennedy Administration's change in strategy, but they attacked it on other grounds.

Traditionalist Mark S. Watson, venerable military critic on the staff of the *Baltimore Sun,* attempted to put this strategic switch in proper perspective when he said: "Routine operating procedure in all services is to replace old with new as rapidly as the new becomes available. Thus in the Air Force the B-17 bomber, a 1941 marvel, was replaced by the far more potent B-29 as soon as possible. This was replaced later by the B-36, and this in turn by today's B-52."

The fact is, Watson concluded, "The United States has a far superior nuclear weapon for the defense of Italy — the sea-based Polaris, newer, better, less vulnerable, and fully capable of reaching the same targets as the shorter-range Jupiter."

Finally, on January 30, 1963, two years and ten days after President Kennedy's inauguration, Secretary of Defense McNamara, accompanied by General Taylor, marched up to Capitol Hill with a fat 161-page justification of the *Defense Budget for 1964 and Review of the Defense Policies, 1964–68.* The word had become both flesh and policy. Two years of zigzag, crises, thaws, threats, and counterthreats had tended to mask the real nature of the Kennedy switch. Secretary McNamara insisted on reading practically his entire statement to the House Armed Services Committee, and for four days he singlehandedly defended his budget and strategy before the Senate Armed Forces Committee. Then the annual parade of generals and admirals, colonels and captains sallied forth from their concrete redoubt in Virginia to confront their "friendly questioners" on the Hill. During these "military posture" hearings the senators, representatives, and press tried to determine the services' real feelings on their appropriations or develop a controversy between the military and the Department of Defense or with the executive branch.

Unhappiest with the McNamara statement were the Military Utopians and their congressional and press friends. The Defense Secretary officially rejected a first strike war-winning counterforce, which he had apparently flirted with at Ann Arbor in June 1962 and adopted instead a second strike capable of retaliating "in a controlled and deliberate way." This "second strike force" would be finite — 1850 missiles and 1000 bombers (for a few years at least) — and it could blast the entire target system in Russia simultaneously, strike back first at missile and bomber bases and other military targets, and "if necessary, strike back at the Soviet urban and industrial complex in a controlled and deliberate way."

McNamara rejected the counterforce argument that because the Soviets also were building an invulnerable deterrent the United States should create a strategic force large enough to destroy Soviet missile power. "We have not found it feasible at this time," the Defense Secretary testified in one of the most important single sentences of government policy of this century, "to provide a capability for insuring the destruction of any very large portion of the fully hard ICBM sites, if the Soviets build them in quantities, or of missile launching submarines." Elaborating further, McNamara said, "It would become increasingly difficult, regardless of the form of attack, to destroy a sufficiently large proportion of the Soviet's strategic nuclear forces to preclude major damage to the United States regardless of how large or what kind of strategic forces we build."

Then answering his Utopian counterforce critics, the Secretary of Defense explained why additional "overkill" was no solution to the defense dilemmas of the sixties and seventies:

Even if we were to double and triple our forces we would not be able to destroy quickly all or almost all of the hardened ICBM sites. And even if we could do that, we know no way to destroy the enemy's missile launching submarines at the same time. We do not anticipate that either the United States or Soviet Union will acquire that capability in the foreseeable future. Moreover, to minimize damage to the United States, such a force would also have to be accompanied by an extensive missile defense and a much more elaborate civil defense program than has thus far been contemplated. Even then we could not preclude casualties counted in the tens of millions.

McNamara further angered the Utopians by denouncing the Skybolt project and rejecting an increase in the present $1,350,-000,000 program for the three test RS–70's. Utopian hopes for space bombers likewise were shot down by Secretary McNamara, who conceded that the Soviets "may now have or soon achieve" the capability of placing H-bomb-laden satellites into orbit. But, he said, there did not appear to be any logical reasons for the Soviets to do this because there are much more efficient ways of delivering nuclear explosives on targets.

Utopian "airpower-is-indivisible" partisans were angered also by the Army's experimental "air assault" division, which would have 460 helicopters and fixed-wing aircraft, backed up by an air cavalry brigade with a mission "much like the horse cavalry of earlier years." This concept was clearly a triumph for General Gavin, who seven years earlier had written his famous article, "Cavalry and I Don't Mean Horses," based on his belief in the need for greater battlefield mobility for the United States Army. McNamara also confirmed for the first time that there were nearly twelve thousand American military in South Vietnam, training and advising Ngo Dinh Diem's troops in the guerrilla warfare against the Communist Viet Cong. In his references to western Europe and NATO, McNamara hit the American and European Utopians in their most sensitive spot: no initial reliance on land-based tactical nuclear weapons. Restating the American government's position since 1945, McNamara declared: "Certainly, a massive attack on Western Europe would have to be met with whatever weapons are required to counter it. That has always been the policy of the Western Alliance. And, I have repeatedly stated before this Committee that 'even in limited war situations we should not preclude the use of tactical nuclear weapons.' "

With this bow to prudence the Secretary forcefully restated the rationale for increased non-nuclear forces:

However, we may well be faced with situations in Europe where it would not be to the advantage of ourselves or our Allies to use even tactical nuclear weapons initially — provided we had the capability to deal with them through non-nuclear means. Nuclear weapons, even in the lower kiloton ranges, are extremely destructive devices and hardly the preferred weapons to defend such heavily populated areas as Europe. Furthermore, while it does not necessarily follow that the use of tactical nuclear weapons must inevitably escalate into global nuclear war, it does present a very definite threshold, beyond which we enter a vast unknown.

Secretary McNamara was criticized for encroaching on the traditional province of the Secretary of State.[2] This criticism is due possibly to the Age of Deterrence, when the most important foreign policy issues are political-military in nature and call for extremely close co-operation between the State and Defense Departments. There was not the slightest shred of evidence to suggest there is any philosophical difference between General Taylor, Secretary McNamara, Secretary Rusk, or President Kennedy, for all are Traditionalists. Certainly Traditionalists could agree with Secretary Rusk's February 13 speech at Los Angeles, where he proclaimed that "our great goal is a peaceful world community of free and independent states, free to choose their own future and their own system so long as it does not threaten the freedom of others. This goal and the Communist goal are incompatible. We shall persevere in this worldwide struggle until freedom prevails. We move into the future not only with resolution but with measured confidence."

Views like this and those that Secretary McNamara expressed in his "competent and confident" exposition of American defense policies, which McGeorge Bundy ratified at Yale on February 16, signified that practically every single Utopian program and philosophical assumption had been rejected, neglected, or stymied by Traditionalist leaders in Defense, State, and the White House: (1) grand strategy (peaceful competition versus liberation or eradication of world Communism); (2) military strategy (mutual deterrence versus pure counterforce); (3) military doctrine (secure strike-second versus ambiguous first strike force); (4) space (defensive and peaceful uses versus offensive bomber satellites and arms race in space); (5) strategic weapons systems (a limited number of Polaris and Minutemen versus unlimited numbers of Minutemen, RS–70's, and Skybolt); (6) tactical weapons systems (upgrading of conventional or non-nuclear weapons versus greater reliance on tactical nuclear); and (7) Vietnam and Cuba (conventional and unconventional limited war versus atomic escalation and nuclear war).

Under these circumstances and especially with Secretary McNamara's hints that even greater changes were in the wind for 1965–1968, Utopians of all varieties apparently decided to launch a co-ordinated offensive counterattack, the likes of which America has seldom seen, against the Traditional strategy that had captured Washington's citadels of power. Neither the B–36 versus supercarrier struggle of 1949 nor the partisan sniping during the Korean War entailed such an across-the-board attack on an Administration's grand strategy. Military and Conservative Utopians singled out Adlai Stevenson on the Mediterranean missile base and restraint in Cuba issues; Military and Liberal Utopians took on Secretary McNamara over Skybolt, RS–70, and nuclear "adequacy"; and Conservative Utopians assailed Secretary Rusk for condemning the extremists who accused the Administration of following a "no-win policy."

Military and Conservative Utopians (in Europe as well as America) lambasted McNamara and "the State Department" for Nassau and the Polaris offer; Military, Conservative, and Liberal Utopians took the Administration's European policy to task. Conservative Utopians adopted the Military Utopian line on offensive military uses of space and blasted McNamara and General Taylor over increasing American commitments and casualties in Vietnam. In this they were aided by Military

Utopians arguing with Military Traditionalists over a Korean War issue: the correct use of tactical air on the Asiatic mainland. Robert Kennedy also was attacked by the Conservative Utopians (and some Conservative Traditionalists who lost their sense of perspective when partisan politics entered the picture) over the bogus issue of "air support" at the Bay of Pigs.

Liberal Utopians within the President's own party were conspicuous in their failure to rally round his new strategy and foreign policy. No wonder the President had problems and history seemed to be gaining on him, for Mr. Kennedy had made deadly enemies of the Military Utopians, who had never really lost a battle in eighteen years. Until recently they have demonstrated astonishing versatility in backing Democrats and Republicans alike as long as appropriations kept flowing into the manned bomber and a related deterrent strategy. The "instant retaliation" of Finletter's *Survival in the Air Age* was blood brother to the massive retaliation of John Foster Dulles and kissing cousin to the counterforce doctrine that reached its highwater mark in the Kennedy Administration with McNamara's pronouncement at Ann Arbor in June 1962. But like the initial Confederate success at Cemetery Ridge, the triumph was illusory and fleeting. For strategic, political, and financial reasons counterforce was killed, but not before its official acceptance had caused a chill in Traditionalist quarters and a thrill in Utopian circles.

In 1963 the stage was set for another epic struggle between the Utopians and Traditionalists. The outcome will probably affect all life on this planet. By late 1963 the Traditionalists, after a decade on the outside, were in the driver's seat. But it was possible, quite possible, that their triumph would be only temporary.

Stating that Traditional strategy has triumphed, if only temporarily, merely means that the Administration has decided to opt for a "strike-second" deterrent force, a buildup of non-nuclear forces, and a willingness to spend fifty to fifty-five billion dollars a year on defense and to fight limited war regardless of the political cost. In other words, the Kennedy Administration has deliberately chosen to stabilize, and keep stabilized, the equilibrium on all three levels of military action by the imaginative construction of spectrum deterrent forces, which are:

Level I	Total War	Polaris and related groups of non-continental mobile-based "true" deterrents
Level II	Limited War	Aircraft carriers for close air support (not dependent on politically sensitive overseas bases); jet air- and sea-lift; expanded conventional ground troops, improved infantry weapons.
Level III	Unconventional or sublimited "wars"	Additional special forces; unique and special equipment aided by conventional forces from the limited war area to help accomplish the traditional diplomatic function of military force.

It is on the third level that the Traditionalist can answer Utopian demands for victory, for here is where the Cold War can be won in the only way possible in the Age of Deterrence. The mutual existence of thermonuclear weapons, although foreclosing total victory, makes it mandatory for the contending nations to develop a total strategy that allows their respective systems the best possible chance to be successful and preserve intact its own revolutionary base, ready to exploit any future weakness in the enemy camp. Any crisis, once the deterrent becomes invulnerable, could end in a twentieth-century Peace of Westphalia. Indeed, it is possible future historians will regard the Korean War as the last great armed conflict between the Communist and non-Communist worlds. Korea was followed by a series of compromise agreements of which Cuba was merely one fragment of a global settlement that might take a decade or two to unfold. The description "Cold War" covered this "neither war nor peace" situation, which can find an analogy only in the religious wars of history. In the coming period of stability, which cannot last indefinitely, economic, political, and ideological concepts of the two blocs will vie for the favor of the third world.

Deterrence can be stabilized only if the *complete* political-military spectrum is relatively "leakproof." Only when this is accomplished will "escalation," death by nibbling, and defeat by default be avoided. There are no quick, easy, or glamorous solutions. The West has been literally paralyzed since Hiroshima, which seemed to open a new era in which our nuclear technology would be sufficient to hold back the brute forces of Eurasia. What is needed now is a radical shift in priorities away from the age of the air offensive and "national defense," when total wars were worth winning and winnable, to the Age of Deterrence, in which "victory" on either the thermonuclear or limited war levels is highly dubious against an atomic-equipped foe that can reach the opponent's homeland. On the third level, Khrushchev's political-military "wars of liberation" must be fought and won, not only by the proper application of military force, which will be more than likely necessary, but by traditional methods of economic, political, and cultural diplomacy.

In sum, the challenge is total, and it can be met only by a strategy that is broad enough to handle all contingencies. Tri-level military stabilization is, in a sense, a unified field strategic theory. It is a Traditional theory because it prefers to use the traditional and diplomatic tools of the fifteenth through nineteenth centuries. Its theoretical opponent, counterforce, is also a unified field strategic theory. It is Utopian because it stresses nuclear weapons primarily, hoping first for total deterrence of all war, but failing that, it looks to escalating all limited wars with nuclear weapons under the protection of a total war winning counterforce.

The struggle with the Utopians is a continuing one, and the long term victor is in doubt basically because the Traditionalists can promise no tidy or quick solutions to really tough problems. Utopians can always promise total victory without defining what the real costs are in terms of cash, casualties, and conscience.

Utopians could be victorious in the short run, which probably would doom Traditionalist concepts, since the Utopians inevitably would adopt a host of destabilizing policies: "liberation," "offensive space race," massive "civilian" defense projects, merger of the military services, and possibly even pre-emptive war.

Traditionalist concepts could be easily discredited by an expanded war in Vietnam, already labeled an "illegal war" by some Conservative Utopians, should it involve increased American casualties. Even now the political obsession with American losses there bears an ominous similarity to the partisan use of Korean War casualty figures that led to widespread public dissatisfaction with "Mr. Truman's war." A 1964 repeat of 1952 is entirely conceivable with another "Republican" general leading the loyal opposition. The American people could become disillusioned with Europe and demand a withdrawal to Fortress America in a spasm of neo-isolationism before Europe is able to protect herself adequately. The worst excesses of nineteenth and twentieth century economic nationalism could return. The presidency could be captured by either Liberal or Conservative Utopians, resulting possibly in unilateral disarmament or a preemptive, controlled thermonuclear war. Increased Pentagon centralization and single service merger *could* set the stage for a *1984,* a *Seven Days in May,* or worse. A single monolithic intelligence network could create a space gap hoax, justify preemptive war, and institute those totalitarian controls over private property, American industry, and the American press needed to "win" a thermonuclear war with "acceptable" losses of merely thirty million Americans!

To prevent these frightening possibilities, it is the task of all Traditionalists — Conservative, Liberal, and Military — to insure that balanced forces, professionalism, and "Americanism" triumph. This can be done by synthesizing the truly conservative ideals of our constitutional checks and balances with the liberal ideals of the Declaration of Independence and the patriotic ideals of our noble military traditions. This new synthesis that knows no traditional political boundaries can help insure that the earth's oldest practicing democracy remains the "world's best hope."

Epilogue

UNFORTUNATELY FOR THE FUTURE OF MANKIND, PRESIDENT Kennedy's Traditionalist strategic policies have barely taken root in the fertile political-military humus created by a quarter century of strategic debate. The Kennedy shift is still a fragile plant that needs the tender loving care of all traditional-minded men if ever it is to bear fruit. By his creation of a truly balanced defense establishment, President Kennedy modified the direction of Western strategy toward the Age of Deterrence and away from the sterile Utopian policies of total victory through nuclear technology and total war.

As the Traditionalists around our former President retire to private life, their places may well be filled by Military Liberal Utopians. When he was a senator, President Johnson, like Senator John Kennedy, supported the Democratic party's position on the bomber and missile gaps and generally was favorable to Utopian weapons systems and strategic concepts. After Sputnik and the Democratic victory in 1960, many of President Johnson's supporters moved across the Potomac to positions of power in the Pentagon. These Liberal Utopians are sympathetic toward a single service and single Chief of Staff, the "military-industrial complex," offensive uses of space, and extensive blast shelters and recuperation networks. In alliance with Conservative Utopians on military weapons and hardware, they are also sympathetic to Conservative Utopian demands for a reduction of conventional ground forces in Europe and a liquidation of our "illegal" commitment to save Vietnam from the Vietcong. They prefer either a neutral solution or expanding the war by atom bombing Hanoi and nuclear interdiction of South China's transportation complex in a repeat of the "No Substitute for Victory" madness of 1952–1953.

President Harry Truman, a Liberal Utopian until the Korean War, bravely fought Utopians within the Democratic and Republican parties who stridently demanded expanding the war to China and Russia. Preventive and pre-emptive warriors were silenced in August 1950 by the firing of Defense Secretary Louis Johnson and again after the dark December days following the defeat of the Eighth Army at the Yalu by Chinese Communist "volunteers."

Thanks to the solid support of Traditionalists, like Secretary of Defense George C. Marshall and Secretary of State Dean Acheson, President Truman was able to wage a successful limited war in Korea against world Communism. However, the Korean War was politically disastrous and in 1952 contributed to President Eisenhower's victory.

President Lyndon Johnson has loyally supported our late Traditionalist President's policies as they developed since Inauguration Day 1961. Johnson's first official address and subsequent actions were very encouraging. The President pledged in his November 27 address to a Joint Session of Congress that "this nation will keep its commitments from South Vietnam to West Berlin"; and he significantly added, "In this age when there can be no losers in peace and no victors in war we must recognize the obligation to match national strength with national restraint. We must be prepared at one and the same time for both the confrontation of power and the limitation of power." By President Johnson's dedication to continuing the struggle to save Southeast Asia, the search for a detente with the U.S.S.R., and the renewal of our commitments to the people of West Berlin and Western Europe, the President is pursuing established Traditional policies.

But Utopian campaign for a reversal of these Traditionalist policies will not be long in coming. In the months before President Kennedy's death, representatives of the Utopian Right and Left and their political-military supporters had begun to exploit apparent weaknesses in the American people: impatience with complicated and hard-to-resolve global problems and a desire to rest on their oars, to be relieved from never-ending foreign aid appropriations and the perpetual manning of freedom's frontiers with their drafted sons. Utopians will continue to exploit this American disenchantment and impatience with the way the world is. Public outcries for letting Europe defend itself before Europe is capable of it and pulling out of Southeast Asia in face of Chinese Communist imperialism may allow China and Russia to do economically and politically what they never could do militarily: absorb those two vital areas into their spheres of influence. A new drive to force the withdrawal from our "outposts," similar to the campaigns to "Bring the Boys Home" in 1945 and "No More Koreas" in 1953, may once again sweep our land, stirring up support for neo-isolationism, economic nationalism, and nineteenth-centuryism.

Predictably, this neo-isolationism will be disguised by a technocratic and highly glamorous New Military Policy, which will rely largely on American thermonuclear weapons (continental- and space-based) to cover all contingencies and will eventually demand the blast shelters and recuperation and patch-up centers to complete the strategic armory. Neo-isolationists and nuclear determinists of all political hues will join forces in the months ahead to try once again to undercut balanced forces and the strategy of spectrum deterrence. Americans will be asked to choose continental-based conventional and strategic nuclear power instead of forward-based sea, land, and airpower. The arguments for a return to the new look and massive retaliation will be ingenious, compelling, and familiar: economic (it will save many billions), military (it is more efficient), political (let Eurasians fight Eurasians), and psychological (nothing deters like massed megatons).

The alternative doctrine of balanced forces is not merely an empty phrase, for it involves flesh-and-blood force levels and mechanical weapons systems. The Kennedy mobilization of 1961–1963 selectively rearmed the United States according to the traditional doctrine of balanced forces. Strategists and commentators who complain of a lack of a "grand national strategy" are blind to this latest rearmament because they do not believe and never have believed in balanced forces, preferring instead to weave an American military doctrine around the use of nuclear weapons in all contingencies. They would quickly launch a first strategic strike if it were necessary to honor our commitments. They would initiate the tactical use of nuclear weapons as a money-saving substitute for increased conventional forces. They would employ the doctrine of nuclear escalation with relative impunity because of our massive strategic superiority. In other words, these nuclear-directed strategists and tacticians would have the United States adopt a grand strategy that necessitates the use of nuclear weapons from the very first incident in any contingency. They are attempting to create a situation of total deterrence, and they reason that even if total deterrence fails, the tremendous nuclear buildup it implies would lead us inevitably to total victory in a thermonuclear exchange.

Opposed to this philosophy was President Kennedy as are Secretary Rusk, Secretary McNamara, and the Joint Chiefs of Staff, who have repeatedly called for a complete range of usable military force to handle all contingencies including total, limited, and unconventional war.

Utopian critics of balanced forces have attempted to label this strategy "unilateral disarmament" and have slandered its supporters. In reality, balanced forces are the end product of the *selective* rearmament of 1961–1963 necessitated by the Kennedy shift. This rearmament compensated for conventional deficiencies produced by the Communist modification of tactics after their failure to "unify" Korea and the revolutionary changes in American defenses necessitated by the Soviet acquisition of the ICBM. Paradoxically, balanced forces, although definitely not a disarmament strategy, is compatible with an arms control policy. For balanced forces aims at controlling the application of military force throughout the entire spectrum of possible challenge from "show the flag" to total thermonuclear war.

The Scylla and Charybdis that Traditionalists must help President Johnson avoid in the months ahead are blind disarmament, which can lead to a repeat of the appeasement-minded decisions of the thirties, and neo-isolationism, which can lead to great political frustrations and consequent demands for pre-emptive war. This desperate move would be counseled by Utopian-minded advisers should the Communists switch tactics in response to a Utopian re-emphasis of unusable strategic thermonuclear forces and once again resume their glacierlike movement out of the Eurasian heartland.

President Kennedy warned against such a historical reversal in his Salt Lake speech of September 1963 when he said: "We cannot adopt a policy which says that if something does not happen or others do not do exactly as we wish, we will return to Fortress America. That is a policy . . . of retreat and not of strength." And it would have consequences, the President predicted, which "would be fatal to our security [for] we would be inviting a Communist expansion which every Communist power would welcome, and all of the efforts of so many Americans for eighteen years would be gone with the wind."

There is grave danger that President Kennedy's courageous and controversial strategic decisions will be undercut in the years ahead as much by his professed friends as by his deadly enemies. It is up to Traditionalists of all political persuasions to help direct this nation and thereby the world into the Age of Deterrence along the path so nobly blazed by our martyred Traditionalist President.

Notes

CHAPTER ONE: *Traditionalists and Utopians in Defense Policy*

[1] Eugene Rachlis, review of *Burn after Reading: The Espionage History of World War II,* by Ladislas Farago, *New York Times Book Review,* December 31, 1961, p. 14.

CHAPTER TWO: *1953 — The Genesis of the New Look*

[1] John W. Spanier, *American Foreign Policy since World War II* (New York: Praeger, 1960), p. 105.

[2] Roscoe Drummond and Gaston Coblentz, *Duel at the Brink: John Foster Dulles' Command of American Power* (Garden City, N.Y.: Doubleday, 1960), p. 114.

[3] Bonner Fellers, "A New Look at War," *Air University Quarterly Review,* VI (Winter, 1953–1954).

[4] Robert J. Donovan, *Eisenhower: The Inside Story* (New York: Harper, 1956), p. 294.

[5] Grover C. Brown, "Concepts and Nature of Air Warfare," *Naval War College Review,* VI (November, 1953), 35.

[6] Fellers, p. 227.

[7] Address by Admiral Radford at the Fifth Annual USMA Student Conference, West Point, New York, December 2, 1953.

CHAPTER THREE: *1954 — Massive Retaliation Full-Blown*

[1] Address by Thomas E. Murray, "The Road Ahead," Duquesne University, November 11, 1953.

[2] Address by Admiral Carney, "Today's Alternatives," to the National Security Industrial Association, New York City, May 27, 1954. Admiral Carney's speech writer, Captain Frank Manson, USN, convincingly argues that the CNO was not advocating preventive war, but, rather, was calling for a rethinking of the traditional strategic options open to a nation which controls the seas. Actually, these strategic alternatives of bringing conventional pressure to bear on Communist China were not real options, as President Kennedy found out in the Laotian crisis of 1961, and would not be valid until sufficient traditional forces were re-created.

[3] Donovan, p. 308. Donovan maintained that the speech had been submitted for clearance by the State Department but not enough time had been allowed for it to reach top officials.

[4] Robert Saundby, "Morality and War: A British View," *Air University Quarterly Review,* VII (Summer, 1954), 10–11.

[5] Address by Secretary Thomas at the Institute of World Affairs, Riverside, California, December 14, 1954.

6 Editorial, *United States Army Combat Forces Journal,* IV (May 1954), 12.

7 Address by General Ridgway, "The Soldier and the Statesman," to the American Assembly, Harriman, New York, July 30, 1954.

CHAPTER FOUR: *1955 — Coexistence Blooms*

1 *New York Times,* January 28, 1955, p. 1.

2 Address by Admiral Radford, "The Technological Race," to the Petroleum Association, Atlantic City, New Jersey, September 15, 1955.

3 Address by General Taylor at Conference of Service Secretaries, Quantico, Virginia, quoted in *Army Combat Forces Journal,* VI (September, 1955), 25.

CHAPTER FIVE: *1956 — The Great Airpower Debate*

1 Hanson W. Baldwin, "The New Face of War," *Bulletin of the Atomic Scientists,* XII (May, 1956), 157.

CHAPTER SIX: *1957 — The Ballistic Missile Comes of Age*

1 *Congressional Record,* 85th Cong., 1st Sess., 1957, Vol. CIII, Part 6, 7674–7678, quoted in *BAS,* XIII (October, 1957), 309.

2 Donald Barry, "The British Navy in the Nuclear Age," *U.S. Naval Institute Proceedings,* LXXXIII (October, 1957), 1071.

3 Hanson W. Baldwin, *New York Times,* May 15, 1957, and "A Military Policy for the Missile Age," *New York Times Magazine,* November 3, 1957.

4 "How U.S. Taps Soviet Missile Secrets," *Aviation Week,* October 21, 1957.

5 Robert Hotz "Why Mr. President?" *Aviation Week,* October 21, 1957, p. 21.

6 *New York Times,* August 15, 1957, p. 2.

7 Address by General Thomas S. Power, Commander of SAC, to the Air Force Association Seminar, Washington, D.C., quoted in *Aviation Week,* December 23, 1957, p. 26.

CHAPTER SEVEN: *1958 — The Birth of the Missile Gap*

1 George F. Kennan, *Russia, the Atom and the West* (New York: Harper & Bros., 1958), p. 54.

2 Address by Admiral Burke to the Society of Naval Architects and Marine Engineers, New York City, November 14, 1958.

3 James Ferguson, "Operational Future of Manned Aircraft," *Air Force,* XLI (April, 1958), 43.

4 Address by General LeMay to the American Newspaper Publishers Association, New York City, quoted in *Air Force,* XLI (June, 1958), 33.

5 Major Alexander P. De Seversky, "On Strategic Organization," *Air Force,* XLI (June, 1958), 87.

CHAPTER EIGHT: *1959 — The Conflicting Strategies Ripen*

1 Address by Admiral Burke to the Chamber of Commerce, Charleston, South Carolina, February 20, 1959.

CHAPTER NINE: *1960 — The Continuing Strategic Debate*

[1] *New York Times,* February 11, 1960, p. 1; *Washington Daily News,* February 15, 1960, p. 3.

CHAPTER TEN: *1961 — The Kennedy Shift*

[1] Stewart Alsop, "Master of the Pentagon," *Saturday Evening Post,* August 5, 1961, p. 45.
[2] *Washington Post,* August 17, 1961, p. A-2.

CHAPTER ELEVEN: *1962 — The Rise and Fall of Counterforce*

[1] This position was similar to one of President Kennedy's eight basic defense principles enunciated in his budget message to Congress on March 28, 1961: "Our strategic arms and defense must be adequate to deter any deliberate nuclear attack on the United States or our allies by making clear to any potential aggressor that sufficient retaliatory forces will be able to survive a first strike and penetrate his defense in order *to inflict unacceptable losses upon him.*" (Italics mine.) U.S. Congress, House, *United States Defense Policies in 1961,* House Document No. 502, 87th Cong., 2d Sess., 1962, p. 9.

CHAPTER TWELVE: *The Cuban Crisis: Theory in Practice*

[1] McGeorge Bundy's speech at Yale University, February 16, 1963, insisted that "some well-intentioned critics [had] hastily misconstrued" McNamara's Ann Arbor speech "as acceptance of a first-strike counterforce theory." Although he did not reject pure counterforce by name, Bundy stated that "nuclear weapons cannot handle the whole duty of defense. No one really believes they can, but almost everyone is tempted by this bizarre hope from time to time. Your government, in the last two years, has firmly rejected this thought."
[2] See Arthur Krock's column, *New York Times,* March 4, 1963, entitled, "Pentagon as a Voice in Foreign Policy." The *Times* pundit sadly lamented the decreasing power and influence of the State Department and the "larger role in announcements and conduct of foreign policy" by McNamara.

Selected Bibliography

T HE ITEMS LISTED IN THIS BIBLIOGRAPHY ARE NOT MEANT
to be an inclusive list of either all the sources utilized or all the
works written on deterrence. Rather, it is a selected bibliography
with major stress on representative Utopian and Traditionalist
statements. The majority of cited addresses, lectures, and miscellaneous material is in the Department of the Navy files, the
custodians of which were so kind as to allow me to use them.
Most of the other research was done at the Navy Library (Main
Navy) and the Army Library (Pentagon).

The majority of cited material is from primary sources, for
such is the nature of a contemporary intellectual history. The
only secondary sources are: Eric F. Goldman, *The Crucial
Decade — and After: America, 1945–60* (New York: Vintage,
1960); Richard Hofstadter, William Miller, and Daniel Aaron,
The American Republic, Vol. II (Englewood Cliffs, New Jersey:
Prentice-Hall, 1959); and John W. Spanier, *American Foreign
Policy since World War II* (New York: Praeger, 1960). Thus
this bibliography is limited to a representative sampling of source
material: books, public documents, articles, newspapers, peri-
odicals, speeches, lectures, and miscellaneous.

BOOKS

Acheson, Dean G., *Pattern of Responsibility,* Edited by McGeorge
Bundy (Boston: Houghton Mifflin, 1952).
Adams, Sherman, *Firsthand Report: The Story of the Eisenhower
Administration* (New York: Harper, 1961).
Amrine, Michael, *The Great Decision: The Secret History of the
Atomic Bomb* (New York: Putnam, 1959).

Aron, Raymond, *The Century of Total War* (Boston: Beacon Press, 1954).

————, *War and Industrial Society* (London: Oxford University Press, 1958).

————, *On War* (Garden City, N.Y.: Doubleday, 1959).

Blackett, P. M. S., *Atomic Weapons and East-West Relations* (Cambridge: Cambridge Univ. Press, 1956).

Blair, Clay, Jr., *The Atomic Submarine and Admiral Rickover* (New York: Holt, 1954).

Borden, William Liscum, *There Will Be No Time: The Revolution in Strategy* (New York: Macmillan, 1946).

Brodie, Bernard, *Strategy in the Missile Age* (Princeton: Princeton Univ. Press, 1959).

Buchan, Alastair, *NATO in the 1960's: The Implications of Interdependence* (New York: Praeger, 1960).

Burnham, James, *Containment or Liberation: An Inquiry into the Aims of United States Foreign Policy* (New York: Day, 1953).

Caidin, Martin, *A Torch to the Enemy: The Fire Raid on Tokyo* (New York: Ballantine, 1960).

De Seversky, Alexander P., *Victory through Air Power* (New York: Simon and Schuster, 1942).

————, *Air Power: Key to Survival* (New York: Simon and Schuster, 1950).

————, *America: Too Young to Die!* (New York: McGraw-Hill, 1961).

Dinerstein, Herbert, *War and the Soviet Union: Nuclear Weapons and the Revolution in Soviet Military and Political Thinking* (New York: Praeger, 1959).

Donovan, Robert J., *Eisenhower: The Inside Story* (New York: Harper, 1956).

Douhet, Guilio, *The Command of the Air*, translated by Dino Ferrari (New York: Coward-McCann, 1942).

Drummond, Roscoe, and Gaston Coblentz, *Duel at the Brink: John Foster Dulles' Command of American Power* (Garden City, N.Y.: Doubleday, 1960).

Earle, Edward Meade (ed.), *Makers of Modern Strategy* (Princeton: Princeton Univ. Press, 1943).

Eliot, George Fielding, *Victory without War, 1958–1961* (Annapolis: U.S. Naval Institute, 1958).

Farago, Ladislas, *Burn after Reading: The Espionage History of World War II* (New York: Walker, 1961).

Fellers, Bonner, *Wings for Peace: A Primer for a New Defense* (Chicago: Regnery, 1953).

Finletter, Thomas K., *Survival in the Air Age: A Report* (Washington: U.S. Govt. Printing Office, 1948).

———, *Power and Policy: U.S. Foreign Policy in the Hydrogen Age* (New York: Harcourt, Brace, 1954).

———, *Foreign Policy: The Next Phase, the 1960's* (New York: Praeger, 1960).

Foot, Michael R. D., *Men in Uniform: Military Manpower in Modern Industrial Societies* (New York: Praeger, 1961).

Frisch, David H. (ed.), *Arms Reduction: Program and Issues* (New York: Twentieth Century Fund, 1961).

Fryklund, Richard, *100 Million Lives: Maximum Survival in a Nuclear War* (New York: Macmillan, 1962).

Gallois, Pierre, *The Balance of Terror: Strategy for the Nuclear Age* (Boston: Houghton Mifflin, 1961).

Garthoff, Raymond L., *Soviet Military Doctrine* (Glencoe, Ill.: Free Press, 1953).

———, *Soviet Strategy in the Missile Age* (New York: Praeger, 1958).

———, *The Soviet Image of Future War* (Washington: Public Affairs Press, 1959).

Gavin, James, *War and Peace in the Space Age* (New York: Harper, 1958).

Graebner, Norman A., *The New Isolationism: A Study in Politics and Foreign Policy since 1950* (New York: Ronald, 1956).

Hahn, Walter F., and John C. Neff (eds.), *American Strategy for the Nuclear Age* (Garden City, N.Y.: Doubleday, 1960).

Halle, Louis J., *Dream and Reality: Aspects of American Foreign Policy* (New York: Harper, 1959).

Higgins, Trumbull, *Korea and the Fall of MacArthur: A Précis in Limited War* (New York: Oxford, 1960).

Holley, Irving B., Jr., *Ideas and Weapons: Exploitation of the Aerial Weapon by the United States during World War I: A Study in the Relationship of Technical Advance, Military Doctrine, and the Development of Weapons* (New Haven: Yale Univ. Press, 1953).

Huntington, Samuel, *The Soldier and the State: The Theory and Politics of Civil-Military Relations* (Cambridge: Belknap Press, 1957).

Kahn, Herman, *On Thermonuclear War* (Princeton: Princeton Univ. Press, 1960).

Kennan, George F., *American Diplomacy, 1900–1950* (New York: New Am. Lib., 1951).

————, *Russia, the Atom and the West* (New York: Harper, 1958).

Kennedy, John F., *The Strategy of Peace* (New York: Harper, 1960).

Kieffer, John E., *Strategy for Survival* (New York: McKay, 1953).

Kissinger, Henry A., *Nuclear Weapons and Foreign Policy* (Garden City, N.Y.: Doubleday Anchor Books, 1958).

————, *The Necessity for Choice: Prospects of American Foreign Policy* (New York: Harper, 1960).

Knorr, Klaus, *NATO and American Security* (Princeton: Princeton Univ. Press, 1959).

Lefever, Ernest W., *Ethics and United States Foreign Policy* (New York: Meridian, 1957).

Liddell Hart, B. H., *Strategy* (New York: Praeger Paperbacks, 1954).

————, *Deterrent or Defense: A Fresh Look at the West's Military Position* (New York: Praeger, 1960).

Mahan, Alfred T., *The Influence of Seapower upon History, 1660–1783* (New York: Sagamore, 1957; first published in 1890: Boston: Little, Brown).

Medaris, John B., *Countdown for Decision* (New York: Paperback Lib., 1961).

Miksche, F. O., *The Failure of Atomic Strategy — And a New Proposal for the Defense of the West* (New York: Praeger, 1959).

Millis, Walter. (ed.), *The Forrestal Diaries* (New York: Viking, 1951).

————, *Arms and Men* (New York: Putnam, 1956).

————, *Arms and the State* (New York: Century Fund, 1958).

Mitchell, William, *Winged Defense: The Development and Possibilities of Modern Air Power — Economic and Military* (New York: Putnam, 1925).

Morgenstern, Oskar, *The Question of National Defense* (New York: Random House, 1959).

Murray, John Courtney, *We Hold These Truths: Catholic Reflections on the American Proposition* (New York: Sheed and Ward, 1960).

Murray, Thomas E., *Nuclear Policy for War and Peace* (Cleveland: World Pub., 1960).

Nagle, William J. (ed.), *Morality and Modern Warfare: The State of the Question* (Baltimore: Helicon Press, 1960).

Newman, James R., *The Rule of Folly* (New York: Simon and Schuster, 1962).

Niebuhr, Reinhold, *The World Crisis and American Responsibility*, edited by Ernest W. Lefever (New York: Assn. Press, 1958).

Orwell, George, *1984* (New York: Harcourt, Brace, 1949).

Osgood, Robert E., *Limited War: The Challenge to American Strategy* (Chicago: Univ. of Chicago Press, 1957).

———, *NATO, The Entangling Alliance* (Chicago: Univ. of Chicago Press, 1962).

Peeters, Paul, *Massive Retaliation: The Policy and Its Critics* (Chicago: Regnery, 1959).

Puleston, William D., *Mahan: The Life and Work of Captain Alfred Thayer Mahan, U.S.N.* (New Haven: Yale Univ. Press, 1939).

———, *The Influence of Force in Foreign Relations* (New York: Van Nostrand, 1955).

Rees, Ed, *The Manned Missile* (New York: Duell, 1960).

Reinhardt, George C. and William R. Kintner, *Atomic Weapons in Land Combat* (Harrisburg, Pa.: Military Service Pub., 1954).

———, *American Strategy in the Atomic Age* (Norman: Univ. of Okla. Press, 1955).

Ridgway, Matthew B., *Soldier: The Memoirs of Matthew B. Ridgway* (New York: Harper, 1956).

Rostow, Walt Whitman, *The Stages of Economic Growth: A Non-Communist Manifesto* (Cambridge: Cambridge Univ. Press, 1960).

Russell, Bertrand, *Common Sense and Nuclear Warfare* (New York: Simon and Schuster, 1959).

Sapin, Burton M., and Richard C. Snyder, *The Role of the Military in American Foreign Policy* (Garden City, N.Y.: Doubleday, 1954).

Schelling, Thomas C., *The Strategy of Conflict* (Cambridge: Harvard Univ. Press, 1960).

———, and Morton H. Halperin, *Strategy and Arms Control* (New York: Twentieth Century Fund, 1961).

Shepley, James R., and Clay Blair, Jr., *The Hydrogen Bomb: The Men, the Menace, the Mechanism* (New York: McKay, 1954).

Sigaud, Louis A., *Douhet and Aerial Warfare* (New York: Putnam, 1941).

Slessor, Sir John C., *Strategy for the West* (New York: Morrow, 1954).

Smith, Dale O., *U.S. Military Doctrine: A Study and Appraisal* (New York: Duell, 1955).

Snow, Sir Charles P., *Science and Government* (Cambridge: Harvard Univ. Press, 1961).

Snyder, Glenn H., *Deterrence and Defense: Toward a Theory of National Security* (Princeton: Princeton Univ. Press, 1961).

Strausz-Hupé, Robert, *et. al., Protracted Conflict* (New York: Harper, 1959).

———, William R. Kintner, and Stefan T. Possony, *A Forward Strategy for America* (New York: Harper, 1961).

Taylor, Maxwell D., *The Uncertain Trumpet* (New York: Harper, 1960).

Teller, Edward, *The Legacy of Hiroshima* (Garden City, N.Y.: Doubleday, 1962).

Truman, Harry S., *Memoirs of Harry S. Truman: Years of Trial and Hope* (Garden City, N.Y.: Doubleday, 1956).

Tucker, Robert W., *The Just War* (Baltimore: Johns Hopkins Press, 1960).

Turner, Gordon B., and Richard D. Challener, *National Security in the Nuclear Age: Basic Facts and Theories* (New York: Praeger, 1960).

Waskow, Arthur, *The Limits of Defense* (Garden City, N.Y.: Doubleday, 1962).

ARTICLES

Baldwin, Hanson W., "Strategy of Restraint or Chaos Unlimited," *United States Army Combat Forces Journal,* IV (January 1954), 10–13.

———, "Nagasaki Plus Nine Years," *Bulletin of the Atomic Scientists,* X (October 1954), 318.

———, "The New Face of War," *Bulletin of the Atomic Scientists,* XII (May 1956), 153–58.

———, "Land Power as an Element of National Power," *Army,* VI (January 1956), 16–21.

———, "A Military Policy for the Missile Age," *New York Times Magazine,* November 3, 1957, pp. 13; 86–88.

———, "Limited War," *Atlantic Monthly,* CCIII (May 1959), 35–43, quoted in Walter F. Hahn and John C. Neff (eds.), *American Strategy for the Nuclear Age* (Garden City, N.Y.: Doubleday, 1960), pp. 249–50.

———, "The Case against Fallout Shelters," *Saturday Evening Post,* March 31, 1962, pp. 8–9.

De Seversky, Alexander P., "Obsolete Thinking — A Greater Danger than Obsolete Aircraft," *Air Force,* XXXIX (January 1956), 39–44.

———, "deSeversky on Strategic Organization," *Air Force,* XLI (June 1958), 83–88.

Hessler, William H., "American Foreign Policy: Patient Courage Pays Off," *United States Naval Institute Proceedings,* LXXXII (January 1956), 9–17.

———, "War: Always an Art," *United States Naval Institute Proceedings,* LXXXIV (April 1958), 23–31.

Loosbrock, John F., "Can We Afford a Second Best Air Force?" *Air Force,* XXXVIII (September 1955), 42.

———, "What about the Next Ten Years?" *Air Force,* XXXIX (April 1956), 36–37.

———, "What Kind of Force for What Kind of War?" *Air Force,* XXXIX (November 1956), 43–47.

———, "The Little World of General Gavin," *Air Force,* LXI (September 1958), 7.

———, "The Delicate Balance of Terror," *Air Force,* XLII (February 1959), 48–56.

———, "Minimum Deterrence is a Phoney," *Air Force and Space Digest,* XLIII (October 1960), quoted in *Survival,* III (March-April 1961), 75, 83.

Miller, George H. "Sea Power of Tomorrow," *United States Naval Institute Proceedings,* LXXVIII (September 1952), 959–68.

———, "Shall We Blow Them Up?" *United States Naval Institute Proceedings,* LXXIX (February 1953), 151–55.

———, "Must We Live in Fear?" *United States Naval Institute Proceedings,* LXXIX (July 1953), 759–66.

———, "Not for the Timid," *United States Naval Institute Proceedings,* LXXV (May 1959), 34–42.

Millis, Walter, "The Place of the Armed Forces in the Making of National Strategy," *Naval War College Review,* V (June 1953), 1–21.

———, "The New Strategy's Unanswered Questions," *United States Army Combat Forces Journal,* IV (March 1954), 13–17.

———, Review of *Atomic Weapons in Land Combat,* by Colonel George C. Reinhardt, USA, and Lieutenant Colonel W. R. Kintner, USA, *United States Naval Institute Proceedings,* LXXX (January 1954), 89–100.

Murphy, C. J. V., "A New Strategy for NATO," *Fortune,* XLVII (January 1953), 80–85; 166–70.

———, "The Hidden Struggle for the H-Bomb. The Story of Dr. Oppenheimer's Persistent Campaign to Reverse U.S. Military Strategy," *Fortune,* XLVII (May 1953), 109–10.

———, "Defense and Strategy," *Fortune,* XLVIII (July 1953), 35–40.

————, "The Atom and the Balance of Power," *Fortune*, XLVIII (August 1953), 97–202.

————, "Defense and Strategy," *Fortune*, XLVIII (August 1953), 75–82.

————, "Defense and Strategy," *Fortune*, XLVIII (September 1953), 75–85.

————, "Defense and Strategy," *Fortune*, XLVIII (October 1953), 55–65.

————, "The U.S. as a Bomber Target," *Fortune*, XLVIII (November 1953), 118–21; 219–28.

————, "Defense and Strategy," *Fortune*, XLVIII (December 1953), 77–84.

————, "Is the H-Bomb Enough?" *Fortune*, XLIX (June 1954), 102–103; 246–54.

————, "America's New Strategic Situation," *Fortune*, L (August 1954), 70–71; 182–86.

————, "The Crisis in the Cold War," *Fortune*, LI (June 1955), 96–98; 223–32.

————, "The New Air Situation," *Fortune*, LII (September 1955), 86–87; 218–30.

————, "The Eisenhower Shift," *Fortune*, LIII (January 1956), 83–87; 206–208.

————, "Defense: The Revolution Gets Revolutionary," *Fortune*, LIII (May 1956), 102–103; 246–56.

————, "Eisenhower's Most Critical Defense Budget," *Fortune*, LIV (December 1956), 112–14; 246–54.

————, "America's Widening Military Margin," *Fortune*, LVI (August 1957), 94–96; 218–26.

————, "The White House since Sputnik," *Fortune*, LVII (January 1958), 98–101; 228–32.

————, "The NATO Alliance Goes Nuclear," *Fortune*, LVII (February 1958), 98–102; 234–36.

————, "Defense: The Converging Decisions," *Fortune*, LVIII (October 1958), 119–20; 227–31.

————, "The Embattled Mr. McElroy," *Fortune*, LIX (April 1959), 147–50; 241–51.

————, "Is the Defense Budget Big Enough?" *Fortune*, LX (November 1959), 114–47; 281–86.

————, "Cuba: The Record Set Straight," *Fortune*, LXIV (September 1961), 92–97; 223–36.

Richardson, Robert C., "Atomic Weapons and Theatre Warfare," *Air University Quarterly Review*, VII (Winter 1954–55), 2–24.

————, "The Nuclear Stalemate Fallacy," *Air Force*, XXXIX (August 1956), 74; 77–78; 80.

————, "The Weapons," *Air Force*, XLI (August 1958), 52–55.

————, "Do We Need Unlimited Forces for Limited Wars?" *Air Force*, XLII (March 1959), 53–56.

Seim, Harvey B., "Naval Power and Deterrence," *United States Naval Institute Proceedings*, LXXVII (December 1961), 61–68.

Walkowicz, Theodore F., and John F. Loosbrock, "How to Live with the H-Bomb," *Air Force*, XXXVII (May 1954), 16, 19.

————, Review of *Power and Policy: U.S. Foreign Policy in the Hydrogen Age*, by Thomas K. Finletter, *Air Force*, XXXVII (November 1954), 68.

————, "Counterforce Strategy," *Air Force*, XXXVIII (February 1955), 25.

Williams, Ralph E., Jr., "National Security and Military Policy," *United States Naval Institute Proceedings*, LXXVII (March 1951), 235–45.

————, "Sea Power and the Western Revolution," *United States Naval Institute Proceedings*, LXXIX (March 1953), 239–49.

————, "The Great Debate: 1954," *United States Naval Institute Proceedings*, LXXX (March 1954), 247–55.

————, "America's Moment of Truth," *United States Naval Institute Proceedings*, LXXXI (March 1955), 245–55.

————, "Task for Today: Security through Sea Power," *United States Naval Institute Proceedings*, LXXXIV (March 1958), 23–30.

PUBLIC DOCUMENTS

U.S., Congress, House, Committee on Appropriations, *Department of Defense Appropriations Bill, 1961*, Report No. 1561, 86th Cong., 2d Sess., 1960.

U.S., Congress, House, Committee on Armed Services, *Hearings, Investigation of National Defense Missiles*, 85th Cong., 2d Sess., 1958.

U.S., Congress, House, Committee on Government Operations, *Civil Defense Shelter Policy and Postattack Recovery Planning*, Report No. 2069, 86th Cong., 2d Sess., 1960.

U.S., Congress, House, *United States Defense Policies in 1959*, House Document No. 432, 86th Cong., 2d Sess., 1960.

U.S., Congress, House, *United States Defense Policies in 1960*, House Document No. 207, 87th Cong., 1st Sess., 1961.

U.S., Congress, House, *United States Defense Policies in 1961*, House Document No. 502, 87th Cong., 2d Sess., 1962.

U.S., Congress, Senate, Committee on Foreign Relations, *Developments in Military Technology and Their Impact on U.S. Strategy and Foreign Policy*, 8th Cong., 1st Sess., 1959.

U.S., Congress, Senate, *Hearings before the Subcommittee on the Air Force of the Committee on Armed Services,* Part II, 84th Cong., 2d Sess., 1956.

U.S., Congress, Senate, *Report of the Subcommittee on the Air Force of the Committee on Armed Services,* Document No. 29, 85th Cong., 1st Sess., February 20, 1957.

U.S., Congress, Senate, Committee on Foreign Relations, *United States Foreign Policy: Developments in Military Technology and Their Impact on United States Strategy and Foreign Policy,* by the Washington Center of Foreign Policy Research, The Johns Hopkins University, 86th Cong., 1st Sess., December 6, 1959.

U.S., Congress, Joint Economic Committee, *Study Paper No. 18: National Security and the American Economy in the 1960's,* by Henry Rowen, 86th Cong., 2d Sess., January 30, 1960.

U.S. *Congressional Record,* 85th Cong., 1st Sess., 1957, Vol. CIII, Part 6.

U.S. *Congressional Record,* 86th Cong., 1st Sess., 1959, CV, Part 6.

U.S., Department of the Air Force, *United States Air Force Basic Doctrine,* Air Force Manual 1–2, April 1, 1955.

U.S., Department of the Air Force, *United States Air Force Basic Doctrine,* Air Force Manual 1–2, December 1, 1959.

U.S., Department of the Army, *Bibliography on Limited War,* Pam 20–60, February, 1958.

U.S., Department of the Navy, *The Department of the Navy and Its Secretary,* July 1, 1956.

U.S., Department of the Navy, *Summary of Major Strategic Considerations for the 1960–70 Era,* (NWG) 11–58, January 22, 1958.

U.S., Department of the Navy, Naval Warfare Analysis Group, *Resumé of Major Strategic Considerations,* (NWG) 62–60, by T. E. Phipps, July 19, 1960, (Revised October 17, 1960).

U.S., Department of the Navy, Office of Information, Internal Relations Division, *Seapower 1960,* February 15, 1960.

U.S., Department of State, *Progress toward a World of Law,* Publication Series S, No. 89, 1960.

NEWSPAPERS (1952–62)

Chicago Sun-Times
Christian Science Monitor
Evening Star and *Sunday Star* (Washington)
New York Herald Tribune

New York Times
St. Louis Post-Dispatch
The Sun (Baltimore)
Wall Street Journal
Washington Daily News
Washington Post

PERIODICALS (1952–62)

Air Force (also listed as *Air Force and Space Digest*)
Air University Quarterly Review
Army (also listed as *United States Army Combat Forces Journal*
    and *Combat Forces Journal*)
Army-Navy-Air Force Register
Aviation Week
Bulletin of the Atomic Scientists
Foreign Affairs
Fortune
Naval War College Review
Newsweek
Life
Nation
New Republic
Saturday Evening Post
Saturday Review
Scientific American
Survival
Time
U.S. News and World Report
United States Naval Institute Proceedings

MISCELLANEOUS

Book-of-the-Month Club *News*, July, 1961.
Brown, Harrison, and James Real, *Community of Fear* (Santa
    Barbara: Center for the Study of Democratic Institutions,
    1960).
Daedalus, Special Issue on Arms Control, *Journal of the American
    Academy of Arts and Sciences*, LXXXIX (Fall, 1960).
*International Security: The Military Aspect: America at Mid-
    Century Series*, Report of Panel II of the Special Studies
    Project [The "Rockefeller Report" on the Problems of U.S.
    Defense] (Garden City, N.Y.: Doubleday, 1958).
Kaufmann, William W., "The Requirements of Deterrence," *Memo-*

randum No. 7 (Princeton: Princeton University, Center of International Studies, 1954), 1–23.

Knorr, Klaus, "Passive Defense for Atomic War," *Memorandum No. 6* (Princeton: Princeton University, Center of International Studies, 1954), 1–32.

Schick, Jack M., "The Limits of War," (unpublished doctoral dissertation, University of Chicago Political Science Department, April 1961).

SPEAKERS AND LECTURERS

Most of this speech material was located in the
OP09D Unclassified Files, Department of the Navy

Anderson, Robert B., Secretary of Navy, 1953–1954

Burke, Arleigh A., Admiral, USN (Ret.)

Carney, Robert B., Admiral, USN (Ret.)

Dulles, John Foster, Secretary of State, 1953–1959

Eisenhower, Dwight D., President

Eliot, George Fielding

Gates, Thomas S., Secretary of Navy, 1957–1959; Secretary of Defense, 1959–1960

Gavin, James, General, USA (Ret.)

Gilpatric, Roswell L., Assistant and Under Secretary of Air Force, 1951–1953; Deputy Secretary of Defense, 1960–

Irvine, Clarence S., General, USAF (Ret.)

Kennedy, John F., Senator and President

Kimball, Dan A., Secretary of Navy, 1951–1953

LeMay, Curtis E., General, USAF

Lincoln, George A., Colonel, USA (Ret.)

McNamara, Robert S., Secretary of Defense, 1961–

Murray, Thomas E., Atomic Energy Commissioner, 1950–1957

Perkins, Dexter, Professor

Power, Thomas S., General, USAF

Raborn, William F., Jr., Admiral, USN

Radford, Arthur W., Admiral, USN (Ret.)

Rickover, Hyman G., Admiral, USN

Ridgway, Matthew B., General, USA (Ret.)

Rostow, Walt W., State Dept.

Smith, James H., Jr., Assistant Secretary of Navy for Air, 1953–1956

Taylor, Maxwell D., General, USA (Ret.)

Thomas, Charles S., Secretary of Navy, 1954–1957

Turner, Gordon B., Professor

Twining, Nathan F., General, USAF (Ret.)
Wade, David, General, USAF
Ward, Chester, Admiral, USN (Ret.)
White, Thomas D., General, USAF (Ret.)
Wilson, Charles E., Secretary of Defense, 1953–1957
Wriston, James, President, Brown University

Acknowledgments

FOR FIRST INTRODUCING ME TO THE ENJOYMENT OF HISTORY nearly two decades ago and for remaining a source of inspiration ever since, I am deeply grateful to Dr. W. W. Black of Findlay College.

For continuing guidance, moral support, and detailed, critical reading of the entire original manuscript, I am greatly indebted to Dr. Walter Johnson, University of Chicago, and Dr. Robert E. Osgood, Washington Center of Foreign Policy Research.

For demonstrating by their examples what military professionalism in a pluralistic society means, I am grateful to a score of heroic active duty naval officers, who, unfortunately, must remain nameless lest their mention here compromise their still useful careers. However, if the United States is militarily more secure today and further away from the perils of pre-emptive war and neo-fascism, then these naval officers deserve a heartfelt "well done" from those who have not lost faith in America and her traditions.

For research assistance I thank especially Lieutenant Commander Arnold Lott (USN, Retired), Commander Russell Bufkins, Lieutenant Commander Paul Gibbons, Mr. Daniel Kimball, Mr. Frederick S. Meigs, and the staffs of the Army and Navy libraries, all of whom have made my task much easier and more productive.

For editorial and secretarial assistance and for successfully surmounting seemingly endless details, I owe the greatest debt to my wife Charlotte, who has contributed so unsparingly of her time and devotion.

The views expressed in this work are my own and should not be attributed to either the Navy or State Departments. For any mistakes, misinterpretations, or omissions, I am solely to blame.

Index

ACHESON, DEAN G., 11, 79, 271, 286
Acheson Plan, 226
Adams, Sherman, 29
"Aerospace," 178; weapons system, 5
Air-atomic force, 75–92
Air Force. *See* U.S. Air Force
Air Force Lobby, 1961 resolutions, 231
Air Force, 37, 75, 80; calls for evolution of "megaton fighter," 82; on the need for initiative, 89; reprints Montgomery speech, 120; on the nuclear stalemate, 145–146; on revised intelligence estimates, 158–159; critical of Eisenhower leadership, 163–165; on the manned bomber and "winning," 180; on McNamara's Ann Arbor speech, 248
Air Force Basic Doctrine, 190
Air Force Manual, 190
Air Force Association, 87; 1954 Omaha Convention, 60–62; 1955 statement of policy, 100–101
Air University Quarterly Review, 32, 37; General White in, 56, 82; supports Utopian doctrine, 75; favors air control, 83; Marshal Saundby in, 85–86; Colonel Richardson in, 92; approves Dulles's brinksmanship interview in *Life*, 125; on strategic missiles, 180
Aircraft carriers, 72–73
Airplane, conflicting views on, 18–19, 20–21
Airpower hearings, 121–124, 128–129, 131, 138–141; committee report, 157–158
Alsop, Joseph, 84, 160; on the ballistic missile race, 163; triggers missile gap controversy, 169, 181–183; popularizes Power's

speech, 205, 206–207; turns on LeMay, 232; misinterprets Kennedy strategy, 233; on Soviet missiles, 274
Alsop, Stewart, 84, 233, 234, 265
America: Too Young to Die!, De Seversky, 81, 236
Amster, Warren, 133
Anderson, Jack, 169, 192
Anderson, General Orville A., 7
Anderson, Robert B., 91
Ann Arbor doctrine, 242–244, 246–248, 250, 259, 260, 281
Apollo Project, 242
Arizona Daily Star, 158–159
Armed services, U.S., competition among, 17–23; proposed unification of, 34, 122, 145, 178, 209
Army, 156–157, 177
Army Association, 74
Army Ballistic Missile Agency, 149
Army-McCarthy hearings, 40
Aron, Raymond, 11, 132, 245
Atkins, Humphrey, 155
Atom bomb, 8
Atomic Energy Commission, 51
Atomic Weapons in Land Combat, Reinhardt and Kintner, 90
Aviation Week, 143, 144; on delivering the H-bomb, 44, 45; on the new look, 49; on preventive war, 58; supports Utopian doctrine, 75; reaction to the H-bomb, 81; on improved air defense, 89; on political aspects of the airpower battle, 143; on Eisenhower's decision to run again, 144; story on U.S. radar bases in Turkey, 160; prints security information, 160

B-36 HEARINGS, 40, 122
B-52, call for increase in production of, 157. *See also* Bombers
B-52 H, 274

Massive retaliation, policy, 30–36,
45, 50–60, 105; political debate
over, 79–92; 1955 debate over
effectiveness of, 100–102; James
Reston on, 107; Colonel Leg-
horn on, 116; attacked by Admiral Burke, 176; updated, 259
Matsu, 113, 118
Matthews, William R., 158, 159
Medaris, General John B., 11, 138,
212
Mercator projection, 175
MIDAS, 275
Miksche, Ferdinand O., 11
Milburn, Dr. Thomas, 171
Miller, Admiral George H., 11,
33–34
Millis, Walter, 11, 32–33, 35, 64,
67, 90
Minuteman missile, 188, 221, 255,
264
Missiles, ballistic, 121, 123, 147,
149–166, 273–274; sea-based,
137, 154–156, 172–173, 175;
Russian intercontinental, 163,
274; Russian, Hanson Baldwin
on, 248–249. See also ICBM,
Jupiter, Minuteman, Polaris, etc.
Mitchell, General William
("Billy"), 6, 7, 20, 22, 39
Montgomery, Field Marshal Ber-
nard, 72, 73, 91, 120
Morgenstern, Oskar, 11
Morgenthau, Hans, Jr., 11
Morse, Wayne, 97, 99
Mundt, Karl E., 214
Murphy, Colonel C. J. V., 7, 38–
42, 150; claims Dulles had
atomic-armed jets sent to Japan,
29–30; discusses Eisenhower
views on weaponry, 45–46; on
the new look, 46–47; credits
Slessor with creating Britain's
new look, 75; proposes variety
of military isolation, 86; on the
tactical use of atomic weapons
in Korea and Indochina, 90; on
Eisenhower's policy, 118; campaign for counterforce bomber
fleet, 118–119; on the roadblock
to counterforce, 144; analysis of
Eisenhower's defense budget,
147; approves modified strategy,
161–162; and the missile gap
controversy, 169, 179–180, 184–
185; on the NATO alliance, 185;
on Air Force justifications for
counterforce strategy, 195–196;
exposé on Cuban invasion, 231
Murray, Thomas E., 51, 53
MRBM, 258

NASSAU PACT, 256, 258, 261, 273
Nasser, Gamel Abdel, 149
National Aeronautics and Space
Administration, 149, 188, 205,
227, 229
National Security Council, deci-
sion to convert to atomic weap-
ons, 45, 47, 54; Childs reveals
existence of study by, 57; rec-
ommends re-examination of U.S.
weapons systems, 123; and the
Cuban crisis, 265
NSC 68, 45
Nautilus, atomic submarine, 64,
71, 73
Naval Warfare Group Study Num-
ber 5, 171
Necessity for Choice, The, Kis-
singer, 223
Nehru, 29
"New Look," first use of term, 46;
Radford spells out, 47–49; Brit-
ain's, 75; partisan political de-
bate over, 79–81
"New new look," 89; scrapping of,
169
New Republic, 207, 248
New York Herald Tribune, 246
New York Times, 60, 91
Newsweek, 202, 205, 207, 249
Nicholas, Colonel Jack D., 126
Nitze, Paul H., 11, 222, 229
Nixon, Richard, 55, 79, 187, 194,
200
Norman, Lloyd, 80, 156
Norris, John, 49
Norstad, General Lauris, 258, 266
NATO, tactical atomic capability,
152, 258; Murphy enthusiastic
about, 185; Richardson on, 210;
and sword and shield concept,
255; multilateral force, 271–272